# AGE, HEALTH, AND EMPLOYMENT

JAMES E. BIRREN,
PAULINE K. ROBINSON,
and JUDY E. LIVINGSTON, Editors

Andrus Gerontology Center
University of Southern California

and
Donna E. Deutchman, Editorial Coordinator

Prentice-Hall, Inc., Englewood Cliffs, New Jersey 07632

*Library of Congress Cataloging-in-Publication Data*

Main entry under title:

Age, health, and employment.

Papers prepared by the Fellows of the Andrew Norman Institute for Advanced Study in Gerontology and Geriatrics at the Andrus Gerontology Center of the University of Southern California.
Includes bibliographies and index.
1. Age and employment. 2. Ability, Influence of age on. 3. Life span, Productive. 4. Aged—Employment—United States. I. Birren. James E. II. Robinson, Pauline K. III. Livingston, Judy E. IV. Andrew Norman Institute for Advanced Study in Gerontology and Geriatrics.
HD6279.A335 1986 331.3 85-12442
ISBN 0-13-018524-8

Editorial/production supervision and
interior design: Cyndy Lyle Rymer
Manufacturing buyer: Barbara Kelly Kittle



Printed in the United States of America
10 9 8 7 6 5 4 3 2 1

ISBN 0-13-018524-8 01

Prentice-Hall International (UK) Limited, *London*
Prentice-Hall of Australia Pty. Limited, *Sydney*
Prentice-Hall Canada Inc., *Toronto*
Prentice-Hall Hispanoamericana, S.A., *Mexico*
Prentice-Hall of India Private Limited, *New Delhi*
Prentice-Hall of Japan, Inc., *Tokyo*
Prentice-Hall of Southeast Asia Pte. Ltd., *Singapore*
Editora Prentice-Hall do Brasil, Ltda., *Rio de Janeiro*
Whitehall Books Limited, *Wellington, New Zealand*

# CONTRIBUTORS

**James E. Birren,** Ph.D. (Chapter 1) is the Dean of the Ethel Percy Andrus Gerontology Center, Director of the Andrew Norman Institute for Advanced Study in Gerontology and Geriatrics, and Professor of Psychology at the University of Southern California. Dr. Birren is also currently a member of the World Health Organization's Expert Advisory Panel on Health of Elderly Persons. He is past President of the Gerontological Society of America, the Western Gerontological Society, and the Division on Adult Development and Aging of the American Psychological Association. In addition, he is a Fellow of the American Psychological Association, the Gerontological Society, the American Geriatrics Society, and the American Association for the Advancement of Science. His many awards include the Brookdale Foundation Award for Gerontological Research, an Honorary Doctorate from the University of Gothenberg, Sweden, and the Gerontological Society Award for Meritorious Research.

**Deborah D. Newquist,** M.S.W.–M.P.A. (Chapter 2) is a Senior Staff Associate at the National Policy Center on Employment and Retirement at the Andrus Gerontology Center, University of Southern California. Her research interests are the health characteristics and behavior of older adults, disability, and cross-cultural aging. She is a past Co-Editor of *Generations,* the quarterly of the Western Gerontological Society. Most recently she has completed a report, "Trends in Disability and Health Among Middle-Aged and Older Persons," for the Administration on Aging. She is a Ph.D. Candidate in Anthropology at the University of California, Los Angeles.

**Erhard Olbrich,** Ph.D. (Chapter 3) is Professor of Psychology at the University of Erlangen, West Germany. He has done research on development in old age, especially on processes of coping with social role losses and with health problems. In recent years, he has tried to combine paradigms of coping and developmental research while studying transitions and critical life events in adolescence and adulthood. Recently, he co-authored a book entitled *Probleme des Jugendalters* (with Eberhard Todt). Dr. Olbrich has published about 40 articles in professional journals.

**Pauline K. Robinson,** Ph.D. (Chapter 4) is the UPS Foundation Research Professor of Gerontology at the Andrus Gerontology Center, University of Southern California, where she directs the Employment and Retirement Division and serves as Co-Director of the National Policy Center on Employment and Retirement. Her recent teaching and writing have been in the area of industrial gerontology, including *Organizational Strategies for Older Workers.* Dr. Robinson's interest in the topic of age, work, and health was furthered when she was a Fellow at the Salzburg Seminar on Health, Productivity and Aging. Another recent publication, *Aging and Technological Advances,* resulted from a NATO Symposium on the same topic which she co-convened with Dr. James Birren at the Andrus Gerontology Center.

**Timothy A. Salthouse,** Ph.D. (Chapter 5) is an Associate Professor of Psychology at the University of Missouri, Columbia, Missouri. His recent publications include a monograph titled *Adult Cognition: An Experimental Psychology of Aging* (1982), chapters in *The Handbook of the Psychology of Aging* (1985) and *Life-Span Development and Behavior* (1983), and research articles in several professional journals. Dr. Salthouse's primary interests are in the cognitive psychology of aging and the nature of human skill.

**Juliene L. Stafford,** Ph.D. (Chapter 1) is Senior Research Analyst at the Department of Psychiatry, General Hospital, Boston, Massachusetts. She is a past Research Fellow of the Gerontological Society of America's Fellowship Program in Applied Gerontology and her past research includes extensive inquiry into skilled problem solving ability and the effects of practice in young and elderly adults. Dr. Stafford received her degree from the Department of Psychology at the University of Southern California in Los Angeles, California.

**Harvey L. Sterns,** Ph.D. (Chapter 6) is Associate Professor of Psychology and Director and Fellow of the Institute for Life-Span Development and Gerontology in the Department of Community Health Science at Northeastern Ohio University's College of Medicine. Dr. Sterns serves as Chairperson of the Ph.D. Program in Industrial Gerontological Psychology and the Northeast Ohio Consortium in Geriatric Medicine and Gerontology. He has contributed numerous chapters and articles in professional books and journals. Among these are chapters in *Life-Span Developmental Psychology: Intervention* and *The Handbook of the Psychology of Aging.* Dr. Sterns has co-edited *Gerontology in Higher Education: Perspectives and Issues* and *Gerontology in Higher Education: Developing Institutional and Community Strength,* and was an Associate Editor for *Aging and Technological Advances.*

**Shelby Stewman,** Ph.D. (Chapter 7) is an Associate Professor of Demography and Sociology at Carnegie-Mellon University, Pittsburgh, Pennsylvania. Recent publications include "Careers and Organizational Labor Markets: Demographic Models of Organizational Behavior" (with S. L. Konda) in the *American Journal of Sociology,* 1983; "Recombinant DNA Breakthroughs in Agriculture, Industry, and Medicine: A Delphi Study" (with E. Cowden, C. Gunn, D. Lincoln, S. Ritter, and S. Wilcox) in *Futures,* 1981; and "The Aging of Work Organizations: Impact on Organization and Employment Practices" in *Aging: Social Change,* 1981. He is currently writing a book entitled *Organizational Demography and Labor* and plans to conduct international comparisons of national labor markets and aging.

**Judith Treas,** Ph.D. (Chapter 8) is Associate Professor and Chair of the Department of Sociology as well as a Research Associate in the Gerontology Research Institute at the University of Southern California. Recent publications include "Trickle Down or Transfers? Postwar Determinants of Family Income Inequality" in the *American Sociological Review* and "Family Aspects of Aging" (with R. Aizenberg) in the *Handbook of the Psychology of Aging.* Her recent interests have included the career cycles of men and women, the family life of the elderly, the determinants of household structure, and demographic influences on the distribution of income.

# CONTENTS

# PREFACE

This volume discusses a number of issues of age, health, and employment. In developed nations today, issues related to employment and health are becoming increasingly important for the field of gerontology and for general policy decisions. Technological developments in the nature of work, increased longevity, early retirement trends, and concern with productivity have directed attention to issues of age, health, and employment. Chapters in this volume focus on the concept of functional age versus chronological age, trends in disability among older workers, age as a factor in coping with stress, age-related health factors in job performance, the training of older workers, an historical view of the institution of retirement, and the age structure of labor markets.

Some chapters in the volume deal with specific topics in the complex relationship either between age and employment or between age and health, while others attempt to deal simultaneously with all three areas of age, health, and employment. The volume presents the authors' attempts to review and consolidate existing studies, to provide new conceptual analyses, to present historical and statistical data to support their theses, and to make specific recommendations for private and public sector policy and for further research.

This is the second in an annual series of volumes devoted to special topics in the field of aging, produced by scholars from the United States and other countries who are Fellows of the Andrew Norman Institute for Advanced Study in Gerontology and Geriatrics at the Andrus Gerontology Center of the University of Southern California. Other volumes in the series include *Cognition, Stress, and*

*Aging; The Dementias: Policy and Management;* and *Education and Aging.* This series reflects a multidisciplinary and multinational approach to complex issues related to aging. The 1982–1983 year of study that produced this particular volume involved Fellows from the disciplines of psychology, medicine, sociology, anthropology, and philosophy and from the countries of the United States, the Federal Republic of Germany, and Australia.

The Andrew Norman Institute for Advanced Study in Gerontology and Geriatrics was established in 1981 at the Andrus Gerontology Center of the University of Southern California, funded by an initial grant from the Andrew Norman Foundation. Fellows of the Institute spend ten months at the Andrus Center doing work related to the year's special topic, meeting in a weekly seminar, and preparing papers for the annual book, as well as pursuing individual research projects.

The goals of the Institute include furthering research in gerontology and geriatrics and encouraging the exchange of information and the development of collaborative research among scholars from the United States and other countries. The "aging of societies" is one of the most important issues facing all nations in the world today; and the field of gerontology is at a point where it can benefit greatly from cross-cultural and multinational exchanges of information and approaches to issues related to aging.

It is our pleasure to acknowledge the generous support of the Andrew Norman Foundation and the Andrew Norman Charitable Trust, whose original gift created and continues to support the Andrew Norman Institute for Advanced Study in Gerontology and Geriatrics, and of Dr. Armand Hammer, who each year has provided financial assistance through Fellowships. We are also grateful to The UPS Foundation, the Xerox Foundation, and the Metropolitan Life Foundation for their contribution to the production of this volume.

We would like to thank Paul Costa, James Dowd, James Fozard, James Fries, Paul Haber, William Hoyer, Irene Hulicka, Alan Jette, Malcolm Johnson, Nathan Keyfitz, Stephen McConnell, Leonard Pearlin, James Schulz, K. Warner Schaie, Donald Shupe, Johannes Siegrist, Hans Thomae, and Harrison White for their assistance in reviewing chapters for this volume. Fellows were ably assisted in their studies by Research Assistants Judy Stryckman and Kristen Norris. Sheri Erickson and Marie Mandel assisted with the production of the manuscript. Donna Deutchman's efforts as Editorial Coordinator of this volume, and of the series of volumes, has been invaluable.

# 1

# CHANGES IN THE ORGANIZATION OF BEHAVIOR WITH AGE

*Implications of Functional Age*

Juliene L. Stafford and James E. Birren

## PURPOSE

The purpose of the present chapter is to address the question: How does the organization of behavior change with age? In the past, the issues raised by such a question have been dealt with under the topic of functional age. It is within that same context that this discussion will be launched. The authors contend, however, that previous theoretical endeavors have been limited both by their conceptual basis and their analytical evaluations. Thus, this enterprise will have two major foci.

First we will review a theoretical framework for the definition of living systems into which aging and behavior must be fitted. Initially, this framework will draw on the thinking of Claude Bernard (1878), Walter Cannon (1929), and Jacques Monod (1971). The views of these scientists, however, will serve only as a background for the conceptualizations of Eugene Yates (1982a). Yates attempts to explain the thermodynamic characteristics of living systems in terms of a general principle of design based on physical considerations. In addition, Yates (1982a) specifically applies this general principle to the process of senescence. It is at that crucial point that the theoretical discussion will once again be united with empirical findings describing adult development and aging.

The second major focus of the paper will then become apparent. The authors will propose a set of structural equations as a first step toward modeling how the organization of behavior changes across the adult life span. We readily admit that this is a formidable task that will raise more questions than this chapter can answer at the present time. It is hoped, however, that the suggestions made will stimulate others to consider the issues at hand and to test out the implications of their theoretical models in a similar manner.

## FUNCTIONAL AGE

The concept of functional age has been with us for several decades; its measurement has catalyzed much discussion, criticism and research in recent years. McFarland (1943) appears to have introduced the term *functional age* in relation to his work in industry. In general, he was concerned with determining the exact age at which past experience and adaptations to offset declining abilities no longer compensate for psychological and physiological deterioration. In particular, he thought it would be important for industry to know the age ranges in which compensation could no longer overcome specific limitations, implying the need for tests to measure how capable individuals may be in meeting the requirements of their job or other life situations. Birren (1959, 1969) systematically introduced the usefulness of nonchronological age scales and contrasted them to the application of chronological age as an index of time elapsed. He defined functional age as a dimension on which individuals could be younger or older than their chronological years. The individual's level of capacities for functioning in society could be compared to other individuals of the same age by a series of measurements comprising operationalizations of biological age, psychological age and social age. An additional assumption of functional age as a concept was that changes occurring in the organism were intrinsically interrelated.

In the present volume Salthouse (Chapter 5) has reviewed three perspectives of functional age that have evolved since the introduction of the concept: occupational functional age, biomedical functional age, and structural organization of human functioning. The first two perspectives tend to be fairly specific in their focus and to be more intimately related to immediate application. On the other hand, the third perspective is more general in nature and allows for theoretical speculation with regard to the interrelationships of various age-related characteristics. It is from this third interpretation of functional age that the present chapter will build.

Similar to Salthouse's perspective, the interest here is in the changes that have occurred in an individual over a lifetime and the mechanism(s) responsible for those changes. In other words, is aging a unitary or multifactor process? Empirically, this fundamental issue has been addressed by representing functional age as an index and as a profile of abilities.

Several investigators have attempted to devise an index of functional age. The work of Jalavisto, Lindquist, and Makkonen (1964) and Furukawa, Inoue, Kajiya, Inada, Takasugi, Fukui, Takeda, and Abe (1975) focused on the development of an index for biological age. Using a similar rationale, Dirken (1972) attempted to assess the functional age of industrial workers in the Netherlands. Many of his measurements were the same as those used by Jalavisto et al. (1964), but there were many additional ones used as well. Initially, Dirken and his colleagues examined 150 variables from psychomotor, sensory, and biomedical domains. They correlated each variable with age and eventually reduced the number of functional variables to 28, which they then intercorrelated and subjected to cluster analysis. Finally, they used eight variables as an index of functional age, and identified a battery of tests that resulted in a regression coefficient with chronological age of approximately .87. These results were remarkably similar to those of Jalavisto et al. (1964).

A final group of studies that adopted this perspective has been carried out by investigators at the Normative Aging Study (Bell, Rose and Damon, 1972). These researchers attempted to define functional age from measurements in six domains: anthropometric, social, auditory, laboratory, personality, and ability measures. In order to estimate the percent of variance in chronological age which could be predicted, the squared multiple correlations for the different domains were calculated. In a follow-up study, Fozard and Thomas (1975) combined the variables from all six domains in a single regression equation predicting chronological age. Their results indicated that 12 variables accounted for about 65 percent of the variance in chronological age (30 to 87 years).

Heron and Chown (1967) represent the major proponents of the use of a functional age profile. They identified eight variables, each showing a linear relationship with chronological age, and subsequently created a functional age profile on these eight separate measures. Although some of their empirical results were similar to Dirken's (1972), Heron and Chown advised against the use of a global index for functional age because they found low intercorrelations between their measures. They thought a functional age profile would allow for greater differentiation of information. More recent discussions of functional age also have concluded that, for the time being, processes measured as indices of functional age should not be culminated in a single index (Costa and McCrae, 1980; Salthouse, 1982). This is not to say that there are not interrelationships among different processes, nor does this recommendation insinuate that the relationships between processes remain stable once determined. Rather, it should imply that the aging process is multidimensional and multidirectional.

## CONCEPTS REGARDING AGING AND BEHAVIOR

Our preference is for the use of multiple measures rather than a global index for describing traditionally defined functional age; we will now show how this perspective might be applied to the structural organization of behavioral change. In this process it is necessary to examine the underlying concepts of aging held by researchers. Earlier, Comfort (1956) sought to examine the mechanisms of senescence and to identify a change in the behavior of the organism with age which leads to a decreased power of survival and adjustment. In Comfort's view, the organism dies of old age because it becomes an unstable system which is provided with no further sequence of operational instructions and in which divergent processes are no longer coordinated to maintain function. Thus, over time the organism regresses from an ordered efficient state to a disordered chaotic state in which predatory influences or stresses might be the terminal influences on its life. Birren (1959) points out that, in order to be useful, explanations of such changes should apply to more than one individual and should represent a property that remains the same under a variety of specified circumstances. In other words, the prediction and, ultimately, the explanation of aging rest on the assumption that patterns or general regularities exist in the structures and functions of living organisms as they move forward in time in the latter part of the life span.

Birren (1959) builds from the earlier work of Medawar (1945) to elaborate on his notions of the general regularities of aging. Basically, he proposes that all systems which age are characterized by limits of size, form, and function, and by principles of irreversibility and cumulation. Thus, with regard to the developing organism, aging may be considered to begin when the forces of growth in size, form and function have arrived at a relatively steady state. This does not mean that individuals do not change after maturity, but instead implies that they change within some boundaries determined by the end of the early adult years. The boundaries, then, are genetically based and limit the adaptability of the organism to the environment. These biologically imposed limitations only become relevant, however, when unusual levels of functioning are demanded of the organism, such as in high or low environmental temperatures. Within some restricted range, functions appear to be relatively autonomous in the healthy normal adult organism. Behavior may be essentially autonomous of the state of the dynamic biological equilibrium except when a critical value of the latter is reached. For instance, in climbing a mountain, one's behavior and clarity of thinking is not limited by oxygen if one has a normal cardiovascular system. However, at high altitudes the oxygen-carrying capacity of the blood is impaired and behavior is less effective. Thus, when a boundary condition or limit is reached, biological aging processes may interact with other aging processes to govern the organism and, ultimately, bring about death. This phenomenon can be illustrated by a number of examples of states with boundary conditions, e.g., vitamin deficiency states, cerebral blood flow, strength, and mobility. Within the normal range, each of these states can vary relatively independent of others. Once they hit an extremely low level of functioning, though, previously independent variations may begin to produce behavioral consequences. Thus, it seems important to consider the nonlinear or the threshold-like quality of biological-behavioral relationships. The concept of thresholds also suggests the possibility of intermittency in behavior. A set of relationships may hold only for a limited time period, after which a new set of behavioral determinants is established. Thus sleeping, eating, playing, and sexual behavior show intermittency, implying that their determinants have different boundary conditions which, if met, result in sudden shifts in behavior. "The behavior or output of the organism in this view would be described as quantum-like, and relationships as probabilistic in nature" (Birren, 1959).

## THEORETICAL BACKGROUND FOR THE DEFINITION OF LIVING SYSTEMS

Many of the concepts discussed by Birren (1959) as characteristics describing the organization of behavior in the aging organism have been elaborated in treatises attempting to define living beings or systems. In Birren's view, aging is regarded as a universal process resulting from the fact that there are irreversible properties of the organism that prevent time from flowing backward.

The notion of irreversibility, according to Birren, implies that the consequences of events proceed unidirectionally, though this does not necessarily imply degradation. "There is nothing inherently incremental or decremental implied by the concept of irreversibility; it imparts only a time direction" (Birren, 1959). An important point with regard to irreversibility is that it is applicable at all levels of analysis–biological, psychological, and social. Thus, when considering aging, attention should be directed at all mechanisms in the hierarchical organization of biological, psychological, and social systems which manifest the quality of irreversibility.

Claude Bernard's (1878) recognition that stability and regulation within the organism are essential conditions for freedom and independence in the surrounding environment stands as a first attempt at a theory of an organism. Bernard maintained that all vital mechanisms are concerned with only one purpose, preserving the conditions of life in the internal environment. Walter Cannon (1929) elaborated on Bernard's notions in his concept of homeostasis. In Cannon's attempt at a theory of the living organism, physiological reactions for obtaining constancy were the focus. Within this framework, regulation in the organism was the central problem for the physiologist. Cannon concluded that an attempt to account for the observed stability of living systems in physical and chemical terms was a task that awaited future developments.

More recently, Jacques Monod (1971) has tried to demonstrate that the molecular theory of the genetic code constitutes a general theory of living systems. In this case, the "theory of the genetic code" includes not only concepts relevant to the chemical structure of hereditary material and the information it conveys, but also the molecular mechanisms for expressing this information morphogenetically and physiologically (Monod, 1971).

Taking as his task the definition of living systems, Monod asserts that there are three characteristic properties that distinguish living beings from all other structures or systems present in the universe. These characteristics are: (1) teleonomy–living systems are objects endowed with a purpose or project, which they simultaneously exhibit in their structure and carry out in their performances; (2) autonomous morphogenesis–structure results from morphogenetic interactions within the object itself, i.e., living beings are self-constructing machines; and (3) invariance–the source of the information expressed in the structure of a living being is always another structurally identical object, i.e., living beings are self-reproducing machines. Note that Monod does not deal explicitly with the organism as a system which is, in part, organized by learning, a characteristic which is so great a feature of the human animal.

Although it remains possible to differentiate these three characteristics, Monod is quick to recognize that they are closely interconnected. "Genetic invariance expresses and reveals itself only through, and thanks to, the autonomous morphogenesis of the structure that constitutes the teleonomic apparatus" (Monod, 1971). With these assertions in mind, Monod can be considered a transition from Cannon's earlier physiological perspective of living systems to Yates' upcoming physical description of living systems.

## A PHYSICAL THEORY OF LIVING SYSTEMS AND AGING

Yates (1982a) has proposed a conceptual scheme based upon a physical theoretic that is thought to apply to living systems at any level and explains their thermodynamic characteristics. Yates, Marsh, and Iberall (1972) believe, as did Monod, that the basic question revolves around determining what physical properties account for the process of organization. On what physical basis can we explain the observation that out of randomness, uncertainty, and dissipative processes, interactions can lead spontaneously to stable forms and behavior? From the perspective of Yates et al., however, Monod does not go far enough. They believe the exhibition of common properties of dynamical systems operating at various scales between molecules and man is an important facet missing from his treatment. Theorists must realize that the common principle behind all hierarchical systems is that the basis for explanation is the same at all levels within the system. It is with this intent that Yates (1982a) attempts to "account for the richness of behavior of organisms, at all their levels of organization, by a level-independent physical theory of self-organization and dynamical stability." That is, Yates asserts that biological systems can be understood via a strictly physical analysis, and proposes homeokinetics as the appropriate physical theory. Homeokinetics is based upon statistical mechanics, nonlinear dynamics, and irreversible thermodynamics. (For a thorough presentation of the application of homeokinetics to physiological systems see Yates, 1982a). The importance of Yates in the present context is the manner in which his approach and conclusions echo and extend the conceptualizations proposed earlier by Birren (1959). To reiterate, the fundamental assumption for hierarchical systems is, in Yates' terms, that at each level in the hierarchy the same physics is renormalized around the scales that apply to that level. As Anderson (1972) points out, it will always appear to an observer that each level has "independent" laws; and, indeed, the equations of change differ in detail from level to level, but not in their dependence on thermodynamic potentials and parameters. This is not to suggest that biology is "nothing but" physics. Yates acknowledges Midgley's (1978) reminder that "all real features of the world can be studied directly on their own terms. They do not have to be approached indirectly, by finding their mirror images in a pattern studied by physicists." However, Yates' hope is to be able to account for the dynamics of life with the fewest *ad hoc* terms and concepts possible.

A second important feature of Yates' description of the dynamics of living systems is the manner in which he suggests that the internal physical processes are manifested. He asserts that internal processes quantize into a set of distinguishable, characteristic external action modes, i.e., behavioral modes. The number of behavioral modes is thought to be finite (less than 25) for any level of a complex system, including man. These modes are grossly equienergetic and represent a regime of marginal stability for the system. It is not difficult to shift from one mode to another, e.g., eating to sleeping, or working to sexual behavior. Not only will the system move from one mode to another, but the system will continually repeat previous modes. Yates maintains that the global stability of an autonomous, complex, persistent system consists of a trajectory through some subset of the possible action modes, with the trajectory itself possessing near-periodic characteristics. There are some behavior modes we use every day, such as elimination or sleeping, which, if not engaged in, would disturb the stability of the global system. Consequently, the cyclic or periodic processes generate a power spectrum of the frequency of action modes that is discontinuous. Thus, like Birren, Yates describes a system that manifests periodicity or regularities in its behavior and exhibits limits on the behaviors which, when exceeded, result in transitions to another behavior.

This movement from one behavior to another appears discontinuous and can be captured by considering the frequency of each behavior.

Recently, Yates (1982b) has begun to think specifically about senescence from the viewpoint of physical stability. He considers senescence to be a normal process and not a disease (where disease implies having a malady or illness of specific causality). In his metaphor based on physical theory, "senescence is a process of progressive loss of dynamical stability. This loss is manifested as a steadily increasing probability of system or component failure on exposure to usual, as well as unusual, environmental fluctuations, particularly those with high frequency power." Although he believes that a physical basis of justification for models of population dynamics (including senescence of individuals and interactions within and between populations) is lacking at the present time, he does suggest that the qualitative characteristics of senescence can be examined. From this perspective Yates, like others, views senescence as a progressive loss of viable autonomy (stability) with time. This loss in stability is conceptualized as the consequence of external environment or fluctuations of the internal environment acting on an individual's given *viability volume* (see Figure 1-1). The notion of viability volume has variously been referred to as vigor (Jalavisto et al., 1964) or vitality (Fries and Crapo, 1981). An organism moves about within the viability volume depending on

**FIGURE 1-1. Senescence as a Progressive Loss of Viability. Reprinted with permission from Yates, F. E. Senescence from the aspect of physical stability. A paper presented to the Research Symposium on Aging: Session 3: "Metaphors in the Study of Cells and Cellular Systems." University of British Columbia, June 19-22, 1982.**

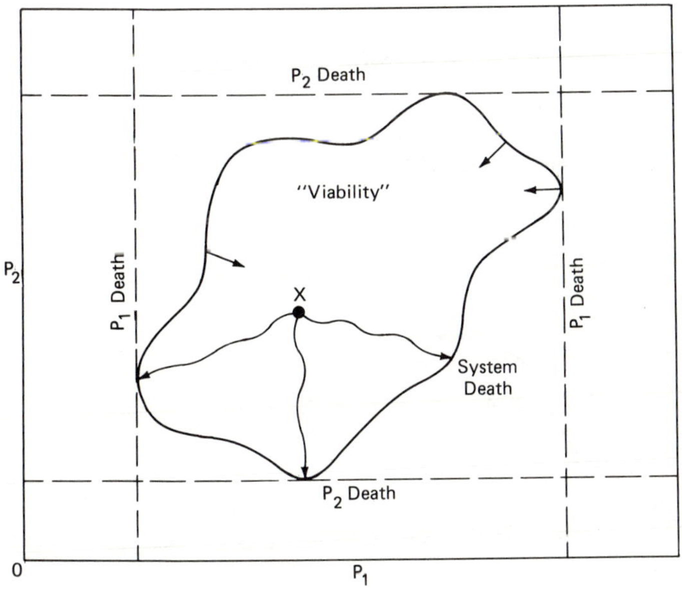

internal and external influences. If the organism reaches or exceeds the boundary of the viability volume, it fails and dies.

The organism can reach the boundary in two ways. The viability volume is surrounded by certain parameters. If the organism reaches the boundary at the extreme of a parameter, it will die due to a specific component failure (e.g., heart, kidney, or liver). However, if the organism reaches a boundary at values of the separate parameters that are not extreme, its death will be due to the combination of the parameters and not the result of a specific component or subsystem failure. According to this metaphor, if the viability volume is large, as in the healthy young adult, it is improbable that the organism will hit the boundary as it responds to the stresses of daily life. As the organism ages, the viability volume shrinks, so there is an increased probability that the organism will hit the boundary and die. This discussion has focused on the qualitative, dynamical view of senescence. The subsequent section will consider viability plotted as a function of time.

## MORTALITY, VIABILITY, AND AGE

Although various curves have been proposed to describe viability across the life span, the data that are available currently tend to endorse one curve in particular (Yates, 1982b). The curve of interest here indicates that human beings are relatively vulnerable at birth, but attain maximal viability in young adulthood, after which point a gradual progressive decline in viability is seen (see Figure 1-2). It is hypothesized that the biological-physical processes that decrease viability are continually operating throughout the life span. These processes do not dominate, however, until after young adulthood. Up until that point, constructive, anabolic processes predominate. In particular, measurements of physiological data appear to fit this curve quite well. After young adulthood, individuals show more or less

**FIGURE 1-2. Curve of Vitality for a Single Individual. Reprinted with permission from Yates, F. E. Senescence from the aspect of physical stability. A paper presented to the Research Symposium on Aging: Session 3: "Metaphors in the Study of Cells and Cellular Systems." University of British Columbia, June 19–22, 1982.**

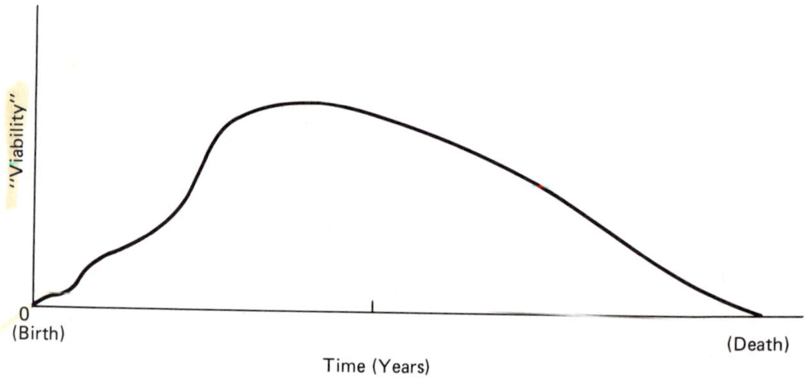

linear declines of various functions with time. One prototypical example would be vital capacity.

The basis for these ideas was captured and expressed as early as 1825 by Benjamin Gompertz, who examined the relationship of human mortality to age. Gompertz focused not on the linear decline of human functioning, but on the logarithmically increasing rate of mortality after young adulthood. Since the Gompertz curve takes into account a denominator denoting the number of persons alive at a given age, it is based on age-specific mortality rate. Although Gompertz was not the only investigator to propose a law representing the relationship between age and the force of mortality (see Benjamin and Haycocks, 1970, pp. 24-25), his is probably one of the simplest mathematical expressions. Gompertz maintained that age-specific mortality rate ($Rx$) increases exponentially with age ($x$). That is, $Rx = Ro^{ax} e$, where $Ro$ is initial vulnerability to disease before the onset of aging and $a$ is a constant depending on the species. Therefore, a straight line occurs for those ages where the law is valid. Gompertz found that the likelihood of death in man doubles about once every eight years after age 30, depending on the specific population. In particular, the equation proposed by Gompertz on physiological grounds describes the mortality rate of homogeneous populations of adult mammals that were maintained relatively free of disease, malnutrition or predation. In fact, the mortality curves for selected populations of mice may be so similar in shape to humans as to be superimposable when adjusted for the species difference in overall life span. Thus, Gompertz's work suggested that it was possible to die of old age, independent of a specific accident or major illness.

In 1867, however, Makeham introduced a constant component in addition to Gompertz's logarithmically–increasing component of the force of mortality. This constant term ($A$) represented chance deaths independent of deterioration due to age. The importance of this term can be realized when primitive societies are considered. In such societies chance deaths work to kill off a species before effects of the biological substrate have an opportunity to be manifested. In contrast, in modern, technologically-sophisticated societies, where the probability of chance death might be drastically reduced, the Gompertz term mandates a fixed, natural life expectancy for a species.

Although there is no absolute *a priori* reason to assign a greater probable validity to one mathematical model of aging than to another that fits the data equally well, there is some advantage to exploring the consequences of the simpler equation first (Strehler, 1977). The simple Gompertz equation may not reflect the interrelationships of time and deteriorative processes with the same precision in specific instances that specifically constructed equations with multiple variables do. More complex equations, however, can be made to approximate almost any monotonically changing variable, provided that a sufficient range of values for variables and coefficients are properly inserted in each separate case or class. It is for this reason that most recent theories of mortality and aging have considered the Gompertz function to be one of the primary observations to be explained.

Strehler and Mildvan (1960) present just such a general theory of aging. They specify that aging refers to those changes in structure and function that usually occur following the attainment of reproductive maturity, resulting in a decreased ability to accomplish the work necessary to overcome environmental or internal challenges, and in an increased probability of death with time. As a precedent to the explication of their theory, Strehler and Mildvan review three observations with which any mathematical theory of mortality should be consistent: (1) the Gompertz function, including the Makeham term, (2) linear decline in physiological functions, and (3) inverse relationship between the slope of the Gompertz function ($a$) and the intercept ($Ro$)–i.e., those countries with a low-standing death rate should possess Gompertz plots whose slopes are greater than those of countries providing poor environments. A major assumption of the theory is that the organism is composed of several independent physiological subsystems continually subject to displacement and fluctuations in the internal and external environment. Energy is then required to overcome displacement and restore homeostasis. The maximum rate at which an organism can expend such energy is referred to as vitality. (Vitality in this context is synonomous with Yates' viability.) Vitality exists for a subsystem and for the organism as a whole. The environment can either challenge the organism without causing lasting damage or, in the case of a harmful environment, produce permanent damage, but may produce little increase in the mortality rate at young ages. Death occurs when the environmental challenge exceeds the vitality of the organism. The increase in the risk of death from all causes is paralleled by a similar increase in the risk of death from most major diseases. These causes of death, however, do not account for the slope of the curve. Even if such cases could be prevented, the resulting curve would lie roughly parallel to the original curve. The constancy of the curve implies the existence of some relatively invariant process of age-dependent deterioration associated with a generally increasing vulnerability to stress, injury, and disease.

## MARKERS OF PRIMARY AND SECONDARY AGING

Thus far in our attempt to reach beyond functional age to a description of the organization of behavior throughout the life span, we have proceeded from the initial philosophical thinking of Bernard, Cannon and Monod to Yates' theoretical application of physics to the design of living systems. Finally, we have reviewed empirically driven mathematical models dealing with the decline in functional processes and the increased mortality rate with age. It seems appropriate now to integrate these ideas with findings in the gerontological literature and to suggest an analytical approach that can attempt to test out applications of some of the previously discussed ideas. Of course, not every change in behavior with age will be described. Instead, the focus will be on those processes that have shown empirically the highest relation to chronological age. It should also be kept in mind that different variables may demonstrate different relationships to chronological age at various points in the life span. To impose some order on these functioning states and the relationships among them, we will adopt Busse's (1969) proposal that there are two major forces driving the aging process: primary aging and secondary aging. Primary aging refers to normal aging processes, while secondary aging refers to disease-related states that happen to be age-correlated.

### Age as a Marker of Aging

The thrust in research on aging is to replace age in the Gompertz function with more differentiated markers of change than chronological age. Here, three ages are discussed: biological age, psychological age, and social age.

*Biological age* can be most clearly defined as an estimate of the present position of individuals with respect to their potential life span. Markers of biological age would be indicated by measurements of the functional capacities of the vital life-limiting organ systems. Biological age would be expected to be correlated with chronological age, but it would be independent of it to a certain degree as well, since biological age must also correlate with the length of life of the individual. A reliable measure of biological age should be able to predict the residual life span of the individual with a smaller error than prediction based on chronological age alone (see Birren, 1959).

*Psychological age* refers to the adaptive capacities of the individual. The focus here is on indexing both the achievements and the potentials of individuals. Do they have the capacity to adapt to changing environmental demands or to modify the environment to meet personal needs? Psychological age, like biological age, would be related primarily to the functioning state of the nervous system and the decision strategies of the individual. This form of aging would involve both cognitive processes and personality traits. In a hierarchy of indices of aging, psychological age would fall between biological and social age.

The third type of human age, *social age*, refers to acquired status and social habits. The interest is in finding markers that indicate how the individual fills the social roles and expectancies of persons in their age category in a particular culture and social group. Both biological and psychological characteristics of individuals influence the societal norms and values.

Clearly, these three kinds of aging overlap and are to a certain extent related to chronological age, but the new thought is that the underlying processes can be relatively autonomous, except at boundary conditions.

### Biological Markers of Primary Aging

There have been five areas of research in which significant biological markers of primary aging have been identified. These have focused on the pulmonary system, the cardiovascular system, blood constituents, sensory processes, and psychomotor processes. Of all of the variables identified, *vital capacity*, the breathing capacity of the lungs, appears to be the most useful index of health, vigor, and musculoskeletal functional capacity. A number of studies have included this variable in their investigations of functional age (Comfort, 1979; Dirken, 1972; Furukawa et al., 1975; Sinnott, 1981). In a recent report on biological markers, Kannel and Hubert (1982) discussed data from the Framingham study and noted that low vital capacity was a valid indicator of premature mortality from all causes of both cardiovascular and noncardiovascular mortality.

There are three variables that have been typically utilized to index aging of the cardiovascular system: oxygen uptake, systolic blood pressure, and left ventricular hypertrophy. Although maximum oxygen uptake has been included in many functional age studies, recent work indicates that normal elderly subjects without evidence of somatic or mental disease, functioning adequately in their communities, should have a normal cerebral blood flow and oxygen uptake up to the age of about 70 years (Birren et al., 1983). Systolic, diastolic, and mean arterial pressure all have been included in studies to measure blood pressure (Clark, 1960; Dirken, 1972; Furukawa et al., 1975; Harbin and Cunningham, 1978; Heron and Chown, 1967; Sinnott, 1981; Webster and Logie, 1976). An extensive literature base has grown solely around the analysis of the implications of various measures of blood pressure. It is not our intent to review this literature here. We will merely conclude that, on the basis of the previous work, systolic blood pressure appears to be the valid, reliable, and convenient index of cardiovascular aging. The third commonly used indicator is left ventricular hypertrophy, a thickening in the wall of the left ventrical and a relaxation in its ability to eject blood (Gerstenblith, 1982). However, Weisfeldt (as cited in Birren et al., 1983, p. 388) asserts that "degeneration in the cardiovascular system does not seem to be due to intrinsic age changes in heart muscle *per se*. The muscle of the pump remains functional with aging. Problems arise from reduced blood flow related to narrowed arteries caused by arteriosclerosis." Thus, in our discussions we will use only oxygen uptake and systolic blood pressure as indicators of cardiovascular aging.

The third source of biological markers of primary aging results from an analysis of blood constituents (i.e., serum cholesterol). Investigations into the Framingham data have indicated that serum cholesterol was not predictive of premature mortality (Kannel and Hubert, 1982). More detailed analyses, however, offer more predictive information. Cholesterol-rich, low-density lipoproteins appear to be indicative of accelerated arteriosclerosis, while high-density lipoprotein has been related to increased longevity and relative absence of arteriosclerosis (Kannel and Gordon, 1980).

The sensory systems that have demonstrated the greatest relation to normal aging processes have been the visual and auditory systems. Sekuler (1982) recommends the use of a multivariate composite including senile miosis (reduction in pupil size), contrast sensitivity, and presbyopia (reduced accommodation for near focus). Although in functional age studies visual acuity has often been tested as an indicator of aging, senile miosis probably accounts for some of the changes seen in visual acuity with age (Sekuler, 1982). In the case of auditory changes with age, pure tone thresholds and pitch discrimination have been used as reliable indices (Clark, 1960; Dirken, 1972; Heron and Chown, 1967). Pure tone thresholds, however, show less variability, and therefore may be more accurate measures of an auditory marker of aging (Corso, 1982).

The final source of biological markers of primary aging are psychomotor variables. Psychomotor variables can be considered a bridge between biological and psychological processes; they typically demonstrate age differences in performance. For example, Salthouse (1982) lists simple reaction time, choice reaction time, crossing off, copying digits, trail making, digit coding, letter substitution, and digit symbol substitution as psychomotor indices of physiological age. In functional age studies, dynamometry (hand-grip strength) is another commonly used indicator of psychomotor performance (Clark, 1960; Comfort, 1979; Dirken, 1972; Furukawa et al., 1975; Heron and Chown, 1967; Sinnott, 1981). The importance of this form of biological marker can be appreciated by considering its dependence on endurance and speed. The effects of these qualities are demonstrated in innumerable behavioral processes (see Birren, Woods, and Williams, 1979).

#### Psychological Markers of Primary Aging

Psychological markers of primary aging have been reviewed extensively in a number of sources (Birren et al., 1983; Birren and Schaie, 1977; Poon, 1980; Salthouse, 1982). In this section we will highlight only those processes which we think indicate the organization of normal aging. Five areas will be briefly outlined: learning, memory, reasoning and problem solving, speed of behavior, and personality.

Research on age differences and changes in learning has demonstrated that older individuals maintain their vocabulary and continue to add to their store of knowledge. In contrast, research using paired-associates learning tasks has found consistent and reliable age differences (Arenberg, 1977; Canestrari, 1968; Hulicka, 1967). Likewise, serial learning tasks demonstrate clear and significant age differences. One explanation for these results has been the episodic/semantic distinction of Tulving (1972), which implies that the older subjects are limited in their ability to learn new, abstract information unrelated to any previous knowledge.

Much of the memory research has been divided into studies on primary and secondary memory. According to Atkinson and Shiffrin (1971), primary memory refers to a set of processes that constitutes the control system for all thinking and remembering and acts to maintain registered material at the focus of attention (Craik, 1977). In contrast, secondary—or long-term—memory refers to the organism's ability to store information. The general conclusion is that there are few age differences in primary memory, however older individuals tend to perform less well than younger individuals in secondary memory tasks (Craik, 1977). In considering the organization of behavioral changes we recommend that both primary and secondary indices be included, as has been done in previous functional age studies (e.g., Dirken, 1972; Heron and Chown, 1967). Digit span tests are the most commonly used measures of primary memory. Research on secondary memory can be broken down into those studies that focus on acquisition and those that focus on retrieval. Immediate recall, delayed recall, and recognition tests have been implemented to measure these psychological processes.

Clear age differences have been seen in research on reasoning ability (Horn and Cattell, 1967; Schaie and Labouvie-Vief, 1974). However, work on problem solving is much more recent, and age-specific expectations have not been fully delineated. Most studies tend to indicate age differences in concept-formation problems (Giambra and Arenberg, 1980; Rabbitt, 1977), but recent work on skill-oriented problems demonstrates that not all aspects of problem solving may decline with age (Charness, 1981; Stafford, 1983). These forms of cognitive abilities appear to be especially important as indices of the ability to view situations in a variety of ways and, therefore, be adaptive.

Slowing in the speed of behavior with age is a well-established behavioral finding and it has been consistently demonstrated that this slowness has a diffuse or general quality governing its influence over other forms of behavior (Birren and Williams, 1980; Birren, et al., 1980). For example, Cunningham (1980) looked at the pervasiveness of slowness of behavior in the performance of complex aptitude tests. He found an increased number of intercorrelations among behavior speed and aptitude factors with age. Cunningham's result once again suggests an increasingly general impact of slowness in behavioral speed with age. Any number of tasks have been identified as indicators of this phenomenon, the most common being simple reaction time, choice reaction time, and digit symbol substitution. However, Botwinick (1977) professes some reservations regarding the digit symbol substitution test as a measure of pure speed.

Generally, the research on personality traits has demonstrated few changes with age (Neugarten, 1977). However, there are two major areas, expected to indicate degree of adjustment, that should be included in any consideration of the organization of behavioral changes with age. The first is defined by the construct of *rigidity,* or cautiousness. Although this construct has instigated a great deal of research in both the cognitive (Angleitner, 1974; Botwinick, 1973; Schaie and Parham, 1976) and personality domains (Angleitner, 1976; Riegel and Riegel, 1960), there still remains some question as to its usefulness. Angleitner (1976) questions the concept that rigidity is related directly to adjustment as a general measure of functional age. Based on findings from the Bonn Longitudinal study, neither a global rigidity score nor a *profile of rigidities* seems to be sufficient to portray the everyday adjustment of the elderly. The second major personality variable is *successful aging* or *life satisfaction.* According to Havighurst (1961), *life satisfaction* is a reliable indicator of adaptation to the conditions that exist in everyday life. Often it is the unchangeable nature of these situations which requires adaptational efforts. The assessment of *successful aging* assumes that "a person who is aging successfully feels satisfaction with his/her present and past life." Life satisfaction is in essence an indicator of the degree with which aged persons cope with their problems. The centrality of life satisfaction as a marker of age within a core of processes defining the aging of personality is not well established.

To the previous variables might be added measures of competence in daily living. These measures represent the extent to which an individual can meet the demands of the environment for independent living. As a group, the measure would represent an outcome of restriction induced by many subsystems and presumably would be a first attempt at operationalizing Yates' concept of the viability volume at the level of overt behavior.

### Social Markers of Primary Aging

In contrast to the work on psychological and biological age, research into the structure of social age has been limited to a study by Rose (1972). Rose defined *social age* as a changing composite of social life styles, attributes, and attitudes at various points in the life cycle. Initially, Rose selected 24 family, occupational, social class, and health variables from the Social Screening Questionnaire administered as part of the Normative Aging Study. Of the original 24 variables, 10 variables resulted in a multiple *R* of .60 with chronological age, and accounted for 35 percent of the variance. The 10 variables were represented by six occupational variables and four family variables. In general, social age was characterized by engagement in community and occupational roles. A man was viewed as socially old before his time if, relative to the respective age norms, he was more settled in his job, put off retirement, had a working wife, did not plan to relocate, and saw less of his relatives. Perceptions regarding future behavior seemed to emerge as the most important elements of social age. Taken together, these results led the investigator to conclude that present status, evaluated in terms of future expectations, was a powerful index of age-related status and that age-related self-evaluations could be made reliably by a respondent.

### Markers of Secondary Aging and Interactions of Lifestyle

As previously mentioned, secondary aging has referred to specific disease states. In the past, this form of aging has been considered somewhat independent of primary aging, which was viewed as due to *natural causes,* where the term *natural causes* represents a decreased ability in the aging organism to withstand any given insult in an increasingly narrow universe of survivable insults (Fries, 1984). That is, a model of population life expectancy based on biological constraints asserts that mortality and morbidity are not necessarily linked and that changing disease risks will not alter the underlying aging rate of the organism (Fries, 1980). Recent research, however, has demonstrated that changes once thought to be irreversible as aspects of primary aging are being shifted into the category of secondary aging. A further consequence is that the boundary between primary and secondary aging is shifting as specific disease states are identified (Siegler and Costa, 1983). This view appears commensurate with Manton's (1982) assertion that an accurate model of human mortality would require that morbidity and mortality be in equilibrium, dynamic, and multidimensional. This perspective of equilibrium would be consistent with the appearance of chronic disease as manifestations of basic age changes, the total prevalence of which would continue to increase due to the aging of human organisms. Thus, as Strehler (1975) warns, "there is no way to increase longevity in a hospitable environment except by improving the health state of all ages." With these thoughts in mind, we turn to a consideration of the most prevalent chronic diseases and some of their related lifestyle factors.

Although mortality due to cardiovascular disease has decreased by more than 30 percent in the past 30 years, cardiovascular disease remains the primary cause of death in the United States (Siegler and Costa, 1983). It is most commonly identified by essential hypertension, often culminating in a heart attack. It is a progressive disease, which has been related to high smoking levels and high intake of cholesterol, the severest effects of which do not usually become apparent until the sixties and seventies.

Malignant neoplasms represent the second major chronic disease possibly resulting in death. The distribution of cancers, however, is relatively more equal across the life cycle, with breast, rectal, colon, head, and neck cancers the most prevalent (Feldman, 1982). In the past 15 years cancer mortality has decreased for those less than 45 years of age, but shows an increase for individuals 45 years and older (Frei, 1982).

Cerebrovascular disease, diabetes, emphysema, and cirrhosis are all chronic diseases that demonstrate significant increases across the life span. Even if these chronic conditions do not lead directly to death, they may contribute to conditions that are lethal.

It would be an exaggeration to conclude that the victim is to blame for his disease. However, it would be a gross error not to consider the potential impact of certain lifestyle patterns in accounting for factors influencing chronic disease. The prominant lifestyle habits that have been identified include exercise, cigarette smoking, excessive alcohol consumption, obesity, and diet. Exercise, in particular aerobic exercise, is considered the key to several of the other risk factors. Aerobic exercise is believed to increase cardiac reserve, improve pulmonary reserve, increase arterial diameter, lower serum cholesterol, increase the high-density lipoproteins, aid in weight control, improve bowel function, add bone and muscle strength, tighten ligaments, improve glucose utilization, and decrease many measures of stress. Cigarette smoking has been tagged as the most harmful of the lifestyle habits. It has been linked with lung cancer and emphysema and serves as a risk factor to potentiate the occurrence of atherosclerosis and respiratory diseases. The major impact of excessive alcohol consumption is cirrhosis of the liver, but it is also associated with the majority of massive hemmorhages from the stomach and duodenum. Obesity increases the risk of Type II diabetes and is also related to high blood pressure, and elevated serum cholesterol and other lipids. Although it is believed that diet composition is an important factor in the maintenance of a healthy organism, diet is so highly correlated with other risk factors that it is difficult to determine if it has any direct causal influence on mortality.

One final set of lifestyle characteristics that very well may influence chronic disease and ultimately longevity is a group of variables that together can be termed socioeconomic status. Palmore (1982) showed that education, income, and occupation all had a significant predictive relationship to longevity. Birren and Bernstein (1978) indicated that socioeconomic status had its greatest impact on mortality during middle age, and a somewhat lesser effect at older ages. In addition, effects of low socioeconomic status on mortality appeared to be disease specific. The influence of socioeconomic variables may be extremely remote and indirect, but their impact should still be considered.

We have reviewed indices of primary aging, secondary aging, and certain interactive lifestyle variables. What has been lacking in the literature has been an integration of these empirical results. What is needed is a manner of depicting the relationships among these conditions and variables and how they change across the life span. It is our intention to offer such an approach to understanding changes in the organization of behavior with age, as well as determine if there are qualitatively different patterns of organization in a given population of individuals. The long-range goal is to determine the changing constellation of conditions and variables and to be able to predict how long an individual is going to live as compared to other individuals of the same chronological age.

## A GENERAL LONGITUDINAL MODEL: THE LISREL APPROACH

A general model for the analysis of longitudinal data has been developed by Jöreskog and Sörbom (Jöreskog, 1979; Jöreskog and Sörbom, 1977). This approach allows for the assessment of changes that occur between successive occasions, and attributes these changes to certain background characteristics and events existing or occurring before the first occasion, and/or to various treatments and developments that occur after the first occasion. The basis for the model is a system of LInear Structural RELations (LISREL) which describes the relationships among sets of observed and unobserved (or latent) variables. The LISREL model has gained support as a method of evaluating cause-and-effect relationships assumed to exist among correlated observed variables when experimental manipulation to achieve causal inference is not possible (see Duncan, 1975; Heise, 1975). In particular, structural equation models appear to be useful for analyzing longitudinal measurements when certain causal sequences are thought to be indicated by the time-structuring of the data (Schaie and Hertzog, 1982).

The focus becomes one of determining the stability of interindividual differences over time and, ultimately, of estimating the consistency of interindividual differences in intraindividual change. Changing patterns of interindividual differences between occasions can be approximated by examining the covariance matrix of the observations. The covariance elements among repeated measures of a variable reflect the extent to which the ordering of individuals about the population mean remains stable from one occasion to the next. Assuming that all tested individuals maintained fixed positions relative to the mean, the covariance between the measure at any two occasions would equal the product of the variances, and the correlation between the two measures would be 1.0. However, if the ordering of individuals about the mean changed from one time of measurement to the next so that there was a systematic increase in variability, interindividual variability in intraindividual change might be indicated. This could be because the increasing dispersion of individuals about the average developmental function might reflect divergence of individual developmental functions from the average developmental function (Schaie and Hertzog, 1982). Clearly, then, the autocorrelation of a given latent variable at a later measurement occasion would be less than the maximum 1.0.

The LISREL model brings together restricted-maximum-likelihood factor analysis and multivariate-structural regression equations (Jöreskog, 1973; Jöreskog and Sörbom, 1978). The factor analysis part of the model specifies how the latent variables or hypothetical constructs are measured in terms of observed variables, and is useful for estimating the measurement properties of the observed variables (reliabilities and validities). The model allows for errors of measurement, which are approximated by analyzing the regressions of latent variables on observed variables. The structural equations model specifies the causal relationships among latent variables. Errors are also allowed in this part of the model. In this case, the errors are referred to as regression residuals–that is, variance not accounted for by the constructs included in the model. These are not errors in measurement.

In the multiple-occasion longitudinal model, a set of variables is measured at several points in time. Time is measured from an arbitrary origin with an arbitrary unit of measurement, and the distance between measurement occasions need not be equal (Jöreskog, 1979). In addition, neither the number of variables nor the variables themselves are required to be the same at all occasions. At each occasion one or more sets of observed variables will estimate one or more endogenous dependent latent variables from one time of measurement to the next. It is important to note that there will be as many structural equations in this causal model as there are endogenous latent variables (Bentler, 1980).

Exogenous independent latent variables may also be included in the model. These variables will also be represented by observed, measurable variables. These variables, however, represent characteristics and conditions existing before the first occasion and assumed to influence the dependent variables. Again, these are assumed to be fallible measures and would be expected to correlate from one time of measurement to the next.

For a detailed specification of the LISREL equations, see Jöreskog, and Sorbom (1978); for a description of the pertinent concerns and procedures for implementing and evaluating the LISREL model, see Schaie and Hertzog (1982). Suffice it to say in the present text that the power of structural equations arises from the fact that the investigator is required to hypothesize a model specifying a causal sequence among the variables. In fact, it is recommended that competing models be specified at the outset (Bentler, 1980). Cliff (1983) has offered some valuable admonitions concerning the application of causal modeling methods. Such cautions should not be taken lightly since they have serious implications for subsequent possible scientific inferences. In particular, Cliff warns that "the possible influence of variables that are not observed must be considered; the well-known difference between correlation and causation is still relevant, even when variables are separated in time; the distinction between measured variables and the theoretical counterparts still exists; and ex post facto analyses are not tests of models."

With these concerns in mind, the final section of this paper will include a description of a LISREL model to test the organization of behavior with age. It is important to realize that this is an initial model. Future investigators should hypothesize competing models based on theoretical extrapolations. Following the description of the model, suggestions will be offered with regard to manageable ways to test this and related models.

## A MODEL OF THE ORGANIZATION OF BEHAVIOR WITH AGE

The proposed model is depicted in Figures 1-3 and 1-4.

As can be seen in the figures, the three endogenous latent variables at each occasion are *biological age, psychological age,* and *social age.* In this model the observed variables will be the same at each time of measurement. Biological age (BA) will be determined by the structure of the relationships of vital capacity, oxygen uptake, systolic blood pressure, low-density lipoprotein, high-density lipoprotein, multivariate visual index, pure tone threshold, dynamometry, and simple reaction time. Psychological age (PA) will be tapped by performance on a vocabulary measure, paired-associate learning task, serial learning task, digit span, delayed recall, recognition, problem solving, choice reaction time, life satisfaction, a measure of cautiousness, and a measure of competence in daily living. Finally, Social age (SA) will be determined by self-perceptions regarding fewer chances for occupational advancement, self-perceptions regarding remaining longer with a company, preference for later retirement, less expectation for relocation, and whether or not the spouse is employed.

The exogenous latent variables will be *socioeconomic status, lifestyle,* and *disease.* Socioeconomic status (SES) will be determined by amount of education, amount of income, and type of occupation. Lifestyle (LS) will be determined by amount of smoking, amount of alcohol consumption, amount of exercise, relative weight, and a measure of dietary habits. The last exogenous variable will be termed disease (DS); its structure will be determined by the presence of cardiovascular disease, malignant neoplasms, cerebrovascular disease, emphysema, and cirrhosis. Measures of these observable variables also will be taken at each time of measurement.

The ideal manner by which to test this model would be to secure a population of normal, healthy individuals in their mid-30s and follow them over the next six decades. That is, when the median age of the population was 35, 45, 55, 65, 75, 85, and 95, the participants would be measured on all the relevant observable variables.

Technically, an *occasion-specific* factor model in which the factor model would characterize the structure of a single occasion would be hypothesized and then extended or replicated to all or some subset of the longitudinal occasions to determine how well it fit the data. When testing the occasion-specific model, it would be expected that several of the observed variables would drop out, since they may be so highly correlated with some of the other measured variables.

It is immediately recognized that few investigators would be able to follow the ideal prescription for testing this model. Abbreviated versions of this model

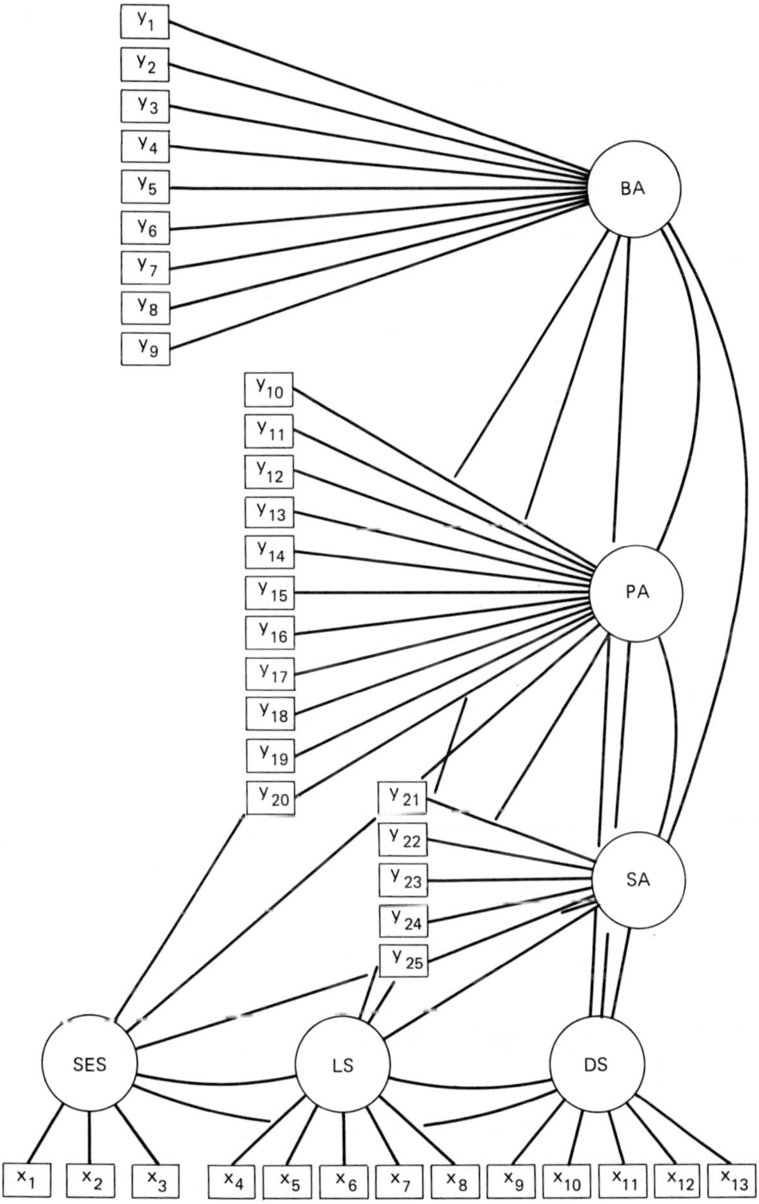


**FIGURE 1-3. Occasion-specific Model.**

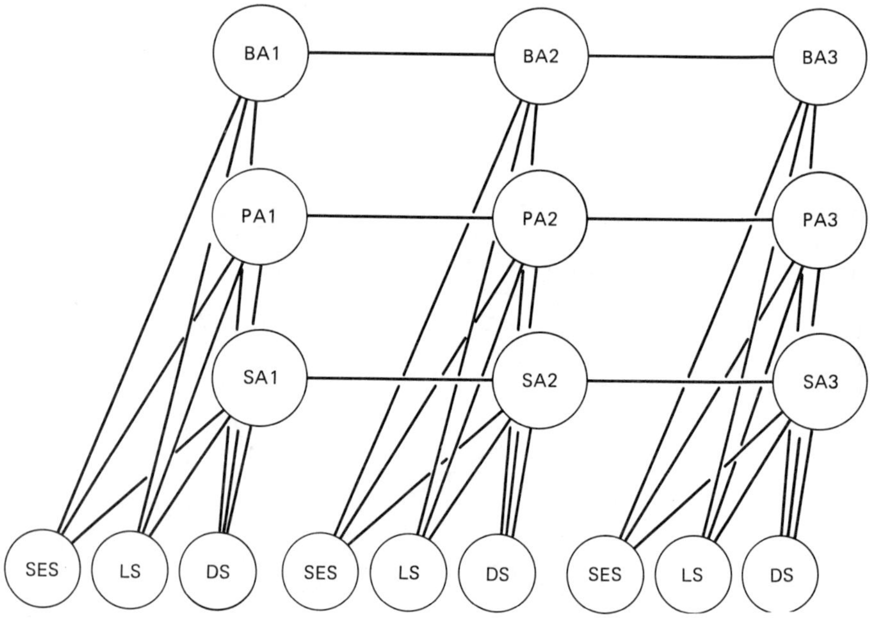


**FIGURE 1-4. Longitudinal Model: First Three Times of Measurement.**

could be tested by independent researchers, however. For example, Cunningham (1981) has already been working on his Cascade Model of Intelligence, which incorporates a subset of the currently discussed ideas. Other investigators could likewise test selected aspects of the basic model. Eventually, interrelationships among the latent variables could be determined reliably and then the predictability of the model over time could be considered. As an increased number of the participants die, model comparisons could be conducted to highlight the antecedent conditions for differential longevity. In addition, as individuals manifest various diseases, models could be hypothesized regarding the development of a specific disease. The relationship of particular age-related diseases to other exogenous variables and the impact of a disease on the endogenous variables can also be cast in hypothesis form and tested. Appendix A offers some initial suggestions for the sorts of relationships that might be expected.

## CONCLUSION

In review of the preceding discussion we would like to leave the reader with four general conclusions. First, we believe that the concept of functional age, as a representation of the structural organization of behavioral functioning with age, is alive and well and has much to offer the interested researcher. In contrast to some investigators (e.g., Costa and McCrae, 1980), we think that the concept of functional age has great potential for explaining the complex interrelationships that describe the aging process.

Second, we have suggested that biological, psychological, and social processes guiding behavioral functioning coexist relatively autonomously for much of the adult life span, adding to the great degree of interindividual variability observed. This variability, however, appears to decrease with age and is particularly apparent as certain boundary conditions in the three domains are reached and the biological, psychological, and social processes become more interrelated. The phenomenon of terminal decline may represent the epitome of this state, when all systems decompensate and dissipate to a chaotic state, and decreased interindividual variability results, because each organism is driven by a limited number of specific vital biological processes. A similar phenomenon has been suggested in the intelligence literature where intellectual abilities are relatively independent in the young adult; but, with age, the abilities become more interrelated—not necessarily that they differentiate, but they may become limited or more closely aligned with some underlying force—for example, the speed of information processing.

The third point we would like to make is that our initial, somewhat vague ideas about aging can begin to be captured and expressed in terms of a physical theoretic. It appears that we are no longer limited to single-variable, physiological descriptions of the living organism. In the long run this should allow for greater understanding of precisely how the organism ages and clues as to how strategic interventions might be made to minimize some of the undesirable accompaniments of advanced age.

Finally, as behavioral scientists, we now have a methodological approach available to us that allows us to propose and test theoretical notions about how behavior is organized over time. Considering the multitude of data indicating that aging is a multidimensional process, it is indeed a great benefit to have a multivariate technique available to test ideas that cannot be captured by the more controlled experimental design. We hope that others will follow up on at least some of the proposed ideas.

## APPENDIX A: EXPECTATIONS FOR RELATIONS AMONG LATENT VARIABLES OF THE MODEL

Assume: Seven times of measurement when the median age of the population is 35 (T1), 45 (T2), 55 (T3), 65 (T4), 75 (T5), 85 (T6), and 95 (T7).

1. Expect the correlation between socioeconomic status (SES) and lifestyle (LS) to increase from T1 to T3, then level off somewhat from T3 to T5 with a potential decrease following T5.
2. Expect the correlation between SES and DS to increase gradually from T1 to T4, after which time it should plateau.
3. Expect the correlation between LS and DS to increase gradually from T1 to T3, increase dramatically from T3 to T5, then to plateau.
4. Expect a moderate relation between SES and biological age (BA) to increase from T1 to T4 or T5, after which time the relation will decrease.
5. Expect a moderate relation between SES and psychological age (PA), but little change across times of measurement, unless there is a slight decrease.
6. Expect a large correlation between SES and social age (SA) with a potential decrease after T3, T4, or T5, depending on retirement views.
7. Expect a moderate correlation between LS and BA to be maintained from T1

to T4, with some decrease after T4, *or* a gradually increasing relation from T1 to T4, with a plateau after T4.

8. Expect a small or no correlation between LS and PA.
9. Expect a small correlation between LS and SA.
10. Expect a moderate correlation between DS and BA, which continues to increase across times of measurement.
11. The relation between DS and PA has not been determined at this point. If the work on hypertension is any indication, however, we would expect little relation until terminal decline sets in.
12. Expect a small correlation between DS and SA.
13. Expect fairly low correlations between BA and PA, BA and SA, PA and SA for T1, T2, and T3.
14. Expect the correlation between BA and SA to increase somewhat at T4 and T5, but the other two relations to stay about the same.
15. Expect the correlations between BA and PA, BA and SA, and PA and SA to increase dramatically at T6 and T7.
16. Expect BA at T1 to T3 to increase gradually in prediction with a dramatic increase from T4 to T6 and possibly a plateau from T6 to T7.
17. Expect PA to show little increase or decrease in prediction across the times of measurement.
18. Not sure what sort of expectation to have for SA.

## REFERENCES

ANDERSON, P. W. (1972). More is different. *Science, 177,* 393–396.

ANGLEITNER. A. (1974). Changes in personality of older people over a 5-year period of observation. *Gerontologia, 20,* 179–185.

ANGLEITNER, A. (1976). In H. Thomae (Ed.), *Patterns of aging.* New York: Karger, Basel.

ARENBERG, D., and ROBERTSON-TCHABO, E. A. (1977). Learning and aging. In J. E. Birren and K. W. Schaie (Eds.), *Handbook of the psychology of aging.* New York: Van Nostrand Reinhold Co.

ATKINSON, R. C., and SHIFFRIN, R. M. (1971). The control of short-term memory. *Scientific American, 224,* 82–90.

BELL, B., ROSE, C. L., and DAMON, A. (1972). The Normative Aging Study: An interdisciplinary and longitudinal study of health and aging. *Aging and Human Development, 3,* 5–17.

BENJAMIN, B., and HAYCOCKS, H. W. (1970). *The analysis of mortality and other actuarial statistics.* Cambridge: University Press.

BENTLER, P. M. (1980). Multivariate analysis with latent variables: Casual modeling. *Annual Review of Psychology, 31,* 332–456.

BERNARD, C. (1878). Lecons surles les phenomenes de la vie. Communs aux animaux et aux vegetaux. Vol. 1. Paris: Balliere.

BIRREN, J. E. (1959). Principles of research on aging. In J. E. Birren (Ed.), *Handbook of aging and the individual.* Chicago: University of Chicago Press.

BIRREN, J. E. (1969). The concept of functional age, theoretical background. *Human Development, 12,* 214–215.

BIRREN, J. E., and BERNSTEIN, L. (1978). Health and aging in our society Perspectives on mortality and the emergence of geriatrics. In *Transactions of the Association of Life Insurance Medical Directors of America, 62,* 135–152.

BIRREN, J. E., MUNNICHS, J. M. A., THOMAE, H., and MAROIS, M. (1983). *Aging: A challenge to science and society, 3, Behavioral sciences and conclusions.* Oxford: Oxford University Press.

BIRREN, J. E., and SCHAIE, K. W. (Eds.). (1977). *Handbook of the psychology of aging.* New York: Van Nostrand Reinhold Co.

BIRREN, J. E., and WILLIAMS, M. V. (1980). Cognitive issues: Speed of behavior. In L. W. Poon (Ed.), *Aging in the 1980's.* Washington, D.C.: American Psychological Association.

BIRREN, J. E., WOODS, A. M., and WILLIAMS, M. V. (1979). Speed of behavior as an indicator of age changes and the integrity of the nervous system. *Brain function in old age: Bayer-symposium VII.* New York: Springer-Verlag, 10–44.

BIRREN, J. E., WOODS, A. M., and WILLIAMS, M. V. (1980). Behavioral slowing with age: Causes, organization, and consequences. In L. W. Poon (Ed.), *Aging in the 1980's.* Washington, D.C.: American Psychological Association.

BOTWINICK, J. (1973). *Aging and behavior.* New York: Springer.

BOTWINICK, J. (1977). Intellectual abilities. In J. E. Birren and K. W. Schaie (Eds.), *Handbook of the psychology of aging.* New York: Van Nostrand Reinhold Co., 580–605.

BUSSE, E. W. (1969). Theories of aging. In E. W. Busse and E. Pfeiffer (Eds.), *Behavior and adaptation in later life.* Boston: Little Brown, 11–32.

CANNON, W. B. (1929). Organization for physiological homeostasis. *Physiological Review, 9,* 399–431.

CANSETRARI, R. E. (1968). Age changes in acquisition. In G. A. Talland (Ed.), *Human aging and behavior.* New York: Academic Press, 169–187.

CHARNESS, N. (1981). Aging and skilled problem solving. *Journal of Experimental Psychology: General, 110,* 21–38.

CLARK, J. W. (1960). Aging dimensions: A factorial analysis of individual differences with age of psychological and physiological measurements. *Journal of Gerontology, 15,* 183–187.

CLIFF, N. (1983). Some cautions concerning the application of causal modeling methods. *Multivariate Behavioral Research, 18,* 115–126.

COMFORT, A. (1956). *The biology of senescence.* London: Routledge and Kegan Paul.

COMFORT, A. (1979). *The biology of senescence.* New York: Elsevier.

CORSO, J. F. (April 1982). Auditory clinical markers of aging. In M. E. Reff and E. L. Schneider (Eds.), *Proceedings of a conference on nonlethal biological markers of physiological aging:* NIH Publication No. 82-2221.

COSTA, P. T., Jr., and McCRAE, R. R. (July 1980). Functional age: A conceptual and empirical critique. In S. G. Haynes and M. Geinleib (Eds.), *Second conference on the epidemiology of aging:* NIH Publication No. 80-969.

CRAIK, F. I. M. (1977). Age differences in human memory. In J. E. Birren and K. W. Schaie (Eds.), *Handbook of the psychology of aging.* New York: Van Nostrand Reinhold Co., 384–420.

CUNNINGHAM, W. R. (1980). Speed, age, and qualitative differences in cognitive functioning. In L. W. Poon (Ed.), *Aging in the 1980's.* Washington, D.C.: American Psychological Association.

CUNNINGHAM, W. R. (1981). The cascade model of intellectual functioning. Presentation at the Annual Meeting of the American Psychological Association, Los Angeles.

DIRKEN, J. M. (1972). *Functional age of industrial workers.* Groningen, Netherlands: Wolters-Noordhoff.

DUNCAN, O. D. (1975). *Introduction to structural equations models.* New York: Academic Press.

FELDMAN, F. (1982). Personal communication.

FOZARD, J. L., and THOMAS, J. C., Jr. (1975). Psychology of aging. In J. G. Howells (Ed.), *Modern perspectives in the psychiatry of old age.* New York: Bruner/Mazel, Inc., 107–169.

FREI, E. (1982). The national cancer chemotherapy program. *Science, 217,* 600–609.

FRIES, J. F. (1980). Aging, natural death, and the compression of morbidity. *New England Journal of Medicine, 303,* 130–135.

FRIES, J. F. (1984). The compression of morbidity: Miscellaneous comments about a theme. *The Gerontologist, 24,* 354–359.

FRIES, J. F., and CRAPO, L. M. (1981). *Vitality and aging.* San Francisco: W.H. Freeman and Company.

FURUKAWA, T., INOUE, N., KAJIYA, F., INADA, H., TAKASUGI, S., FUKUI, S., TAKEDA, H., and ABE, H. (1975). Assessment of biological age by multiple regression analysis. *Journal of Gerontology, 30,* 422–434.

GERSTENBLITH, G. (April 1982). Cardiovascular aging. In M. E. Reff and E. L. Schneider (Eds.), *Proceedings of a conference on nonlethal biological markers of physiological aging:* NIH Publication No. 82-2221.

GIAMBRA, L. M., and ARENBERG, D. (1980). Problem solving, concept learning, and aging. In L. W. Poon (Ed.), *Aging in the 1980's.* Washington, D.C.: American Psychological Association, 253–259.

GOMPERTZ, B. (1825). On the nature of the function expressive of the law of human morbidity; And on a new mode of determining the value of life contingencies. *Philosophical Transactions, 115,* 513.

HARBIN, T. J. and CUNNINGHAM, W. R. (1978). Influence of contextual variables on blood pressure in the elderly. *Experimental Aging Research, 4,* 521–534.

HAVIGHURST, R. J. (1961). The nature and values of meaningful free-time activity. In R. W. Kleemeir (Ed.), *Aging and leisure.* New York: Oxford University Press.

HEISE, D. R. (1967). *Casual analysis.* New York: John Wiley.

HERON, A., and CHOWN, S. (1967). *Age and function.* London: Churchill.

HORN, J. L., and CATTELL, R. B. (1967). Age differences in fluid and crystallized intelligence. *Acta Psychologia, 26,* 107–129.

HULICKA, I. M. (1967). Age differences in retention as a function of interference. *Journal of Gerontology, 22,* 180–184.

JALAVISTO, E., LINDQUIST, C., and MAKKONEN, T. (1964). Assessment of biological age III: Mental and neural factors in longevity. *Annales Academiae Scientiarum Fennicae, 106,* 3–20.

JÖRESKOG, K. G. (1973). A general method for estimating a linear structural-equations system. In A. S. Goldberger and O. D. Duncan (Eds.), *Structural equations models in the social sciences.* New York: Seminar Press.

JÖRESKOG, K. G. (1979). Statistical estimation of structural models in longitudinal developmental investigations. In J. R. Nesselroade and P. B. Baltes (Eds.), *Longitudinal research in the study of behavior and development.* New York: Academic Press.

JÖRESKOG, K. G., and SÖRBOM, D. (1977). Statistical models and methods for analysis of longitudinal data. In D. S. Aigner and A. S. Goldberger (Eds.), *Latent variables in socioeconomic models.* Amsterdam: North Holland Publ., 285–325.

JÖRESKOG, K. G., and SÖRBOM, D. (1978). *LISREL IV; Analysis of linear struc-*

*tural relationships by the method of maximum likelihood.* Chicago: National Educational Resources.

KANNEL, W. B., and GORDON, T. (1980). Cardiovascular risk factors in the aged: The Framingham study. In S. G. Haynes and M. Feinleig (Eds.), *Second Conference on the epidemiology of aging:* NIA Publication No. 80–969.

KANNEL, W. B., and HUBERT, H. (April 1982). Vital capacity as a biomarker of aging. In M. E. Reff and E. L. Schneider (Eds.), *Proceedings of a conference on nonlethal biological markers of physiological aging:* NIH Publication No. 82-2221.

MANTON, K. G. (1982). Changing concepts of morbidity and mortality in the elderly population. *Milbank Memorial Fund Quarterly, 60,* 183–224.

McFARLAND, R. A. (1943). The older worker in industry. *Harvard Business Review, Summer,* 505–520.

MEDAWAR, P. B. (1945). Size, shape, and age. In W. E. Le Gros Clark and P. B. Medawar (Eds.), *Essays on Growth and Form,* Oxford: Clarendon Press, 156–187.

MIDGLEY, M. (1978). *Beast and man: The roots of human nature.* New York: Cornell University Press.

MONOD, J. (1971). *Chance and necessity.* New York: A. A. Knopf.

NEUGARTEN, B. L. (1977). Personality and aging. In J. E. Birren and K. W. Schaie (Eds.), *Handbook of the psychology of aging.* New York: Van Nostrand Reinhold Co., 626–649.

PALMORE, E. B. (1982). Predictors of longevity difference: A 25 year follow–up. *The Gerontologist, 22,* 513–518.

POON, L. W. (1980). *Aging in the 1980's.* Washington, D.C.: American Psychological Association.

RABBITT, P. (1977). Changes in problem solving ability in old age. In J. E. Birren and K. W. Schaie (Eds.), *Handbook of the psychology of aging,* New York: Van Nostrand Reinhold Co., 606–625.

RIEGEL, K. F., and REIGEL, R. M. (1960). A study of changes of attitudes and interests during later years of life. *Vita Human, 3,* 177–206.

ROSE, C. L. (1972). The measurement of social age. *Aging and Human Development. 3,* 153–168.

SALTHOUSE, T. A. (April 1982). Psychomotor indices of physiological age. In M. E. Reff and E. L. Schneider (Eds.), *Proceedings of a conference on nonlethal biological markers on physiological aging:* NIH Publication No. 82-2221.

SALTHOUSE, T. A. (1982). *Adult cognition: An experimental psychology of human aging.* New York: Springer-Verlag.

SCHAIE, K. W., and HERTZOG, C. (1982). Longitudinal methods. In B. B. Wolman (Ed.) *Handbook of developmental psychology.* Englewood Cliffs, NJ: Prentice-Hall, Inc.

SCHAIE, K. W., and LABOUVIE-VIEF, G. (1974). Generational versus ontogenetic components of change in adult cognitive behavior: A fourteen-year cross-sequential study. *Developmental Psychology, 10,* 305–320.

SCHAIE, K. W., and PARHAM, I. A. (1976). Stability of adult personality: Fact or fable? *Journal of Personality and Social Psychology, 34,* 146–158.

SEKULER, R. (April 1982). Vision as a source of simple and reliable markers of aging. In M. E. Reff and E. L. Schneider (Eds.), *Proceedings of a conference on nonlethal biological markers of physiological aging:* NIH Publication No. 82-2221.

SIEGLER, I., and COSTA, P. (1985). Health behavior relationships. In J. E. Birren and K. W. Schaie (Eds.), *Handbook of the psychology of aging.* New York: Van Nostrand Reinhold Co.

SINNOTT, J. (1981). Presentation at the Annual Meeting of the Gerontological Society, Toronto.

STAFFORD, J. L. (1983). Skilled problem solving ability and the effects of practice in young and elderly adults. University of Southern California, DAI 44 (9): 2917 B.

STREHLER, B. L. (1975). Implications of aging research for society. *Proceedings of the 58th annual meeting of federation of American societies for experimental biology, 34,* 5–8.

STREHLER, B. L. (1977). *Time, cells, and aging.* New York: Academic Press.

STREHLER, B. L., and MILDVAN, A. S. (1960). General theory of mortality and aging. *Science, 132,* 14–21.

TULVING, E. (1972). Episodic and semantic memory. In E. Tulving and W. Donaldson (Eds.), *Organization of memory.* New York: Academic Press, 381–403.

WEBSTER, I. W., and LOGIE, A. R. (1976). A relationship between functional age and health status in female subjects. *Journal of Gerontology, 31,* 546–550.

YATES, F. E. (1982a). Outline of a physical theory of physiological systems. *Canadian Journal of Physiology and Pharmacology, 60,* 217–248.

YATES, F. E. (1982b). Senescence from the aspect of physical stability. Presented at the Research Symposium on Aging: Session 3, "Metaphors in the Study of Cells and Cellular Systems." University of British Columbia, June 19–22.

YATES, F. E., MARSH, D. J., and IBERALL, A. S. (1972). Integration of the whole organism: A foundation for a theoretical biology. In J. A. Behnke (Ed.), *Challenging biological problems: Directions towards their solutions.* New York: Oxford University Press, Inc.

# 2

# TOWARD ASSESSING HEALTH AND FUNCTIONAL CAPACITY FOR POLICY DEVELOPMENT ON WORK-LIFE EXTENSION

Deborah D. Newquist

## INTRODUCTION

Retirement-age practices are on the threshold of change. Whereas over the past several decades we have witnessed a steady decline in labor force participation by older people, concerted efforts are now being directed toward reversing this trend. These efforts can be seen in several arenas. Legislation has been enacted to raise the Social Security retirement age. Age criteria in personnel policies are being challenged, including challenges to BFOQs (Bona Fide Occupational Qualifications) through age discrimination suits. The total elimination of mandatory retirement is being promoted. In addition, both the public and private sectors have undertaken steps to expand employment opportunities for older workers; and finally, older people themselves express interest in continued labor force participation, whether because of financial need or other reasons (Robinson and Sanford, 1982). Taken as a whole, these trends point to a growing movement to extend the work life for older persons willing and able to work. *Work-life extension* is a term used to describe these trends; it refers to increasing the labor force participation of older adults through delayed retirements or labor force reentry by retirees.

A recurrent theme raised in discussions of work-life extension is that of the health of the older population. Policy makers are concerned about the health implications of extended work life as they relate to issues of labor supply, productivity, employee health costs, and health maintenance. Certainly health is only one of several variables which affect the behavior of workers; nevertheless, it is a major concern of government leaders (see, for example, U.S. House of Representatives, 1983).

Questions about the functional capacity of older persons are particularly at issue in discussions of work-life extension. If work-life extension is directed toward those who are "willing and able" to work, policy and practice may depend on determining whether or not people are able to work. Assessments of work capacity or disability are traditionally conducted on an individual basis by health and vocational specialists (Gilbert and Peters, 1983; Keith, 1984). They are micro-level assessments. The question for policy makers is how to assess the working capacity of the older population. This constitutes a macro-level assessment and requires analysis of survey data rather than clinical data.

The purpose of this chapter is to discuss some of the issues involved in analyzing survey data in order to assess health and functional capacity among the older population. This chapter offers something of a "shoppers' guide" for government decision makers and their staff, for researchers, and for business leaders who participate in the various debates surrounding work-life extension. It provides a set of considerations to take into account when making or evaluating statements about health and work capacity or disability among the older population.

## HOW IS HEALTH MEASURED?

It is only recently that the health status of the population has been a subject of extensive study. Historically, the health of the population was assessed by means of mortality rates alone. The Survey of Sickness, initiated in 1943 in the United Kingdom and conducted annually until 1952, was the first attempt ever to gather annual morbidity data representative of a national population (Sullivan, 1966). In the United States, it was not until July 1957 that a similar endeavor was undertaken with the launching of the Health Interview Survey. The Health Interview Survey, the Health Examination Survey launched full-scale in April 1961, and the Health Records Survey inaugurated in April 1962, form the tri-part National Health Survey authorized by Congress in the National Health Survey Act of 1956. Prior to the passage of this act and the inauguration of the National Health Survey, information about morbidity in the American population was limited to *ad hoc* reports derived from specialized, localized health studies; physicians' reports of communicable diseases required by state laws; and various reports from hospitals, insurance companies, and other health organizations. No ongoing, uniform, valid measure of the nation's health level, beyond that revealed by mortality statistics, was available (National Center for Health Statistics, 1963).

Much progress has since been made in the conceptualization and measurement of the complex phenomenon we call health. Today, health measures are used as direct and indirect indicators of health status. An extensive literature discusses various health concepts and measurement issues (Caplan, Englehardt, and McCartney, 1981; Murnaghan, 1981; Wilson and Drury, 1984). Health measures include *health indicators,* defined as statistics which summarize a larger body of data; and *indices,* which are more complex, multidimensional measures or scales. Indices are often composed of a number of health indicators (Murnaghan, 1981).

The most commonly used health indicators measure poor health rather than good health—that is, they document the presence of disease or disability, or the occurrence of death. In regard to work-life extension, this means that standard health indicators are more able to measure *disability* than functional capacity. Disability can be assessed by an individual's behavior, by observed performance or nonperformance. Functional capacity, on the other hand, is more difficult to assess, and its evaluation requires technical skill (Murnaghan, 1981).

*Mortality-based indicators* are probably the most commonly used indirect measures of health (Wilson and Drury, 1984). Death rates, infant mortality rates, and life expectancy have historically been used to assess the health of the population. The assumption underlying the use of these measures is that mortality mirrors morbidity and disability levels, and thus indicates health as well.

Arguments concerning the working capacity of the older population are replete with references to mortality statistics. A few examples will illustrate.

The National Commission on Social Security (1981), when discussing proposals to raise the retirement age, stated:

> Although 65 may have been the most acceptable age for retirement in 1935, it cannot be assumed that it will be the most appropriate age for normal retirement in the year 2000. . . . the commission anticipates that increased longevity will be accompanied by a corresponding increase in active life (124–126).

The Work in America Institute (1980, page 5) goes even further, extrapolating from mortality rates to potential work life:

> It should be emphasized that today's older workers differ markedly from those of previous decades: they are healthier so that age 50 today corresponds to age 40 or 45 in 1970. . . . With the marked decline in death rates, the potential length of productive working life has increased greatly.

Lastly, mortality rates and their appropriate use and meaning are central topics in the Kingson-Myers debate on the health of very early retirees and the eligibility criteria for Social Security disability. Kingson asserts that the eligibility criteria should be liberalized because some early retirees are as unhealthy as disability beneficiaries, yet do not receive benefits. He bases his assessment of their health levels on their mortality rates, degree of functional limitation, and duration of reported work limitations (Kingson, 1981, 1982, 1983). Myers has challenged Kingson's mortality analysis and believes that nonbeneficiaries do not have higher mortality rates than beneficiaries, which is what Kingson found (Myers, 1982, 1983).

Recently, the relationship between mortality and morbidity has come under scrutiny (Butler, 1983; Feldman, 1983; Fries, 1980; 1984; Gruenberg, 1977; Manton, 1982; Myers and Manton, 1984; Verbrugge, 1983). The results are not yet in, but there is growing sensitivity to the fact that mortality rates are only indirect indicators of health, particularly for those persons with chronic conditions.

The most common direct measures of health are indicators that assess the *incidence* or *prevalence* of disease (Wilson and Drury, 1984). These measures focus on the occurrence of *specific* diseases, rather than on how frequently a person is sick. Often chronic diseases are reported separately from acute diseases. Included within the category of chronic diseases are impairments such as visual or hearing deficits.

Other health indicators measure *disability,* which refers to the restriction of a person's activity because of illness or impairment (Murnaghan, 1981). Disability can be either short-term or long-term. Short-term disability is often measured by *event-type* indicators such as bed days, work-loss days, school-loss days, or days when a person's usual activity is restricted because of illness or injury (Wilson and Drury, 1984). Short-term disabilities involve *interruptions* in a person's normal routine, in contrast to long-term disabilities, which necessitate *permanent alterations in that routine.*

Long-term disability is often measured in reference to a person's *normal* activities. The National Center for Health Statistics' measure of chronic activity limitation is an example. There, limitation of activity is assessed in reference to normative life activities for different age groups. Thus children are assessed according to their ability to play or attend school, and adults according to their ability to work or do housework.

Other measures assessing capacity for "essential" activities have been developed in an effort to provide a more objective, stable referent for evaluating long-term disability. Indicators measuring *activities of daily living* (such as independence in eating, dressing, or bathing) or functional capacity (such as ability to stand for long periods of time, or lift ten pounds) are examples (see Haber, 1977; Katz and Akpom, 1976; Posner, 1981). Functional capacity measures typically place a heavy emphasis on *physical* functioning. They do not usually include indicators of social or mental functioning. Furthermore, pain, distress, or prognosis are rarely incorporated directly in disability measures (Murnaghan, 1981).

Yet another measure of long-term disability focuses on mobility limitations. These assess whether or not a person is bedridden, confined to the house, or needs assistance in getting around inside or outside the house.

*Self-assessed health status* is another indicator used in several surveys. Typically this indicator asks the respondent, "Would you say that your health in general is excellent, very good, good, fair or poor?" (Wilson and Drury, 1984, page 88). There has been much discussion in the literature about the meaning and reliability of self-reported health (La Rue, Bank, Jarvik, and Hetland, 1979; Maddox and Douglass, 1973; McCrae, Bartone, and Costa, 1976; Tissue, 1972; Wolinsky, Coe, Miller, and Prendergast, 1984). Some researchers consider it to be a good indicator of health (Kaplan and Camacho, 1983; La Rue, et al., 1979; Mossey and Shapiro, 1982), while others feel it needs to be augmented (Wolinsky, et al., 1984). Overall, however, self-rated health is considered a reasonably reliable measure of global health.

Finally, *utilization of medical care* and *indicators of risk factors for disease* are two other measurement areas included in most comprehensive discussions of health status. Specific indicators in the former category include the average number of doctor visits per person per year; the average number of short-stay hospital days in the past year; and the average number of short-stay hospital episodes per person per year. In the latter category, indicators include health practices regarding cigarettes, exercise, and nutrition (Wilson and Drury, 1984).

## WHAT ASPECTS OF HEALTH ARE CENTRAL WHEN MEASURING DISABILITY?

Before choosing among the available health measures, it is important to know exactly what it is you want to measure. An understanding of the logic of health and disability is important here because it will guide the choice of health measures.

Health may be defined in several ways. The World Health Organization (1958) has offered a global definition: "Health is a state of complete physical, mental, and social well-being, and not merely the absence of diseases and infirmity." Sigerist (1971) defined health as "not simply the absence of disease: it is something positive, a joyful attitude toward life; and a cheerful acceptance of the responsibilities that life puts on the individual" (100). In discussing health in old age, Atchley (1980) employs the following definition: "It refers not merely to the absence of disease or disability, but also to more positive things, such as mental, physical, and social well-being. It is more useful to look at health as a continuum" (108). This continuum places good health opposite poor health and the absence of disease or impairment opposite death due to illness (Figure 2-1). In contrast to Atchley, Murnaghan (1981) states: "Healthfulness–or the lack of it–is not a unidimensional state of being or continuum from some ideal state of perfect health to the point of death. The method used to describe and measure ill health depends on the cultural background, point of view, understanding, and purposes of the observer, and on the conditions under which observations are made" (329). For Murnaghan, then, health is a relative concept.

Two fundamental criteria of good health in all these definitions (with the exception of Murnaghan's) are the absence of disease and, secondarily, the absence of disability or impairment. Furthermore, these definitions go on to assert that good health is *more* than the mere absence of disease and disability. Viewing health in this way is characteristic of *positive health* definitions according to Sullivan (1966), who states: "Positive health . . . generally implies existence of identifiable levels of health among those free of apparent morbidity" (2).

Positive health is a goal of the World Health Organization (Murnaghan, 1981). For health planning purposes this is appropriate. For employment planning, however, this definition of health is too restrictive. If applied to the older population, it would lead to the conclusion that most older people are unhealthy, since the majority have some form of chronic condition. More appropriate for employment purposes would be a functional definition of health which recognizes the loose relationship that can exist between disease, sickness, impairment, and functioning.

Illnesses involve different dimensions of experience. As described by Kleinman, Eisenberg, and Good (1978), disease and sickness are ontologically distinct phenomena. A *disease* is a medical concept, a label which identifies a set of pathological somatic processes. *Sickness,* on the other hand, is the individual's subjective experience of feeling unwell. While the experience of sickness may closely track a disease state, it is not axiomatic that this be so. The hypertension experience is a case in point. An individual may be diagnosed as hypertensive and yet feel no symptoms, signs, or other manifestations of ill health. Similarly, a cancerous growth may develop for some time unbeknownst to the afflicted in-

**FIGURE 2–1. Stages of the Health Continuum. Source: Atchley, 1980:109**

| **Good Health** | | | | | | | **Poor Health** |
|---|---|---|---|---|---|---|---|
| Absence of disease or impairment | Presence of a condition | Seeks treatment | Restricted activity | Restricted in major activity | Unable to engage in major activity | Institutionalized | Death |

dividual. These asymptomatic individuals will not feel sick, and yet each has a disease.

Going beyond disease and sickness distinctions, Nagi breaks out the concepts of impairment and disability. He first identifies pathology as a state "associated with mobilization of the body's defenses and coping mechanisms, and [which] may be the result of infection, metabolic imbalances, degenerative disease processes, traumatic injuries, or other etiology." He distinguishes pathology from *impairment,* which he defines as "a physiological or anatomical loss or other abnormality, or both," and further, he distinguishes these from sickness, which he identifies as "forms of behavior that evolve when the presence of pathology is perceived." Finally, he differentiates these concepts from *disability,* which he defines as "a pattern of behavior that evolves when impairments impose limitations upon the individual's capacities and levels of functioning." As stressed by Nagi, *disability* is a social behavior and not all pathologies, impairments, or sicknesses result in disabilities (Nagi, 1969, 9–12).

These distinctions are particularly important in regard to chronic disease. With acute conditions, the dimensions of disease, sickness, and disability are usually experienced, and frequently they are experienced simultaneously. With chronic diseases this is often not the case.

An example will illustrate how these relationships operate differently with acute versus chronic conditions. Person A has pneumonia, an acute condition. That person has an objective medical condition (disease), verifiable through a diagnostic examination. That person will also *feel* sick. He or she may have a temperature, feel weak, or have other symptoms. Thus the person will experience a state of sickness concomitant with the state of disease. Finally, the person will usually respond to pneumonia by going to bed or reducing his or her usual activities. Hence the person will evidence functional disability as a result of the pneumonia. Figure 2-2 illustrates this set of relationships.

**FIGURE 2-2. Acute Medical Conditions and the Experience of Disease, Illness, and Disability. (Note: Figure not drawn to scale to represent proportionate relationships.)**

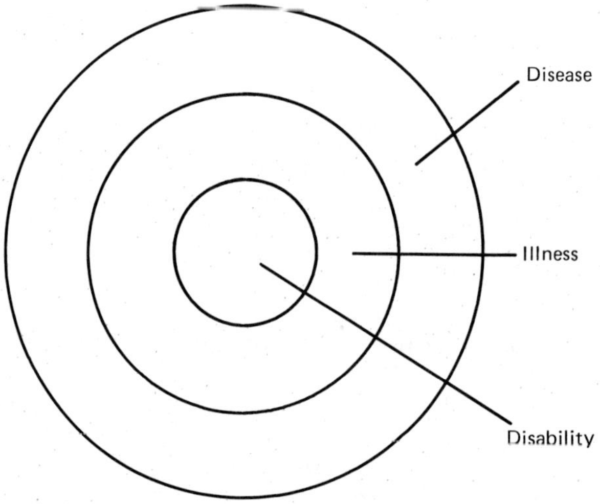

Now consider someone who has a chronic condition. Person B has arthritis, a chronic disease. That person may or may not feel sick or unwell as a result of the arthritis. Depending on the seriousness of the disease, its location, and its pattern of periodicity, the person will experience pain frequently, intermittantly, or not at all. Thus the person need not experience a state of sickness concomitant with the presence of the disease. Similarly, the person's response to the disease may vary: The person may have the disease, yet feel no pain, and function normally; or the person may feel pain and continue to function; or the person may feel pain and reduce functioning. Thus, with the chronic condition, disease, illness, and disability may be loosely related and are not necessarily concomitant experiences (see Figure 2-3).

The difference between acute and chronic illnesses in this regard is one of degree. Certainly not all people who experience a cold, for instance, respond by going to bed. Many go to work and continue to function normally, although they may not feel well in the process. The experience of disease, sickness, and disability varies depending upon the particular condition, the individual's coping style, and other factors. The point is that these experiences are distinct and need not always occur together. Moreover, this is particularly true with chronic conditions.

Mortality risk may also differ dramatically between chronic and acute conditions. This fact underlies the recent scrutiny of the relationship between mortality, morbidity, and disability noted earlier.

The distinctions between disease, sickness, impairment, and disability are important in regard to work-life extension because they highlight the fact that disability or functional capacity is not directly tied to the presence of a disease or impairment, or to an experience of sickness. Thus, *health measures that focus only on the presence of specific diseases are not the most appropriate indicators for assessing functional capacity.* As stated by Haber (1977): "It is apparent from a number of studies that evaluation of disability based on anatomical loss or medical impairment alone is clearly inadequate" (1).

Closer examination of the relationship between mortality, morbidity, and disability is also important because it illuminates the fact that functional disability

**FIGURE 2-3. Chronic Medical Conditions and the Experience of Disease, Illness, and Disability. (Note: Figure not drawn to scale to represent proportion of events falling within each category.)**

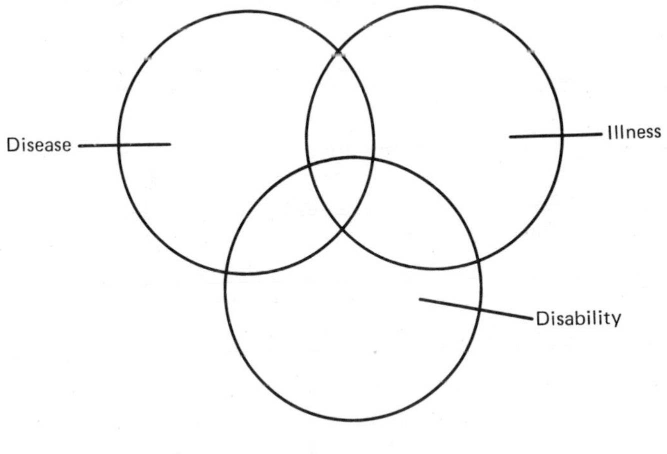

need not be associated with death. Someone can be disabled for years but not be at risk of dying because of his or her condition. On the other hand, someone can function at a maximal level and yet die suddenly of a myocardial infarction.

The Kingson-Myers debate could benefit by closer attention to these distinctions. For example, Myers (1983) thinks it is "impossible" that Social Security Disability (SSDI) nonbeneficiaries could have higher mortality than beneficiaries, which is what Kingson asserts. Yet a close look at the SSDI guidelines shows that heavy emphasis is accorded to *functional* limitations (Francis, 1983; Gilbert and Peters, 1983; Social Security Administration, 1980). The regulations state:

> To receive disability benefits, a person must have a severe impairment. We deny a disability if we find that a person does not have a severe impairment. . . . An impairment is not severe if it does not significantly limit your physical or mental abilities to do basic work activities. . . . When we talk about basic work activities, we mean the abilities and aptitudes necessary to do most jobs. Examples of these include—(1) Physical functions such as walking, standing, sitting, lifting, pushing, pulling, reaching, carrying or handling; (2) Capacities for seeing, hearing, and speaking; (3) Understanding, carrying out, and remembering simple instructions; (4) Use of judgement; (5) Responding appropriately to supervision, co-workers and usual work situations; and (6) Dealing with changes in a routine work setting (Social Security Administration, 1980: 55566, 55588).

The SSDI regulations do grant a disability if a person has a condition that is severe enough to result in death. A list of these conditions and their pathological criteria is provided in the regulations. That list is referred to as "The Listings." It is assumed that any condition of such severity automatically leads to disabilty.

It is possible, however, for someone to be denied disability and yet have a disease severe enough to cause early death. The SSDI regulations are very restrictive in their definition of severe pathology. Furthermore, the disability application process is sequenced so that severe impairment must be proven *before* disease severity is considered. To quote the regulations again: "We follow a set order to determine whether you are disabled. We review any current work activity, the severity of your impairment(s), your residual functional capacity and your age, education, and work experience. If we can find that you are disabled or not disabled at any point in the review, we do not review further" (Social Security Administration, 1980: 55588). Francis (1983) explains that Social Security provides a sequential process for making disability determinations. That process involves five fundamental questions. If the claimant does not meet the criteria at any one of the steps in the process, he or she is denied disability and the remainder of the steps are not followed. The five questions are:

1. Is the worker engaged in Substantial Gainful Activity (SGA)?
2. Does the worker have a severe impairment?
3. Does the impairment meet The Listings?
4. Does the impairment prevent past relevant work?
5. Does the impairment prevent other work (Francis, 1983, Chap. 11)?

It is possible for a person to have a severe disease and yet not experience a severe impairment as an immediate result of the disease. Since the definition of severe impairment stresses physical functioning, this is even more possible. For example, a person could have severe heart disease and yet be able to lift a ten-pound weight or perform some other physical tasks. Such a person would be denied disability on the basis that he or she did not have a severe impairment. The denial would be made even before questions were raised about the severity of the disease. That same person could die shortly thereafter from the disease. The person could die before an appeal was made (this occurred in an actual case).

To the extent that Social Security stresses functional limitations over pathology, and also adheres to very restrictive pathology criteria, it is entirely possible for nonbeneficiaries to have higher mortality rates than beneficiaries. Thus Myers's view that such a finding is "impossible" is not supported.

Kingson's (1981) argument that nonbeneficiaries are as unhealthy as beneficiaries could also benefit from a greater consideration of disease, sickness, disability distinctions.[1] Kingson based his conclusion on three health measures: mortality, degree of functional limitation, and duration of reported work limitation. He describes his measure of functional limitation as "constructed from detailed questions concerning *physical limitations* and their effect on the ability to work" (Kingson, 1981, 16, emphasis added). He does not address the fact that if the groups were measured on another dimension–sickness–they might not be as similar. In other words, his measures of health may not fully tap the health dimensions relevant in the etiology of work disability. The Social Security Disability program considers signs of sickness (e.g., pain, vertigo, numbness, work absences) when making disability evaluations (Gilbert and Peters, 1983). Thus it is possible that beneficiaries are actually less healthy than nonbeneficiaries, but that Kingson's measures did not tap all the relevant dimensions and so would not detect this. Whether Kingson's unhealthy retirees are *unhealthy enough* to be granted benefits is another issue. That issue centers on the focus and stringency of SSDI eligibility criteria.

There are various pathways to disability. Some involve the direct impact of disease on physical functioning and, hence, work capacity. Arthritis could be an example. In other cases, frequent experiences of sickness could impair work ability. Here physical limitations would only be indirectly involved, if at all. In still other cases, such as blindness, an impairment could disable and yet not result in abnormal sickness episodes or even physical limitations such as ability to sit or stand for long periods of time, or ability to lift ten or twenty pounds. Finally, cognitive and psychological problems, such as dementia or alcoholism, can be disabling and yet not physically limiting.

Imminently life-threatening diseases are also grounds for disability benefits in some programs such as Social Security. These illnesses may not always bring physical limitations or even sickness episodes in their early stages. Ultimately, however, they are disabling and lethal.

## WHAT MEASURES BEST ASSESS DISABILITY?

As discussed earlier, common health indicators include those that measure mortality; the incidence or prevalence of disease or impairment; the prevalence of long-term disability and functional limitations; the incidence of short-term disability

[1] Kingson does acknowledge these distinctions (1982), but his analysis does not incorporate them conceptually.

such as bed days or work-loss days; and self-assessed health status. Indicators of the utilization of medical care and of risk factors for disease have also been used to examine the health of the population.

Self-reported statements of work disability or inability to perform one's major activity are one form of indicator that can be used by policy makers. However, these measures have been criticized by some as unreliable (Chirikos and Nestel, 1981; Myers, 1982). Others disagree, though, and remain convinced that self-reported health provides useful information because it correlates significantly with subsequent mortality (Andrisani, 1977).

In an attempt to provide more objective ratings, some researchers in this area use measures which address specific functional limitations, such as ability to bend, reach, or lift (Berkowitz, 1978; Chirikos and Nestel, 1981; Lambrinos, 1981). These measures have four major drawbacks: (1) they have not been routinely incorporated in national surveys of the general population (Wilson and Drury, 1984); (2) they rarely incorporate direct measures of sickness (Murnaghan, 1981); (3) they often fail to measure unstable or episodic limitations; and (4) they frequently do not adequately assess stamina or work hardiness. Since disability can evolve from these experiences, and yet not result in specific physical limitations, these measures can underestimate disability levels.

Further research is needed to develop an index of disability which incorporates measures of sickness, impairment, pathology, and physical and mental limitations. This index would avoid some problems of subjectivity and questionable reliability associated with self-reported disability measures.

In the interim, policy makers can look to self-reports of disability such as those used in the Health Interview Survey (HIS) of the National Center for Health Statistics, and the disability surveys conducted by the Social Security Administration. They can augment the data from that indicator if they choose by looking at (1) the frequency of work-loss days for the employed population, and bed days or restricted activity days for the total population; (2) the prevalence of specific impairments which they would assume cause work disabilities, such as blindness or severe paralysis; and (3) the prevalence of specific chronic diseases which are known to be highly disabling, such as neurological disorders. These data are available from the National Center for Health Statistics. They could be used to construct a current disability profile of the population similar to that undertaken by Nagi (1976) and Sullivan (1971) but based on different analytical criteria.

## HEALTH STANDARDS AND EVALUATION PERSPECTIVES

Aside from life-over-death issues, health is a relative concept whose meaning is derived through a consideration of the standard against which it is assessed and the perspective from which it is viewed. The armed forces, for example, reject as "unhealthy" millions of men who go on to lead normal, productive lives. Are these men truly unhealthy? Or rather, are they not healthy enough to meet the standards set by the military establishment, standards which presumably are tied to particular role-performance requirements?

How healthy must a person be in order to participate in the economic pursuits of our society? How healthy must that person be to perform at acceptable levels? How is that level of health to be assessed?

For analytical purposes, health may be viewed from three perspectives: the particularist, the comparative, and the idealist. The *particularist* focus concerns a group's experience of sickness or well-being as evaluated in comparison to that group's health history. The perspective from which health is assessed is the individual group's: Does the group evidence more sickness or more disease than it did in the past?

This might be thought of as the ipsative longitudinal approach to health assessment. It assumes that repeated evaluations are taken on the same group over time. (The group can be an age cohort or the same cohort followed through time.) The approach is sensitive to *changes* in health status. Poor health would mean declining health, regardless of where the group started healthwise or how it compared to other groups on the assessment outcome.

From an employment point of view, when concerns shift to issues of health maintenance or performance decline, the particularist perspective would be most useful for evaluating older persons. It could also be used in assessing the health of age cohorts over time.

The second health perspective is the *comparative.* This perspective is concerned with the level of a group's health relative to other groups' health at a fixed point in time: Is the group sick more or less often than other groups in the population?

From this perspective, it matters little whether the group's health has declined or improved, or whether it is basically bad or good. Poorer health using this model would describe groups who experience significantly greater numbers of health problems, significantly more serious health problems, or significantly more of certain types of health problems than other groups in the population. This relative approach to health is sensitive only to differences between groups or individuals.

The comparative perspective is very common in survey research on the health status of population groups. It is also often used by policy analysts who raise questions about the health of older workers. They ask how the health of older workers compares to that of younger workers.

But what standards are they to use in assessing these health differences? What health scores will be considered good or bad? When compared, both groups could evidence similar health profiles; the health of older persons could be the same as that of younger persons. But this finding would not tell policy makers if that health level is acceptable. It only tells them that the groups are the same. A standard for distinguishing good health from bad health must be applied to these findings if they are to be useful.

A critical characteristic of both the particularist and the comparative health perspectives is that they are *standard free.* Each user must determine which measure and standards to use with these comparative equations, which factors are meaningful or have validity for the user's particular needs.

The *idealist* health perspective, the third type of assessment focus, measures health against a fixed standard. The standard often used with this perspective is that of positive health, which, as described earlier, specifies that individuals be more than free of disease and impairment in order to be considered healthy. Deviation from the ideal, as seen from this perspective, constitutes impaired health. Furthermore, some people go further to assume that impaired functioning will follow if the ideal is not met.

Many employers, for example, have traditionally used the positive health standard when making hiring decisions. They have sought persons free of disease or impairment and excluded those who did not meet the ideal. Preemployment physical examinations have often been used to identify and screen out job applicants with chronic conditions. As a result, persons with chronic conditions have experienced discrimination in the work place regardless of their productive capacity (American Heart Association, 1976; Hager, 1982).

The Rehabilitation Act of 1973 was enacted to combat practices such as these. The act prohibits discrimination on the basis of handicap. Employers may no longer use preemployment medical examination data to speculate on the risk of future work disability posed by an applicant with a particular health condition. Rather, job applicants can only be evaluated on their *current* mental and physical ability and on whether their handicap makes them unable to perform a specific job or "creates a substantial risk of imminent danger to self or others" (Mitchell, 1982, 267). Despite these protections, however, impaired workers (those who fall short of the health ideal) continue to encounter employment barriers.

The positive health standard is not an appropriate standard against which to judge the working capacity of individuals or groups. Use of this standard underestimates the functional capacity of individuals with chronic conditions and ample evidence documents their productive potential (Cobb, 1973; Dunn, 1981; Dunham, 1978; Felton, Perkins, and Lewin, 1966; Ferron, 1981; Franco, 1965; Leckey, 1966).

Consideration of the health of the population as it pertains to work-life extension necessitates the use of the idealist health perspective. The standard used with that perspective should not be that of positive health, however. Instead, analysts need to apply a *functional* standard. They need to focus on job performance as the standard against which health is measured. It matters little from an employment perspective whether worker A has arthritis and worker B does not, *unless* worker A feels unwell and risks health impairment through employment, performs poorly, and/or costs the company more than worker B because of the arthritis. This would not necessarily be the case.

Job performance standards need to be developed. These standards would specify what levels of health are acceptable and unacceptable from an employment perspective. For example, attendance is an important factor in productivity. A job performance standard could incorporate this factor and specify that work loss greater than *X* days per year, in conjunction with other factors, indicates work disability risk. Functional capacity measures, discussed earlier, incorporate a standard of physical functioning deemed relevant for job performance. But for other measures of health, such as bed disability days, no such standards exist. These standards are needed if objective assessments of disability are to be derived from health measures, in addition to those that focus on physical limitations.

## EVALUATING HEALTH DATA

In addition to assessing the availability, reliability, and validity of health measures as recommended by Ware and his associates (Ware, Brook, Davies, and Lohr, 1981), it is important to critically examine how data are reported and whether they can answer the questions you want answered. Two primary limitations should be noted. The first is the lack of age detail in most reports on health and the older population; the second is the frequent use of averages in standard health reports.

### Disaggregating "the Aged"

Published reports on the health of the elderly almost universally treat the older population as one homogeneous age group. Information is almost nonexistent which describes this population in any way more refined than merely reporting on them as one group aged 65 and over.

This method of reporting can distort the reality of health and aging. First, it fails to show the often small health differences between adjacent age groups. Second, it does not account for the growing size of the very old (those 85 years and over) among the aged population. This very old group typically experiences many more health problems than persons 60-70 years old. By averaging the health patterns of the younger old (65-74), the older old (75-84), and the very old (85+), and attributing the result to the younger group, a biased perspective can be obtained. Published reports on the health of the aged do not discuss the range of the distribution within the elderly population, nor the standard deviation from the mean. The result is that the younger old, those for whom work-life extension is most relevant, can be portrayed as less healthy than they actually are.

### The Tyranny of the Average

Another problem with extant health data is its frequent use of averages (specifically, the arithmetic mean) in reporting levels of health. This approach is often inappropriate for use on the older population.

It is widely acknowledged that the aged are a diverse group. This characteristic of diversity holds in regard to health levels as well. Two persons of the same age may evidence markedly different health profiles. One may be free of disease and disability, while the other may have numerous health problems, experience repeated hospitalizations, and be severely limited in functional ability.

The problem with using the mean as descriptive of the central tendency of a group is that the mean unduly reflects cases at the extremes of the distribution (unlike the median or mode). It is quite possible that this is what happens with health data on the elderly. The mode and median of health data distributions are typically not reported in published materials.

An example will help to illustrate. Figure 2-4 presents two hypothetical profiles of the rate of bed disability among two groups of older persons. The average number of bed days per person per year is six for both groups. For Group A, this average clearly misrepresents the experiences of the group for whom one third had no bed day episodes at all in the year, and one third had at least 33 percent fewer bed days than represented by the average. The poor health of two members (one third of the group) skewed the average upward. Consequently, the entire group is portrayed as less healthy than the majority of its members actually are.

Turning to Group B, we find a different situation. There, the average of six bed days per person per year closely represents the health experiences of the members of the group. For Group B, then, the average is a true representative measure; it is not skewed by the extremes of a few members.

The marked variability within the aged population, both between age groups and even within age groups, indicates that health data reported only in averages may misrepresent the health experiences of many older persons. This fact should be borne in mind by those who seek to use such reports.

| GROUP A HOSPITAL DAYS PER PERSON PER YEAR | | GROUP B HOSPITAL DAYS PER PERSON PER YEAR | |
|---|---|---|---|
| Person 1: | 20 days | Person 1: | 6 days |
| Person 2: | 2 days | Person 2: | 7 days |
| Person 3: | 0 days | Person 3: | 5 days |
| Person 4: | 0 days | Person 4: | 4 days |
| Person 5: | 4 days | Person 5: | 8 days |
| Person 6: | 10 days | Person 6: | 6 days |
| Total | 36 days | Total | 36 days |
| Average Rate of Hospital Utilization (average number of hospital days per person per year) | 6 days | Average Rate of Hospital Utilization (average number of hospital days per person per year) | 6 days |

**FIGURE 2-4. Averages and the Representativeness of Populations: Hypothetical Hospital Utilization Rate Profiles.**

## SUMMARY AND CONCLUSION

As national leaders seek ways to extend the working lives of older Americans, they often encounter questions about the health implications of different retirement age policies. These questions center around issues of labor supply, productivity, employee health costs, and health maintenance. Questions about the functional capacity of older persons are particularly at issue with work-life extension policies because they are directed toward persons who are "willing and able" to work.

The purpose of this chapter was to discuss some of the issues involved in analyzing survey data for the purpose of assessing health and functional capacity among the older population. It has provided a set of considerations for government decision makers and their staff, for researchers, and for business leaders when they make or evaluate statements about health and the working capacity or disability of older persons.

The chapter reviewed the most commonly used measures of health. These include mortality-based indicators; measures of the incidence or prevalence of disease and impairments; indicators of disability, including measures of short-term and long-term disability; self-assessed health measures; and indicators of medical care utilization and of risk factors for disease. Next, it discussed the appropriateness of these measures for functional capacity questions through a consideration of the dimensions of illness and their saliency for disability evaluations. Examples from ongoing policy debates were used to illustrate how conceptual blurring can cause difficulty. The health indicators identified as most appropriate for assessing disability were self-reports of disability augmented by indicators of sickness; the prevalence of specific impairments thought to be commonly disabling, such as blindness; and the prevalence of specific diseases which are known to be highly disabling, such as neurological disorders. These data are available through the National Center for Health Statistics. Further research is needed, however, to develop a comprehensive index of disability.

Once the appropriate health measures have been selected, attention shifts to choosing the evaluation perspective and health standard best suited for the particular task. Because their concerns differ from those of the health care establishment, employment analysts need to use functional standards for judging acceptable levels of health. The standards used by the medical community, which focus on disease and impairment, are not the most appropriate for employment analyses. Analysts must be wary of assuming a one-to-one relationship between disease, sickness, and disability, particularly where chronic conditions are concerned. Furthermore, they must be cautious with data that aggregate the elderly into one group, usually those aged 65 and over. Data reported in this way may distort the health profile of younger aged persons (those between the ages of 65 and 70 or 74) who would be the target population for most work-life extension proposals. Similarly, data that are reported only in averages can distort the experiences of older persons. The recognized variability that exists within the older population calls into question the representativeness of the mean as an accurate descriptor of the experiences of the group members.

Only recently has attention begun to focus on older workers. The very concept of the *working aged* is new to our contemporary cultural orientations. As a policy goal, work-life extension catches us ill-prepared informationally. Much needs to be learned if we are to proceed on this policy course in a better than haphazard manner. This chapter has attempted to help employment decision makers best utilize the health information that is available to them for their policy deliberations on work-life extension.

## *REFERENCES*


AMERICAN HEART ASSOCIATION. (1976). Report of the committee on stress, strain and heart disease. Special report. *News from the American Heart Association.* Dallas: American Heart Association.

ANDRISANI, P. J. (1977). Effects of health problems on the work experience of middle-aged men. *Industrial Gerontology, 4* (2), Spring 1977, 97–112.

ATCHLEY, R. C. (1980). *The social forces in later life: An introduction to social gerontology.* Third edition. Belmont, CA: Wadsworth Publishing Company, Inc.

BERKOWITZ, M. (1978). The search for a health variable. *Policy analysis with Social Security research files,* Proceedings of a workshop held March 1978 at Williamsburg, Virginia. U.S. Social Security Administration, Washington, D.C.: U.S. GPO., 411–431.

BUTLER, R. N. (1983). The relation of extended life to extended employment since the passage of Social Security in 1935. *Milbank Memorial Fund Quarterly/Health and Society, 61* (3), 420–429.

CAPLAN, A. L. ENGLEHARDT, H. T., JR., and McCARTNEY, J. J. (Eds.).

(1981). *Concepts of health and disease: Interdisciplinary perspectives.* Reading, MA: Addison-Wesley.

CHIRIKOS, T. N., and NESTEL, G. (1981). Impairment and labor market outcomes: A cross-sectional and longitudinal analysis. *Work and Retirement.* Cambridge, MA: MIT Press.

COBB, A. B. (1973). *Medical and psychological aspects of disability.* Springfield, IL: Charles C. Thomas.

DUNHAM, J. R. (1978). Blindness and visual impairment. In Robert M. Goldenson (Ed.) *Disability and rehabilitation handbook.* New York: McGraw-Hill, 249–303.

DUNN, D. J. (1981). Vocational rehabilitation of the older disabled worker. *Journal of Rehabilitation, 47* (4), 76–81.

FELDMAN, J. J. (1983). Work ability of the aged under conditions of improving mortality. *Milbank Memorial Fund Quarterly/Health and Society, 61,* 430–444.

FELTON, J. S., PERKINS, D. C., and LEWIN, M. (1966). *A survey of medicine and medical practice for the rehabilitation counselor.* Washington, D.C.: U.S. Department of Health, Education and Welfare.

FERRON, D. T. (1981). Changes in selected characteristics of the disabled, 1966–72. In D. T. Ferron (Comp.), *Disability survey, 72, disabled and nondisabled adults.* Department of Health and Human Services, Social Security Administration. Washington, D.C.: U.S. GPO., 309–321.

FRANCIS, R. E. (1983). *Social Security disability claims. Practice and procedure.* Wilmette, IL: Callaghan & Company.

FRANCO, S. C. (1965). Re-employment or retirement. *Archives of Environmental Health, 11,* 835–845.

FRIES, J. F. (1980). Aging, natural death, and the compression of morbidity. *The New England Journal of Medicine, 303* (3), 130–135.

FRIES, J. F. (1984). The compression of morbidity: Miscellaneous comments about a themes. *The Gerontologist, 24* (4), 354–359.

GILBERT, R. R., and PETERS, J. D. (1983). *Social Security disability claims.* New York: The Lawyers Co-operative Publishing Co., San Francisco: Bancroft-Whitney Co.

GRUENBERG, E. M. (1977). The failure of success. *Milbank Memorial Fund Quarterly/Health and Society, 55* (1), 3–24.

HABER, L. D. (1977). The epidemiology of disability: II. The measurement of functional capacity limitations. In *Compilation of Social Security survey of the disabled population: 1966.* Report 10, Social Security Administration, DHEW (SSA). 77-11713. Washington, D.C.: U.S. GPO.

HAGER, P. (1982). Court takes broad view of law on infirm. *Los Angeles Times,* 19, part 1. October 22.

KAPLAN, G. A., and CAMACHO, T. (1983). Perceived health and mortality: A nine year follow-up of the Human Population Laboratory Cohort. *American Journal of Epidemiology, 117,* 292–304.

KATZ, S., and AKPOM, C. A. (1976). Index of ADL. *Medical Care, 14* (suppl. 5), 116–118.

KEITH, R. A. (1984). Functional assessment measures in medical rehabilitation: Current status. *Archives of Physical Medicine and Rehabilitation, 65,* 74–78.

KINGSON, E. R. (1981). The health of very early retirees. *Aging and Work, 4* (1), 11–12.

KINGSON, E. R. (1982). Critique of early retirement study disputed. *Aging and Work, 5* (2), 93–110.

KINGSON, E. R. (1983). Still more on early retirement. *Aging and Work, 6* (2), 111–115.

KLEINMAN, A., EISENBERG, L., and GOOD, B. (1978). Culture, illness, and care: Clinical lessons from anthropologic and cross-cultural research. *Annals of Internal Medicine, 88* (2), February, 251–258.

LAMBRINOS, J. (1981). Health: A source of bias in labor supply models. *Review of Economics and Statistics,* May, 206–212.

LaRUE, A., BANK, L., JARVIK, L., and HETLAND, M. (1979). Health in old age: How do physicians' ratings and self-ratings compare? *Journal of Gerontology, 34* (5), 687–691.

LECKEY, R. G. (1966). Pre-employment examination—a pointed study. *Journal of Occupational Medicine, 8,* 532–536.

MADDOX, G. L., and DOUGLASS, E. B. (1973). Self-assessment of health: A longitudinal study of elderly subjects. *Journal of Health and Social Behavior, 14,* 89–93.

MANTON, K. G. (1982). Changing concepts of morbidity and mortality in the elderly population. *Milbank Memorial Fund Quarterly/Health and Society, 60* (2), 183–244.

McCRAE, R. R., BARTONE, P. T., and COSTA, P. T. (1976). Age, anxiety, and self-reported health. *International Journal of Aging and Human Development, 7* (1), 49–58.

MITCHELL, J. W. (Ed.). (1982). Occupational medicine forum. Committee on occupational medical practice. *Journal of Occupational Medicine, 24* (4), 262, 266–267.

MOSSEY, J. M., and SHAPIRO, E. (1982). Self-rated health: A predictor of mortality among the elderly. *American Journal of Public Health, 72* (8), 800–808.

MURNAGHAN, J. H. (1981). Health indicators and information systems for the year 2000. *Annual Review of Public Health, 2,* 299–361.

MYERS, G. C. and MANTON, K. G. (1984). Compression of Mortality: Myth or reality? *The Gerontologist, 24* (4), 346–352.

MYERS, R. J. (1982). Why do people retire from work early? *Social Security Bulletin, 45* (9), 10–14.

MYERS, R. J. (1983). More about the controversy on early retirement study. *Aging and Work, 6* (2), 105–109.

NAGI, S. Z. (1969). *Disability and rehabilitation.* Columbus, OH: Ohio State University Press.

NAGI, S. Z. (1976). An epidemiology of disability among adults in the United States. *Milbank Memorial Fund Quarterly, 54* (4), 439–467.

NATIONAL CENTER FOR HEALTH STATISTICS. (1963). Origin, program, and operation of the U.S. National Health Survey. *Vital and Health Statistics.* Series 1, No. 1, Washington, D.C.: U.S. GPO.

NATIONAL COMMISSION ON SOCIAL SECURITY. (1981). *Social Security in America's future.* Final report of the National Commission on Social Security, Washington, D.C.: U.S. GPO.

POSNER, I. (1981). Functional capacity limitations and disability, 1972. In *Disability survey 72: Disabled and nondisabled adults—a monograph.* Office of Research and Statistics, Social Security Administration (SSA) 13-11812, 69–75.

ROBINSON, P. K., and SANFORD, M. J. (1982). *The availability of older workers to the labor market.* An unpublished report by the Employment and Retirement Division, Andrus Gerontology Center, University of Southern California, Los Angeles, CA.

SIGERIST, H. E. (1971). *Medicine and human welfare.* New Haven: Yale University Press.

SOCIAL SECURITY ADMINISTRATION. (1980). *1980 Annual report of the board of trustees of the federal old-age and survivors insurance and disability insurance trust funds.* House Document No. 96-332. Washington, D.C.: U.S. GPO.

SULLIVAN, D. F. (1966). Conceptual problems in developing an index of health. *Vital and Health Statistics.* Series 2, No. 17. Washington, D.C.: U.S. GPO.

SULLIVAN, D. F. (1971). Disability components for an index of health. *Vital and Health Statistics.* Series 2, No. 42. Washington, D.C.: U.S. GPO.

TISSUE, T. (1972). Another look at self-rated health among the elderly. *Journal of Gerontology, 27,* 91–94.

U.S. HOUSE OF REPRESENTATIVES. (1983). *Threats today against tomorrow's Social Security retirees.* Hearing before the Select Committee on Aging, Ninety-eighth Congress, First session, March 8, 1983. Washington, D.C.: U.S. GPO.

VERBRUGGE, L. M. (1983). Longer life but worsening health? Trends in health and mortality of middle-aged and older persons. Paper presented at the Population Association of America Meetings, Pittsburgh, PA, April 1983.

WARE, J. E., JR., BROOK, R. H., DAVIES, A. R., and LOHR, K. N. (1981). Choosing measures of health status for individuals in general populations. *American Journal of Public Health, 71* (6), 620–625.

WILSON, R. W., and DRURY, T. F. (1984). Interpreting trends in illness and disability: Health statistics and health status. *Annual Review of Public Health, 5,* 83–106.

WOLINSKY, F. D., COE, R. M., MILLER, D. K. and PRENDERGAST, J. M. (1984). Measurement of the global and functional dimensions of health status in the elderly. *Journal of Gerontology, 39* (1), 88–92.

WORK IN AMERICA INSTITUTE. (1980). *The future of older workers in America, new options for an extended working life.* Scarsdale, NY: Work in America Institute.

WORLD HEALTH ORGANIZATION. (1958). *The first ten years of the World Health Organization.* Geneva: World Health Organization.

# 3

# COPING IN OLD AGE

Erhard Olbrich

*Coping* is a rather new concept in the gerontological literature. Since 1966 an increasing number of studies have used it as a central term; but while our knowledge about the coping process and about its adaptive or developmental consequences has grown, we still know little about coping in old age.

The purpose of this chapter is to review the basic conceptualizations of the coping process which have been developed within psychoanalytic, cognitive, and cognitive-behavioral theories of adaptation and development and which, although not elaborated very clearly, form the basis for our present understanding. Further, two competing hypotheses concerning age-related changes in coping will be discussed, and an integrative conceptualization will be proposed. Empirical work in support of this integrated concept, based on studies of health and work in old age, will be presented.

## COPING: THE CONCEPT AND ITS RELEVANCE FOR DEVELOPMENT

The term *coping* refers to a form of adaptive behavior. The formulations of White and Lazarus are representative of current definitions of coping. White (1974) puts coping, defense, and mastery under the superordinate category of adaptation; he differentiates coping from other processes in the following manner: "It is clear that we tend to speak of coping when we have in mind a fairly drastic change or problem that defies familiar ways of behaving, requires the production of new behavior, and very likely gives rise to uncomfortable affects. . ." (p. 48). Lazarus, whose work will be explained at greater length later in this chapter, has defined coping as efforts to manage demands, efforts that include emotion-focused as well as problem-focused processes. Both definitions intimate that there can be development through coping, but they do so only in a very general way. They include cognitive as well as positive and negative affective components. Neither formulation distinguishes between situational and personal, between stimulus and processing qualities of coping, nor do they define an adaptive outcome as a constituting element. However, both definitions seem to address ambiguity experienced in the face of jeopardizing or promising demands or of taxed adaptive resources, and in situations with an open outcome. The situation that requires coping has characteristics of a developmental transition that can lead to new forms of behavior and thus to productive adaptation; but it can, of course, also lead to failure.

### Theoretical Conceptualizations of Coping

In order to provide a basis for the understanding of coping processes and their relation to development, we will summarize some well-known theories of adaptation and development, with an emphasis on how they explain actual and diachronic (i.e., over-time or developmental) adaptive processes.

1. One of the best-known roots of coping theory is *psychoanalysis.* Psychoanalytic ideas about defense mechanisms have influenced our understanding of personality processes and of development since the beginning of this century (Freud, 1905). They have quite obviously become incorporated in *neo-analytical* conceptualizations of coping, which emphasize conscious control mechanisms more strongly. A helpful distinction between defensive and coping processes was proposed by Blos (1962), and later clarified by Kroeber (1963) and by Haan (1963). These authors felt the need to conceptually "represent the rational, logical, wise, civil, loving, playful and sensual aspects of people's ego actions" (Haan, 1977, 36), and to distinguish these coping modes from more defensive ones.

> Coping involves purpose, choice, and flexible shift, adheres to intersubjective reality and logic, and allows and enhances proportionate affective expression; defensiveness is compelled, negative, rigid, distorting of intersubjective reality and logic, allows covert impulse expression, and embodies the expectancy that anxiety can be relieved without directly addressing the problem (Haan, 1977, 34).

Coping processes are adaptive and, since "they continue an open system," allow development, while "defenses produce particular closures of the system" (p. 34).

In Haan's view, coping is an adaptive ego process, integrating the cognitive and motivational as well as the social, moral, and value orientations of the individual. All these responses are usually elicited by new demands. Developmental consequences of coping are discovered in more effective programs for person-environment interactions; these represent the individual's ego resources. Defense is likely to occur when the person encounters demands that go beyond his/her capacities and the developmental consequences of defending are assumed to be disruptive in nature, since they do not represent the individual's adaptive potentials but actually distort them. From this theoretical perspective, challenging or threatening demands, life transitions, or even crises and conflicts are prerequisites for coping. These must not, however, exceed an individual's resources.

2. Lazarus's (1966, 1974, 1980) *cognitive conception,* possibly the most important contribution to our knowledge of coping, was based on his stress research, where from "its humble beginnings as a footnote to stress theory, the concept of coping has grown to occupy a central place in current theoretical models of stress and emotion" (Roskies and Lazarus, 1980, 45). Lazarus, both in his early work on stress and performance as well as in his recent work on stress and health, found *facilitative* as well as *impairing* effects of stress on the individual. It is likely that this differentiation can be explained by different forms of coping with the stressor. A panel report on psychological assets and modifiers of stress, presented by the Institute of Medicine and by the National Academy of Science, expresses the potential positive effects of coping:

> Individuals who have faced severe life stressors also may find that they have increased self-esteem, are able to perform better in similar situations at a later time, learn empathy, or can take advantage of new opportunities. Certain stressors are inevitable throughout the life course, yet most people do not appear to suffer from adverse effects (Cohen, 1982, 153).

Whether stressful demands will lead to growth, temporary difficulty, or trauma in the individual is a function of (1) the pervasiveness and persistence of the stressor, (2) the timing of the event, (3) the individual's personal resources available for dealing with the stressor, (4) the opportunities available to act on the environment and to receive social support (Dunkel-Schetter and Wortman, 1981), and (5) the meaning given to the experience (Benner, Roskies, and Lazarus, 1980). A developmental outcome appears to be a function of situational demands, the individual's perception and processing of these situational demands, and social support. This is in accordance with theoretical conclusions reached in a review of the literature on stressful occupations (Elliott and Eisdorfer, 1982). Above all, cognitive representations of stressful factors and their appraisal seem to be the most relevant determinants of outcomes. In general, scientists and practitioners in the fields of personality and clinical psychology have developed the conviction that, more than the impact of stress per se, it is how people *cope* with stress that is important for their adaptation, their health, and their development (Coelho, Hamburg, and Adams, 1974; Filipp, 1981; Goldfried, 1977; Kaplan, 1983; Meichenbaum, 1977; Moos, 1976, 1977; Murphy and Moriarity, 1976).

Lazarus has developed a transactional model of coping. He views the person as an active organizer of the stress experience and an active responder to the demanding environment; a transaction occurs when the stressor and the person mutually influence each other. This conceptualization "offers a new level of discourse in which separate variables are now lost or changed" (Lazarus, 1980, 37). It is on the level of cognitive representation and cognitive appraisal that situational components and personal factors seem to meet. "Because appraisal is a function of both situational and personal variables, this unit expresses the transaction between the person and the environment in terms of the cognitive processes by means of which a given type of person processes and evaluates information about the environment" (Lazarus et al., 1974, 307).

Lazarus conceptually distinguishes between primary, secondary, and tertiary appraisal. Primary appraisal is basically an evaluative perception and a judgment of what the demands mean to the person. In secondary appraisal this perception is brought together with the individual's resources for dealing with the demands. Secondary appraisal can be compared to a cognitive extrapolation of how personal resources can be employed in order to meet aspired goals or to reach foreseen effects of planned actions. Secondary appraisal can be understood as the part of the coping process that contributes most to the development of plans for action. Prospective cognitions come into play. Finally, tertiary appraisal, or reappraisal, refers to a new perception and evaluation that is reached after possible reactions to the encountered demands have been constructed. In this conceptualization, coping is called for whenever habitualized programs of behavior are insufficient to meet a demand. If coping results in mastery of the demand, it contributes to the development of new behavioral programs. Failure, on the other hand, will have adverse effects on cognitive functioning, performance, health, morale, and self-esteem.

3. The *cognitive-behavioral* conceptualization of coping was developed by Thomae (1951, 1968, 1984), who believes that behavior is usually thematically structured. Themes result from specific constellations of environmental presses and personal needs; however, these do not interact mechanically. Thomae speaks of open thematic structures—he realizes that individually developed personal potentials for perceiving and experiencing come into play, as do personal intentions and tendencies toward self-realization. In thematically structured behavior, motivation is not only directed toward better homeostasis, but growth tendencies are often incorporated in interactions between environmental presses and personal needs.

A second important concept in the cognitive-behavioral conceptualization is that of *daseinstechniken* (coping techniques). These instrumental techniques are used by the individual in order to attain a thematically defined goal behavior. Thomae (1984) distinguishes between techniques of performance, adaptation, defense, evasion, aggression, and others. *Daseinstechniken* are used in accordance with the individual's perceptions of situational demands as well as of his/her personal needs and resources. They are integrated within the individual's personal framework of meaningful behavior, which is set by his/her themes. Through *daseinstechniken,* prospective elements come into play as factors determining adaptation and development.

4. Another conceptualization of the coping process should be mentioned briefly. Schönpflug (1979) has proposed a *biocybernetic* conception of the coping process, which states that following stress or disregulation of behavior a reprogramming of old or a development of new regulatory processes can begin, which may lead to a new form of behavioral organization. This theoretical approach will not be elaborated here since little or no research on coping in old age has yet been conducted using it as a basis.

In summary, all of the basic conceptualizations of coping are based on an active-organism model. They emphasize productive adaptation and development instead of drive reduction and striving for homeostasis. They describe processes, rather than static variables, as important for transactions and behavior. Cognitive constructions and preconstructions (plans) of behavior are emphasized. Success or failure of adaptation and development appear as basic functions of coping. The crucial role of the coping process in actual adaptation and in development has already been emphasized in personality theory and developmental theory (Thomae, 1968), in studies on coping with stress or with everyday hassles (Folkman and Lazarus, 1980), in clinical work (Caplan, 1964), in studies on critical life events (Filipp, 1981), in studies on crisis and conflict management (Matteson and Ivancevich, 1982; McLean, 1979; Moos, 1976, 1977), and in developmental work on periods of transition (Olbrich, 1981).

### Short and Long-term Perspectives of Coping

Throughout this paper a distinction has been made between actual adaptive processes and diachronic adaptation or development. Actual or short-term processes regulate adaptive functions of the person in specific encounters with immediate situational demands. We have emphasized analysis of the process of coping with taxing, challenging, or threatening demands, since these appear to be situations in which a person can no longer rely on habitualized forms (or programs) of behavior; a reprogramming or restructuring is required. In this framework, personality is understood as a system of programs, not as a "pattern of traits" (Guilford, 1957). Programs can be cognitive, emotional, biological, or interactional. They are, of course, constructs inferred from directly observed personality processes.

Diachronic or long-term processes, like those which regulate adaptive functions over time, are developmental processes, emphasizing interactions between later processes and former ones or formerly developed programs.

To advance our theoretical model of coping, a combination of paradigms for the study of immediate adaptation (coping) with those for the study of adaptation over time (diachronic adaptation or development) is required. Here, the concepts of *crystallization* and *fluidization* are proposed in order to link short-term (coping) and long-term (developmental) perspectives. It is assumed that a person who repeatedly encounters a set of specific demands and whose behavior proves to effectively meet these demands will crystallize programs (and corresponding manifest processes) leading to successful adaptation. In cases of inadequate behavior or maladaptive actions, successful adaptation will not be reached. On the other hand, it can be assumed that whenever new demands must be met, one or several of the individual's commonly used programs will have to be rendered fluid in the sense that the programming becomes malleable. Change or even development of new programs can occur. Thus we can assume interactions will occur between short-term and long-term processes in such a way that those which have become crystallized over time may become fluid again through actual demands that require their change. But immediate adaptive processes also depend on former ones, whether crystallized or otherwise developed over time. The development of adaptive processes can thus be conceptualized as an interaction between short-term (coping) and long-term (developmental) processes. This is a conceptualization of personality and personality development that recognizes continuous interactions between a person's adaptive resources and situational demands; it combines person-situation interactions with interactions over time. Finding an answer to the question of how coping changes over the adult years thus seems even more crucial in light of the possible association between coping and development.

## COPING AND AGING: TWO HYPOTHESES AND AN INTEGRATION

The literature about coping in the later years is limited. Many of the existing studies were not planned in order to analyze age changes of coping processes; therefore, frequently results come only from clinical observations. A review of available research, together with insights gained in the few systematic studies (cf. Lazarus and Olbrich, 1983; Lieberman, 1975; McCrae, 1982; Pfeiffer, 1977; Renner and Birren, 1981; Thomae, Lehr, and Schmitz-Scherzer, 1981) provide an overview as well as a possible answer to the question of how coping changes in old age.

### The Regression Hypothesis

McCrae (1982) distinguished between two different hypotheses concerning the changes related to coping and age. One is the regression hypothesis, presented, for example, by Pfeiffer (1977) in his work on psychopathology and social pathology in aging. This hypothesis states that, with increasing age, failures to adapt to challenging or threatening demands will occur more frequently. Pfeiffer bases his theory on the assumption that demands to which older people have to adapt differ substantially from those faced by younger adults. The elderly have to deal with more frequent and, possibly, more severe losses–of persons, relationships, work, roles, recognition, mobility, and health. The older individual has to cope with the necessity to remain active and to retain functions. In addition, a quite different task of the older adult which must be dealt with is the identity review.

Presenting data on adaptation to various losses, Pfeiffer concentrates on those elderly (approximately 15 percent) who suffer from some moderate to significant form of psychopathology, and who indeed often fail to adapt. He concedes that "some older persons continue to use the entire range of adaptive mechanisms," but stresses that many return to the use of more primitive mechanisms, which are often defensive in nature. "Thus, unmodified anxiety, depression-withdrawal, projection, somatization, and denial are the preponderant mechanisms used." Pfeiffer specifies that "in those instances where failure of adaptation has occurred, the mechanisms outlined are used with great regularity" (Pfeiffer, 1977, 651), but only in those instances. It should be added that regression does not occur in the majority of those aged who successfully adapt to the taxing demands encountered in their life. It therefore appears that Pfeiffer's study does not present convincing universal (i.e., overindividual) and general (i.e., oversituational) evidence for a regression hypothesis.

Gutman (1977; 1980) argues that as active mastery diminishes with age, and passive or even magical mastery becomes prevalent, coping capacities seem to decrease. This can be called regression, but only as far as the performance and mastery of achievement demands are concerned. This is, of course, important in work life, especially in technologically oriented societies. Gutman presents evidence that judgment, wisdom, and contemplative functions do not deteriorate with aging. Thus, again, no general evidence for a regression hypothesis is found; rather, evidence of regression can only be confirmed in connection to specific circumstances.

### The Growth Hypothesis

Vaillant (1977) observed that immature defense mechanisms–such as projection, schizoid fantasies, passive-aggressive behavior, and acting out–decrease with age, whereas mature mechanisms–such as altruism, humor, sublimation, and anticipation–increase. Based on data gathered in a study of a healthy and well-adapted group of middle-age men, Vaillant proposed the *growth hypothesis.* This hypothesis, however, also is not generally and universally accepted in that a definite positive relationship between age and successful adaptation has not been confirmed.

In order to explain such discrepancies, we should mention that the samples studied by Pfeiffer are very different from those of Vaillant and others with regard to education, health status, socioeconomic situation, and psychological variables. Moreover, measures of coping and forms of data analysis are not directly comparable. A lengthy discussion of methodological issues would not be useful here, since so little relevant research has been done to date. At the present time, theoretical and substantive considerations appear to be more fruitful approaches to the regression-growth controversy. We should focus our attention on the following facts: (1) With ongoing age, individuals encounter life situations and demands that are new and qualitatively different from those in younger years. (2) We have data about changes in an aging person's energies and personal resources, in her or his types of activity and in commitments. And (3) as demands and personal potentials change, transactions between them undergo qualitative change. These considerations lead our attention away from the controversy between regression and growth and direct our attention toward understanding the coping individual in his/her situation within his/her life course.

It seems unlikely that universal or general evidence for age-related change in coping can be found if the active view of coping held by Lazarus or by Thomae is correct. In this view, an individual perceives, cognitively appraises, represents, and then processes the demands of a specific situation. Individual influences that have been developed in the biography come into play and modify general (situational) and group-specific or universal (personal) factors.

While idiosyncratic analyses of coping with age-specific demands in different periods of an individual's life are goals, we are aware that they cannot currently be attained. However, differentiations which take situational variations into account can be developed, and distinctions can be considered between individuals' perceptions of their personal resources to deal with the demands of subjectively appraised stressful situations. The remainder of this section will focus on data concerning differences in demands encountered during different periods of the adult life cycle, changes in coping potentials over the adult years, and conclusions about their interactions in order to provide evidence for a "differential" model of coping and age.

### Age-related Changes in Stressors and Demands

Age-related changes in stressors and demands have been isolated in work on normative and non-normative transitions encountered during the family life cycle and the work life (cf. Datan and Ginsberg, 1975; Kohli, 1978; Olbrich, 1983). McCrae (1982) reports that older people have to deal with a disproportionately larger number of *exit events,* while younger persons have to adjust to more *entrance events.* After comparing data from subjects between 24 and 91 years of age, McCrae concluded that challenges decrease with age, losses occur at all ages with about equal frequency, and threats increase. The latter are most often related to health. Folkman and Lazarus (1980) found in their sample that older participants between 45 and 64 years of age reported more health-related problems, while younger people more often mentioned work and family-related difficulties.

### Age-related Changes in Coping Potentials

Looking at personal coping potentials, some of the best information available again comes from the work of McCrae (1982). His cross-sectional comparisons of coping styles did not reveal evidence for either the regression or the growth hypothesis. Using analysis of covariance, McCrae then corrected his data for different stressors encountered during the single periods of the life span. He concluded:

> These analyses again offer no support for the regression hypothesis, but they partly support the growth position. . . None of the theoretically mature mechanisms shows a cross-sectional decline, whereas some of the theoretically immature mechanisms do. There was, however, no evidence that the use of theoretically mature mechanisms increased with age (1982, 457).

Lesser, Lazarus, Wilson, et al. (1981) found more psychotic defense mechanisms among demented elderly, but no age effects for normal subjects. Kirscht and Rosenstock (1979) explicitly emphasized the differential perspective when reporting that older persons who have a greater belief in internal control have more efficient coping styles. In a study by Quayhagen and Quayhagen (1982), older people scored lower on problem-solving coping styles and higher on negative affectivity. Help seeking increased between 40 and 70 years, and this increase was larger for men than for women. No differences were found for other coping variables. In the Gleason, Karuza, and Zevon (1981) study, older participants assumed less responsibility and used more mechanisms by which they relied on others and profitted from their support and discipline. It seems that a lack of social support and reduced attributions of personal control seem to gain more and more relevance with ongoing age.

The studies cited differ with regard to selection of samples, measures, and techniques for the assessment of coping and, most importantly, they differ with regard to theoretical frameworks. Nevertheless, the fact that such different results were obtained tends to support our view that neither situational nor personal variables alone can satisfactorily explain coping, which is by definition an ongoing transaction between situational demands and an *actively* perceiving, appraising, and acting individual.

### Demands and Resources: Changing Interactions Over Time

When we conceive of coping as a transaction between situation and person, we are required to direct our attention to the "unit" that consists of situational demands and personal resources, which are both cognitively represented and which, on this level of representation, both form the basis of an individual's plan of action and his/her plan for ensuing behavior. Turning from the actual to the diachronic perspective, we must recognize that objectively identical demands can be perceived differently by different individuals (cf. Olbrich and Thomae, 1978; Roskies and Lazarus, 1980). There is also evidence that, over the lifetime, a reordering of priorities, a relegation of no-longer-relevant roles to the periphery of importance and an investment into activities more in tune with present commitments occur (Lazarus and Olbrich, 1983). Therefore, a description of differences in demands or in coping potentials leads to only a partial understanding of coping processes. In order to come to a better explanation of coping in old age, we should take the person with his/her cognitive, emotional-motivational, physical, and social potentials in his/her situation in each period of his/her biography as a unit of analysis, and try to understand the processes in the personality system that are integrated over time in biographical development.

### Coping and Social Support

In addition to the coping potentials of the person, social and other external influences must be considered. Work on cognitive behavior modification has frequently shown that processes of perceiving and appraising demands can be influenced in much the same way as the planning of behavior (cf. Baade, Borck, Kroebe, and Zumvenne, 1980; Meichenbaum, 1977). For example, cognitive strategies and processes of problem solving can be improved in educational programs (Labouvie-Vief and Gonda, 1976; Plemons, Willis, and Baltes, 1978; Willis, Blieszner, and Baltes, 1981). Studies have shown that coping strategies, which dampen or eliminate disturbing emotional responses to challenging or threatening situational demands, can be learned (Baade et al., 1980; Roskies and Lazarus, 1980). Psychoanalytic techniques of therapy or counseling are recommended by McLean (1979) as a kind of "Rolls-Royce" in a person's progress toward effective functioning; they strengthen ego processes, improve accurate recognition of situational demands as well as personal resources, and facilitate coordinated use of cognitive, affective, moral, and social schemas (Haan, 1977). In this view, development is enhanced by coping skills that are learned in counseling or in psychotherapy.

Not only exacting techniques that are applied by trained professionals are effective in strengthening coping skills; everyday helpful interactions and social support measures also seem to influence coping positively. House (1981), as well as Dunkel-Schetter and Worthman (1981), offer hypotheses concerning the effects of instrumental, informational, emotional, and appraisal support for the aging. In our context of coping and development, the role of appraisal support and of instrumental support will be briefly reviewed. Appraisal support relates directly to personal coping and refers to help given an individual in order to adequately interpret an encountered demand (cognitive appraisal). It also refers to exchanges that take place while communicating cognitive and affective experiences and receiving validation that these are understood by others who are or have been in a similar situation. In its cognitive elements, appraisal support is related to informational support, since it incorporates the giving and receiving of accurate information about demands as well as about older persons' capacities to deal with them. The adaptive and developmental effects of both forms of social support come into play in the cognitive appraisal of stresses or demands and in the individual's processing of them.

## COPING WITH PROBLEMS OF HEALTH AND WORK IN OLD AGE

In the Bonn Longitudinal Study on Aging (BLSA), data was collected longitudinally pertaining to the transactions between situational demands and personal potentials. In that study (Thomae, 1983), a sample that was fairly representative for the social middle class of Western Germany ($n = 222$) was studied between 1965 and 1981. Participants had been born between 1890 and 1910. Psychological, social, medical, and ecological variables were assessed at seven measurement points, and extensive interviews, observations, and medical examinations were made in an attempt to represent the real-life situation of the elderly. Each of the assessment periods lasted about one week. In a three-hour interview, a fairly complete account of stresses experienced due to health, occupation, and other factors was obtained. Participants were also asked to describe how they had perceived the various stresses in their lives and how they had reacted to them.

### The Perception and Cognitive Representation of Demands

In his cognitive theory of personality and aging, Thomae (1970) formulated the postulate that the *perception of change* rather than *objective change* is related to subsequent adaptations in personal behavior. Using data on health status derived from objective assessments made by physicians, on subjectively rated stress due to health problems, and on health-related activities, Olbrich and Thomae (1978) tested the hypothesis that path coefficients on health-related activities from objective health scores (e.g., degree of heart insufficiency or degree of sclerosis) would be smaller than those from stress experienced due to health. Results of path analyses confirmed the hypothesis.

### Coping Styles and Their Development

Within the BLSA, a system of categories was developed in order to describe coping styles *(Daseinstechniken)*. This system was used in order to score interview information. The following table presents patterns of coping with occupational problems in 1948 (as measured by retrospective accounts) and in 1965 (as mea-

**FIGURE 3-1. Influences of "heart insufficiency" on the cognitive representation of the health situation (Stress (Health)) and on behavior in reaction to these (Activity (Health)). From Olbrich, Erhard and Thomae, Hans, "Empirical Findings to a Cognitive Theory of Aging,"** ***International Journal of Behavioral Development,*** **1, 1978, 67–82.**

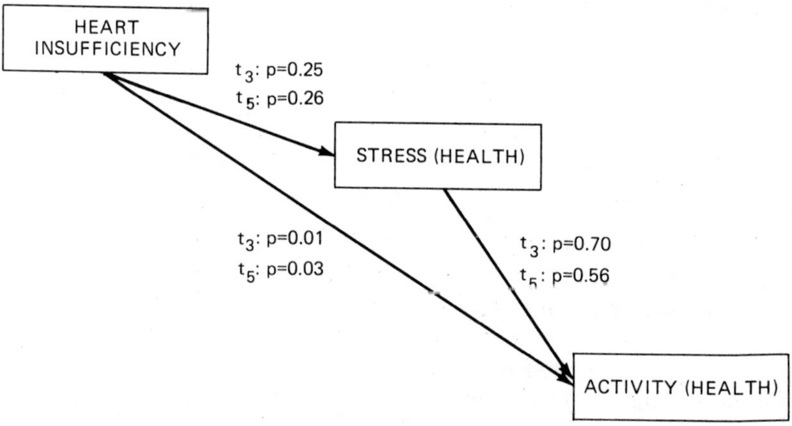


Influences of 'Heart insufficiency' on the cognitive representation of the health situation (Stress (Health)) and on behavior in reaction to these (Activity (Health)).

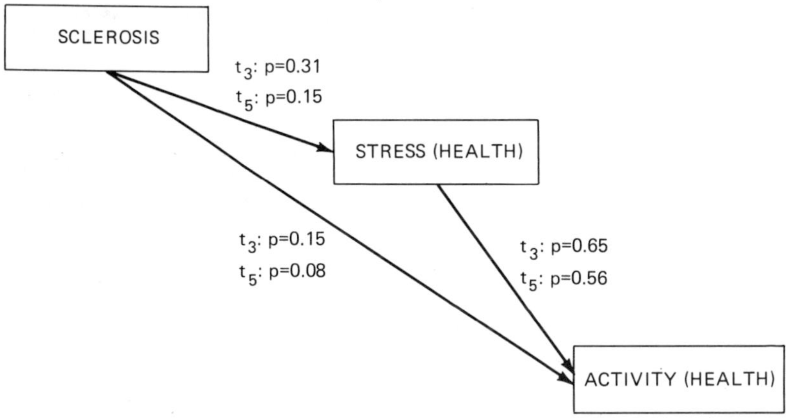


Influences of 'Sclerosis' on the cognitive representation of the health situation (Stress (Health)) and on behavior in reaction to these (Activity (Health)).

**FIGURE 3-2. Influences of "sclerosis" on the cognitive representation of the health situation (Stress (Health)) and on behavior in reaction to these (Activity (Health)). From Olbrich, Erhard and Thomae, Hans, "Empirical Findings to a Cognitive Theory of Aging,"** ***International Journal of Behavioral Development,*** **1, 1978, 67–82.**

sured by actual descriptions). Only data from men born between 1890 and 1895 are presented.

Participants may have reconstructed their information about 1948 when interviewed in 1965 and thereby distorted it (cf. Field, 1981). But there is evidence that the intensity of subjective experiences made by Germans during the currency reform in 1948 and after World War II allowed for rather accurate recollections.

The data in Table 1 express changes in coping styles that show a meaningful cognitive and behavioral restructuring in our aging participants. Due to the 1948 currency reform in Germany, most people had lost most of their savings and had only DM 40 to start anew. People had to rely on chance opportunities in their jobs (and, of course, in other areas, such as the black market). The average pattern of coping seemed to require a good deal of adjustment to institutionalized aspects of the situation (e.g., finding out about governmental compensations for damages suffered during the war). On the other hand, people could not follow an evasive pattern of behavior, they had to build new careers, and had to activate achievement-related behavior. Identification with the goals and/or the successes of children and grandchildren could become stronger in 1965, after the situation had changed occupationally as well as with regard to the family situation of participants, who were between 70 and 75 years of age at that time.

More general evidence supporting a coping theory of adjustment to aging comes from a study of changing social-role activities and satisfaction. Olbrich (1976) showed that for the BLSA sample between the years 1965 and 1974, in the areas of close social interaction—for example, in the role of parent, grandparent, or spouse—little or no decrease occurred in scores measuring activity and satisfaction. There were decreases, however, in areas which are relatively psychologically dis-

**TABLE 1: Rank-ordered styles of coping with occupational problems (arrows indicate significant differences in rank order of coping styles; translated from Lehr, 1977). Used with permission.**

| 1948 | 1965 |
|---|---|
| 1. Achievement-related behavior | 1. Identification with children's goals and life |
| 2. Establishing social contacts | 2. Achievement-related behavior |
| 3. Adjusting to others | 3. Establishing social contacts |
| 4. Adjustment to institutional aspects of the situation | 4. Adjusting to others |
| 5. Accepting situation as it is | 5. Internal distancing from the situation |
| 6. Using chances | 6. Accepting situation as it is |
| 7. Active resistance | 7. Evasive reaction |
| 8. Hope for change | 8. Depressive reaction |
| 9. Relying on others | 9. Adjustment to institutional aspects of the situation |
| 10. Asking for help | 10. Relying on others |
| 11. Aggressive reaction | 11. Using chances |
| 12. Depressive reaction | 12. Hope for change |
| 13. Identification with children's goals and life | 13. Active resistance |
| 14. Postponing own needs | 14. Aggressive reaction |
| 15. Evasive reaction | 15. Asking for help |
| 16. Internal distancing from the situation | 16. Postponing own needs |

tant to the aging person, e.g., in the citizen role, the role of club member, and, of course, in the worker role. These results confirm the theory that a reordering of priorities and a change in the thematic structure of role behavior seems to occur in the later years. While institutionalized activities decrease in relevance, the informal ones that fulfill the aging individual's needs remain important. Rosow's (1976) differential description of the importance of institutionalized, informal, and tenuous roles over the life span is also confirmed by these data.

### Health-related Problems

Degrees of subjectively perceived stress and coping increase over time with regard to health (see Figure 3-3). There is, however, a decrease in these parameters with regard to economic and housing problems. Stress due to the family situation did not change.

Comparisons of preferred and less-preferred styles of coping with health problems encountered over the time span of the BLSA seem to indicate that the aging

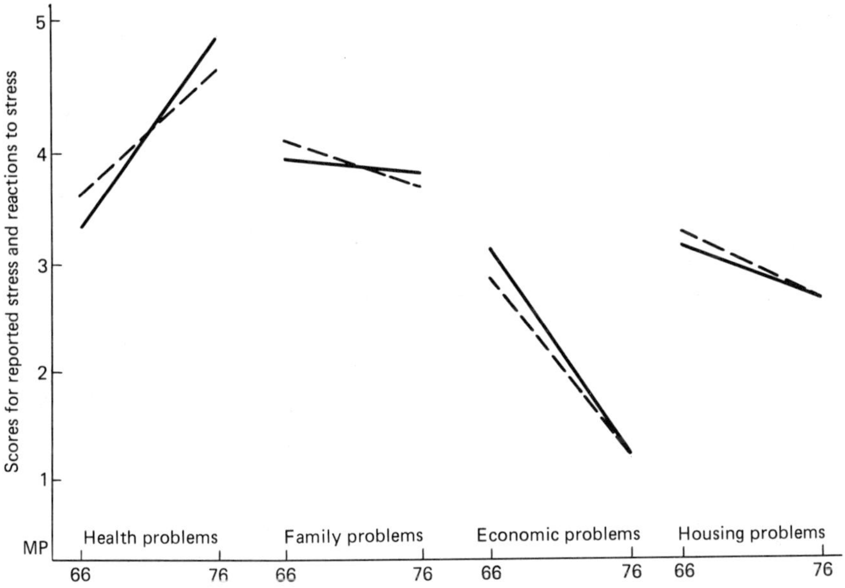


**FIGURE 3-3. Degree of perceived stress (——) and intensity of coping (– –) in different areas, 1966 and 1976. From Thomae et al., 1981.**

persons structured their situations in a way that allowed them to deal meaningfully with loss and failure. We have to repeat that objective health problems of the sample increased over the years 1966 to 1976. Data from medical examinations show that vision, hearing, and mobility became increasingly impaired. Symptoms of heart insufficiency and of sclerosis, as well as of high blood pressure, were significantly more frequent in 1976 than a decade before. Table 2 shows how participants in 1966 and 1976 coped with their health-related situation. Rank orders of *daseinstechniken* are given. We have to add that the overall intensity of coping increased over the time observation.

Before interpreting their reactions to health problems, we have to explain that each person showed an idiosyncratic pattern of *daseinstechniken* (coping styles) when dealing with the demands. Scores for many styles were low, but differences became evident when *daseinstechniken* were rank-ordered for the group and shifts from earlier to later times of assessment were analyzed. Data in Table 2 show evidence of a considerable consistency in reactions to health problems. This seems to indicate that averaged patterns of coping remain quite constant for well-functioning aging persons.

The two techniques of coping that were preferred in 1966 and in 1976 deserve particular attention. They are both forms of active behavior. "Adjustment to the institutional aspects of the situation" in the area of health behavior refers to activities like finding the best doctor or getting the best treatment, to endeavors directed at getting the most out of health insurance, or to efforts to find financial support for recreation, for example, in a spa. It also includes active adjustments to the regulations of a hospital or rehabilitation center. *Achievement-related behavior* is defined by any expenditure of energy or effort in order to obtain a goal. This

**TABLE 2: Rank order of the ten most important styles of coping with health-related problems in 1966 and in 1976 (data from all participants of the BLSA; reprinted from Thomae et al., 1981). Significant differences in ranks are indicated by arrows.**

| 1966 | 1976 |
|---|---|
| 1. Adjustment to institutional aspects of situation | 1. Achievement-related behavior |
| 2. Achievement-related behavior | 2. Adjustment to institutional aspects of situation |
| 3. Depressive reaction | 3. Accepting the situation as it is |
| 4. Hope for change | 4. Depressive reaction |
| 5. Accepting situation as it is | 5. Revision of expectations |
| 6. Relying on others | 6. Relying on others |
| 7. Active resistance | 7. Asking for help |
| 8. Using chances | 8. Using chances |
| 9. Asking for help | 9. Hope for change |
| 10. Revision of expectations | 10. Active resistance |

could be work in one's garden because it is "healthy," physical activities or efforts recommended by one's physician.

Irrational reactions like "hope for change" apparently lost their relevance over the decade observed, since they may have turned out to be ineffective in dealing with demands related to maintaining health in older age. Another *daseintechniken,* active resistance, shifted from rank 7 in 1966 to rank 10 in 1976. This indicates that resistance against recommendations to take medical examinations (or to undergo surgery) was given up. The aging persons also offered less resistance to a recommended diet or to advice concerning reduction of alcohol or cigarette consumption.

Changes in coping with housing problems, economic troubles, and family conflicts cannot be reported here. It must suffice to say that for many individuals a remarkable consistency of *daseintechniken* over the ten-year period could be observed. Achievement techniques did not decrease. Relying on others became more important. But while old parents took support from their social environment, they also continued to support financially the household of their children and to give care.

## CONCLUSION

The intention of this paper is to analyze work on coping processes in a developmental framework. An attempt has been made to proceed from a process-oriented view of personality to show how personality processes interact with developmental processes. We argue that examination of coping behavior might show actual change in personality processes and give evidence of their diachronic effects.

Older people can deal successfully with threatening, challenging, or otherwise taxing demands. Data on coping with health- and work-related demands provide evidence for the assumption that cognitive processes play a major role when the aging individual is confronted with these demands. Cognitively appraised demands are not simply isomorphic representations of the taxing situations encountered; they are, in part, constructed by an actively perceiving and appraising individual. An activistic conceptualization of personality is supported.

Interaction between actual and developmental processes can be inferred on the basis of the results from the BLSA. The concepts of crystallization, fluidization, and theme help us to understand ongoing change over time. With repeated experiences of a deteriorating health status, for example, not only perceptions of health and health-related problems change, but also the constellation of personal needs and situational presses, i.e., the thematic structure of the aging person's cognitively represented life space. This interpretation follows Thomae's conceptualization of personality development. In terms of Haan's theory, we would emphasize that as disequilibration of thematic structures occurs, the person's adaptational programs can undergo accommodation. We find that aging individuals in general cope in order to restructure and to reach a reequilibration of assimilative and accommodative processes. Haan would not stress the thematic structure of such a development as clearly as Thomae.

The BLSA data show that older people "meaningfully" restructure their programs of adaptation. Although we cannot speak of a consistency of coping styles, we can claim evidence of consistency of their efficacy. The hypothetical processes of fluidization and crystallization seem to allow productive adaptation in old age which is based on personal potentials as well as on situational demands in that period of development.

## REFERENCES

BAADE, F. E., BORCK, J., KROEBE, S., and ZUMVENNE, G. (1980). *Theorien und methoden der verhaltenstherapie.* Mitteilungen der DGVT, Sonderheft II.

BENNER, P., ROSKIES, E., and LAZARUS, R. S. (1980). Stress and coping under extreme conditions. In J. E. Dimsdale (Ed.), *Survivors, victims, and perpetrators: Essays on the Nazi holocaust.* Washington, D.C.: Hemisphere, 219–258.

BLOS, P. (1962). *On adolescence.* New York: The Free Press.

CAPLAN, G. (1964). *Principles of preventive psychiatry.* New York: Basic Books.

COELHO, G. V., HAMBURG, D. A., and ADAMS, J. E. (Eds.). (1974). *Coping and adaptation.* New York: Basic Books.

COHEN, F. (1982). Panel report on psychosocial assets and modifiers of stress. In G. R. Elliott and C. Eisdorfer (Eds.), *Stress and human health: Analysis and implications for research.* New York: Springer, 147–188.

DATAN, N., and GINSBERG, L. H. (Eds.). (1975) *Life-span developmental psychology: Normative life crises.* New York: Academic Press.

DUNKEL-SCHETTER, C., and WORTHMAN, C. B. (1981). Dilemmas of social support: Parallels between victimization and aging. In S. B. Kiesler, J. N. Morgan, and V. K. Oppenheimer (Eds.), *Aging: Social change.* New York: Academic Press, 349–381.

ELLIOTT, G. R., and EISDORFER, C. (Eds.). (1982). *Stress and human health: Analysis and implications for research.* New York: Springer.

FIELD, D. (1981). Retrospective reports by healthy intelligent elderly people of personal events of their adult lives. *International Journal of Behavioral Development, 4,* 77–97.

FILIPP, S. H. (Ed.). (1981). *Kritische lebensereignisse.* Munchen: Urban und Schwarzenberg.

FOLKMAN, S., and LAZARUS, R. S. (1980). An analysis of coping in a middle-aged community sample. *Journal of Health and Social Behavior, 21,* 219–239.

FREUD, S. (1905). *Drei abhandlungen zur sexualtheorie.* Wien: Deuticke.

GLEASON, J., KARUZA, J., JR., and ZEVON, M. A. (1981). Personal responsibility in coping. Paper presented at the Meeting of the Gerontological Society of America, San Diego.

GOLDFRIED, M. R. (1977). The use of relaxation and cognitive relabeling as coping skills. In R. B. Stuart (Ed.), *Behavioral self-management: Strategies, techniques and outcome.* New York: Brunner and Mazel, 82–116.

GUILFORD, J. P. (1959). *Personality.* New York: McGraw-Hill.

GUTMAN, D. (1977). The cross-cultural perspective. In J. E. Birren and K. W. Schaie (Eds.), *Handbook of the psychology of aging.* New York: Van Nostrand, 302–326.

GUTMAN, D. (1980). Observations on culture and mental health in later life. In J. E. Birren and B. Sloane (Eds.), *Handbook of mental health and aging.* Englewood Cliffs, NJ: Prentice-Hall, 429–447.

HAAN, N. (1963). Proposed model of ego functioning. Coping and defense mechanisms in relation to IQ change. *Psychological Monographs, 77,* no. 8.

HAAN, N. (1977). *Coping and defending.* New York: Academic Press.

HOUSE, J. S. (1981). *Work stress and social support.* Menlo Park, CA: Addison-Wesley.

KAPLAN, H. B. (Ed.) (1983). *Psychosocial stress. Trends in theory and research.* New York: Academic Press.

KIRSCHT, J. P., and ROSENSTOCK, I. M. (1979). Patient's problems in following recommendations of health experts. In G. C. Stone, N. E. Adler, et al. *Health psychology: A handbook.* San Francisco: Jossey-Bass.

KOHLI, M. (1978). *Soziologie des lebenslaufs.* Darmstadt/Neuwied: Luchterhand.

KROEBER, T. C. (1963). The coping functions of the ego mechanisms. In R. White (Ed.), *The study of lives.* New York. Atherton.

LABOUVIE-VIEF, G., and GONDA, J. N. (1976). Cognitive strategy training and intellectual performance in the elderly. *Journal of Gerontology, 31,* 327–332.

LAZARUS, R. S. (1966). *Psychological stress and the coping process.* New York: McGraw-Hill.

LAZARUS, R. S. (1980). The stress and coping paradigm. In L. A. Bond and J. C. Rosen (Eds.), *Competence and coping during adulthood.* Hanover: University Press of New England, 28–74.

LAZARUS, R. S., AVERILL, J. R., and OPTON, E. (1974). The psychology of coping: Issues of research and assessment. In G. V. Coelho, D. A. Hamburg, and J. E. Adams (Eds.), *Coping and adaptation.* New York: Basic Books, 249–315.

LAZARUS, R. S., and OLBRICH, E. (1983). Problems of stress and coping in old age. In M. Bergener, U. Lehr, E. Lang, and R. Schmitz-Scherzer (Eds.), *Aging in the eighties and beyond.* New York: Springer, 272–287.

LEHR, U. (1977). *Psychologie des alterns.* Heidelberg: Quelle & Meyer.
LESSER, L., LAZARUS, L., WILSON, R., COHLER, B., SCHWEON, C., KASZNIAK, A., and FOX, J. (1981). Psychological defense mechanisms in normal and demented elderly. Paper presented at the meeting of the Gerontological Society of America, San Diego.
LIEBERMAN, M. A. (1975). Adaptive processes in later life. In N. Datan and L. H. Ginsberg (Eds.), *Life-span developmental psychology: Normative life crises.* New York: Academic Press, 135–159.
MATTESON, M. T., and IVANCEVICH, J. M. (1982). *Managing job stress and health.* New York: The Free Press.
McCRAE, R. R. (1982). Age differences in the use of coping mechanisms. *Journal of Gerontology, 37,* 454–460.
McLEAN, A. (1979). *Work stress.* Reading, MA: Addison-Wesley.
MEICHENBAUM, D. (1977). *Cognitive behavior modification.* New York: Plenum Press.
MOOS, R. (Ed.) (1976). *Human adaptation: Coping with life crises.* Lexington, KY: Health.
MOOS, R. (Ed.) (1977). *Coping with physical illness.* New York: Plenum.
MURPHY, L. B., and MORIARTY, A. E. (1976). *Vulnerability, coping and growth.* New Haven and London: Yale University Press.
OLBRICH, E. (1976). *Der altere mensch in der interaktion mit seiner sozialen ümwelt.* (Ph.D. thesis) Bonn.
OLBRICH, E. (1981). Normative ubergange im menschlichen lebenslauf: Entwicklungskrisen oder herausforderungen? In S. H. Filipp (Ed.), *Kristische lebensereignisse.* München: Urban und Schwarzenberg, 123–138.
OLBRICH, E. (1983). Übergange im jugendalter. In R. Silbereisen und L. Montada (Eds.), *Entwicklungspsychologie. Ein handbuch in schlüsselbegriffen.* München: Urban und Schwarzenberg, 89–96.
OLBRICH, E., and THOMAE, H. (1978). Empirical findings to a cognitive theory of aging. *International Journal of Behavioral Development, 1,* 67–84.
PFEIFFER, E. (1977). Psychopathology and social pathology. In J. E. Birren and K. W. Schaie (Eds.), *Handbook of the psychology of aging.* New York: Van Nostrand, 650–671.
PLEMONS, J., WILLIS, S., and BALTES, P. (1978). Modifiability of fluid intelligence in aging: Short term longitudinal training approach. *Journal of Gerontology, 33,* 224–231.
QUAYHAGEN, M. P., and QUAYHAGEN, M. (1982). Coping with conflict. Measurement of age-related patterns. *Research on Aging, 4,* 364–377.
RENNER, V. J., and BIRREN, J. E. (1980). Stress: Physiological and psychological mechanisms. In J. E. Birren and R. B. Sloane (Eds.), *Handbook of mental health and aging.* Englewood Cliffs, NJ: Prentice-Hall, Inc., 310–336.
ROSKIES, E., and LAZARUS, R. S. (1980). Coping theory and the teaching of coping skills. In P. O. Davidson and S. M. Davidson (Eds.), *Behavioral medicine.* New York: Brunner and Mazel, 38–69.
ROSOW, I. (1976). Status and role change through the life-span. In R. H. Binstock and E. Shanas (Eds.), *Handbook of aging and the social sciences.* New York: Van Nostrand.
SCHÖNPFLUG, W. (1979). Regulation und Fehlregulation im Verhalten. I and II, *Psychologische Beiträge, 21,* 174–202 and 597–621.
THOMAE, H. (1951). *Persönlichkeit.* Bonn: Bouvier.

THOMAE, H. (1968). *Das individuum und seine welt.* Göttingen: Hogrefe.

THOMAE, H. (1970). Theory of aging and cognitive theory of personality. *Human Development, 13,* 1–16.

THOMAE, H. (1983). *Alternsstile und altersschicksale.* Bern, Stuttgart, Wien: Huber.

THOMAE, H. (1984). Formen der auseinandersetzung mit konflikt und belastung im jugendalter. In E. Olbrich and E. Todt (Eds.), *Probleme des jugendalters,* Heidelberg: Springer, 89–110.

THOMAE, H., LEHR, U., and SCHMITZ-SCHERZER, R. (1981). Research on aging in behavioral sciences in the Federal Republic of Germany. *Zeitschrift für Gerontologie, 14,* 204–223.

VAILLANT, G. E. (1977). *Adaptation to life.* Boston: Little Brown.

WHITE, R. W. (1974). Strategies of adaptation. In G. V. Coelho, D. A. Hamburg, and J. E. Adams (Eds.), *Coping and adaptation.* New York: Basic Books, 47–68.

WILLIS, S., BLIESZNER, R., and BALTES, P. (1981). Intellectual training research in aging: Modification of performance on the fluid ability figural relations, *Journal of Educational Psychology, 73,* 41–50.

4

# AGE, HEALTH, AND JOB PERFORMANCE

Pauline K. Robinson

This chapter addresses two questions related to the effects of age on health and thus on job performance. The first question is both a conceptual and an empirical one: "Is the job performance of middle-aged and older workers adversely affected by age-related health factors?" The second question stems from a more applied approach: "If so, how can these age-related effects be minimized through work-place interventions?" The applied approach directs attention in the chapter to the perspective of decision makers in the arena in which job performance is most relevant, that of business management. The term *older workers* will be used to denote middle-aged and older workers up to retirement age.

Due to fewer young persons entering the workforce, the maturation of the sizable baby boom cohort, and the continuing early retirement trend, the work force is becoming distinctly middle-aged (Robinson, Coberly, and Paul, 1985). This demographic trend is attracting increasingly greater interest from several sectors—government, business, and academic research. Table 1 shows the increase in the proportion of 35- to 54-year-old workers in the labor force from about one third to one half by the year 2000.

The swelling of the ranks of middle-aged workers signals a need for employers to pay greater attention to the relationship of aging to the health and performance of the work force. If conditions in the work place are responsible for some health and performance decrements over the span of employees' careers, management needs to try to correct these conditions. If it is possible to promote the good health, and thus performance, of a middle-aged and older work force, management

**TABLE 1. Labor Force Changes, 1982-2000. Percent of the Labor Force by Age Group.**

| | 1982 | 2000 |
|---|---|---|
| 18-24 | 20% | 15% |
| 25-34 | 28 | 22 |
| 35-54 | 35 | 49 |
| 55-64 | 11 | 9 |
| 65+ | 3 | 2 |

Source: Derived from data in Morrison, M.H. (1983).

needs to examine the costs and benefits of health promotion programs. Management policies of hiring, training, job redesign, and retirement age all rest on assumptions about the capabilities of middle-aged and older workers to perform their jobs adequately.

It is especially in periods of economic downturn and high unemployment, when reductions in the work force are widespread, that the health and job performance of older employees come under scrutiny. Chronological age is of course not permissible as a criterion for termination or other personnel decisions (from age 40 up to age 70 in most jobs) under the Age Discrimination in Employment Act. Early retirement incentives, however, are permissible and constitute a management option that will continue to reflect assumptions about the health and job performance of older workers.

Job performance is not only of interest to employers; it is also important to broad national interests and to the well-being of individual employees. In recent years, international trade competition has focused national concern on economic productivity, one factor of which is individual productivity (job performance). An increase in the average age of the work force, therefore, creates apprehension about the effects of this aging phenomenon on individual productivity (Fox, 1951; Robinson, 1983; Welford, 1976).

Public concern about the impact of age on job performance is particularly acute in reference to occupations in which public safety is involved—for example, airline pilots. It is beyond the scope of this chapter to discuss the special class of jobs deemed in law to be bona fide occupational qualification jobs because of the public safety factor, but national attention to such cases has focused attention on the effects of age-related health changes on job performance and on the ability of testing procedures to predict future performance.

In addition, the health and employment status of older workers is a national concern because of the serious demand that can be placed on alternative sources of income, such as Social Security retirement, disability, unemployment compensation, etc., when job performance declines and workers leave the labor force prematurely.

Individuals themselves may be concerned about their health and their ability to perform their jobs as they move into their middle and later years, because of the importance of work in their lives and the implications for their current and lifetime earnings.

A distinction should be made between the issue of disability that keeps individuals out of the labor force, or limitations on the kind of work that can be performed, on the one hand, and the issue addressed in this chapter: the effects of age-related health factors on the performance of jobs in which individuals are actively engaged. A great deal more attention has been paid to the former issue of disability (Andrisani, 1977; Lando, Cutler, and Gamber, 1982). Early retirement and other forms of termination remove most older workers from the work force before they are incapable because of health reasons of performing their jobs, and early retirement is especially prevalent in heavy manufacturing jobs, which place the greatest demands on aging workers. This chapter is concerned with the health and job performance of those middle-aged and older workers who are actively participating in the labor force.

## AGE-RELATED CHANGES IN HEALTH AMONG MIDDLE-AGED AND OLDER WORKERS

In order to address the question of whether age-related health changes affect job performance in the middle and later years of the work life, it is first necessary to investigate the nature and extent of health-related changes during this period.

The dominant changes in health that accompany aging can be attributed to a number of causes, namely: genetic predisposition; lifelong environmental influences, e.g., nutrition and toxins; individual lifestyle and behavior; stress; and intrinsic processes of aging. All age-related health changes are relevant to the discussion of job performance, regardless of their source. Appropriate data for observing age-related health changes relevant to job performance would be longitudinal data on individuals who are active in the work force. Unfortunately, we often rely on population data on health in order to study age differences in the health of active workers, thereby introducing an error due to the *healthy worker effect*; this term reflects the relatively favorable health status of the employed population due to (1) the selection, self-selection, and retention of healthy workers in the labor force and (2) the more favorable conditions associated with employment, such as higher income, access to medical care, and, perhaps, healthier lifestyle (Wen, Tsai, and Gibson, 1983).

The differences between the total population and the population in the labor force are substantial. For example, the labor force participation rate of men aged 55 to 64 is only 71 percent and only 41 percent for women aged 55 to 64; many of the remaining percent are out of the labor force for health reasons. One out of four persons aged 55 to 64 is unable to work regularly or unable to work at all due to disability (Social Security Administration, 1982). Population health data, then, exaggerate the prevalence of illness and impairment in the working population.

Since longitudinal data on the health of workers active in the labor force are not readily available in published form, all that we can usually observe are age *differences* in cross-sectional data on the health of the working-age population. These cross-sectional differences reflect an additional problem, the confounding of two kinds of age effects: first, the individual aging effects discussed above; and second, differences at a given point of time between younger and older cohorts as a result of (1) different generational experiences (e.g., nutrition, health care, lifestyle) and (2) selective survival. Other issues in interpreting available health data in relation to work are discussed in detail in Chapter 2.

Bearing in mind the limitations of the available data, it is possible to state some generalizations about age differences in health in the working-age population:

1. Of the ten chronic conditions most prevalent in the population, most occur more frequently in the middle and later than in the younger years—hypertensive disease, heart conditions, diabetes, varicose veins, arteriosclerosis, and hernia of the abdominal cavity (U.S. Public Health Service, 1981).

2. Among the population aged 55 to 64, the most prevalent chronic conditions occur as follows (rate per thousand): arthritis, 306; hypertensive disease, 263; heart conditions, 167; and chronic sinusitis, 177 (U.S. Public Health Service, 1984). (Some portion of these rates represents individuals who have been included in more than one category.)

3. Physical impairments rise sharply with increased age. Included in this category are visual, hearing, and back impairments (Newquist and Robinson, 1983[1]; U.S. Public Health Service, 1981).

4. Days of restricted activity due to illness per year increase from 16 days for 25 to 44-year-olds to 26 days for 45 to 64-year-olds (U.S. Public Health Service, 1981).

These four statements emphasize health decrements with age. On the other hand, the following generalizations place data on health decrements in some perspective:

1. The incidence of *acute* conditions is lower in the fifties and sixties than in younger age groups (U.S. Public Health Service, 1982).

2. The great majority of older adults (81 percent of 45 to 54-year-olds and 71 percent of 55 to 64-year-olds) in the community report no limitation of activity due to chronic conditions, and only 4 percent (45 to 54) and 9 percent (55 to 64) report that they are unable to perform their major activity (employment or housework) (U.S. Public Health Service, 1984).

3. Forty percent of persons aged 45 to 54 and 32 percent of persons aged 55 to 64 rate their health as excellent; only 5 percent of those aged 45 to 54 and 8 percent of those aged 55 to 64 rate their health as poor (U.S. Public Health Service, 1984).

4. No single physical impairment (e.g., visual, hearing, or back impairment) is experienced by more than 10 percent of the 54 to 64 age group (U.S. Public Health Service, 1984). (Some individuals may have more than one impairment.)

5. Longitudinal studies have shown only a gradual decline of function with aging

[1]The Newquist and Robinson (1983) paper contains unpublished cross-sectional data from the National Center for Health Statistics, with cross tabulations by narrower age categories than are generally available in published data.

in most organ systems in the absence of disease up to about age 75 (Birren, Butler, Greenhouse, Sokoloff, and Yarrow, 1971; Palmore, 1970, 1974; Weg, 1975).

Certain qualifications need to be added to these observations. First, it is extremely important to note that most health data are based on samples of the total noninstitutionalized population, including individuals who are outside the labor force for health-related reasons, as discussed previously. Secondly, individuals of the same age differ widely on measures of health and functional capabilities, and this variability increases with age up to at least age 70 (Svanborg, Landahl, and Mellstrom, 1982). Third, limited and highly summarized statistics on chronic conditions and other health limitations, such as those cited above, do not portray the severity of limitations or effects on the ability to perform in particular jobs.

Given that there are changes in health during the working years, the second question to be addressed is whether age-related health changes affect work capacity and job performance.

## EFFECTS OF AGE-RELATED HEALTH CHANGES ON WORK CAPACITY AND JOB PERFORMANCE

Solomon (1984) has reviewed the available data on age-associated changes in health from the perspective of work performance; a few of his observations follow.

**1.** As far as the cardiovascular system is concerned, changes with aging per se are modest. Although cardiac output at rest does not decline with age in carefully screened normal subjects, changes in cardiac function in response to exercise begin by age 40. These changes in normal aging functions are not a serious problem in most work situations, but serious problems do arise with the occurrence of coronary artery disease. Hypertension, the chief risk factor in coronary artery disease, is found in 30 percent of the population aged 60 to 65 and in 40 percent of those over 65.

**2.** Changes in the respiratory system with age decrease the efficiency and increase the effort of breathing. These changes are not usually a problem with ordinary exertion at sea level. These changes do become problematic, however, with the onset of diseases such as carcinoma of the lung, emphysema, chronic bronchitis, asthma, pulmonary infections, and pulmonary emboli.

**3.** Most gastrointestinal and liver diseases do not increase with age, and do not result in major impairment of working ability in late middle age.

**4.** The bones, muscles, and joints become progressively more fragile, less supple, and more a source of pain with aging, contributing to partial disability in many individuals after the age of 55.

**5.** Although kidney functions decline steadily after age 30 (almost 10 percent per decade), the direct effects are minimal because of the reserve of the kidney. The reduction in renal reserve, however, makes older persons more vulnerable to drug toxicity and dehydration or overhydration. In addition, damage to the kidneys due to high blood pressure increases with age. The conclusion Solomon draws from the evidence he reviewed is as follows:

> On the average, physical, cognitive, and psychological function do decline with advancing age. However, each of these trends begins only slowly and has small impact in the later phase of the usual working lifetime, ages 55 through 65. Although it is undeniable that the percent of the work force disabled rises detectably, the remaining workers are not significantly impaired. I would suggest that health first becomes a major factor only in the subsequent decade, 65 through 74. Only at 75 and above, when very few remain in the work force, does health become a really dominant consideration in the work situation (1984, 1).

Age differences in physical work capacity were observed by Shephard (1969) in a sample of Canadian men and women in various occupations. Shephard's data are important in that his sample was drawn from a working population. On a measure of aerobic power, men showed a drop between the ages of 16 and 60, an effect which Shephard considers significant for performance in some work circumstances. Excessive weight was observed to be much more prevalent among men and women employees over the age of 40, and its effect on increased risk of morbidity and mortality as well as on the energy cost of some forms of industrial work was noted by Shephard. No real decline in strength (hand grip) was observed among males until after age 50.

A later study by Shephard of a specific occupation, marine surveying, showed that the arduous work of inspecting vessels and cargo challenged the speed and accuracy of performance and aerobic power of men in their mid-sixties (Shephard, 1983). The conclusions, which supported the retirement of marine surveyors at age 65, were not based on objective evidence of slowing down of the older surveyors, but rather on impressions of their performance and on observations of the specific job demands relative to the maximum oxygen intake of an unfit 65-year-old. Shephard based his conclusions on the public safety aspects of marine surveying, and noted that exceptional older employees might be identified by careful testing.

An appropriate set of data for analyzing the relationship of age differences in health to job performance would be observations of individuals within particular occupations on both health status and job performance, comparing across age categories. Although many companies have data available on both health and job performance—for example, through annual performance evaluations—they do not ordinarily analyze their data in this way, and if they do, they do not ordinarily publish the results.

An approximation of this kind of analysis can be found in the periodically published data on the incidence and duration of disability among the office and sales personnel of the Metropolitan Life Insurance Company. Disability in this analysis refers to absence from work due to illness lasting between one week and 26 weeks. If we are willing to accept relatively short-term illness absences as an indirect indicator of both health loss and reduced job performance, then these data are relevant to the issue of the effects of age-related health factors on job performance.

Illness absences of over a week to 26 weeks are more common among Metropolitan Life Insurance Company office personnel between 45 and 54 than among younger office personnel, and are still higher for those aged 55 to 64. For example, the 1980–1981 annual incidence (per 1000) of these illness absences among males was 81 for 17 to 24-year-olds, 74 for 25 to 44-year-olds, 180 for 45 to 54-year-olds, and 191 for 55 to 64-year-olds. For females the incidence was 176 (17 to 24), 179 (25 to 44), 204 (45 to 54), and 230 (55 to 64). The age differences among male sales personnel are similar to those of male office workers, but are reversed for female sales personnel, due in part to absences among the younger personnel for maternity and related conditions (Disability among Metropolitan employees in 1980–1981, 1983). (Since shorter illness absences are not included in these data, it is not known how the total number of days absent due to illness varies by age.) The causes of illness-related absence that accounted for the greatest age differences were diseases of the circulatory system (including diseases of the heart).

Statistics on the same work force on duration of disability show that, in general, older employees were absent for a longer time than younger employees. Among male office employees on disability, the proportion who returned to work within three months decreased somewhat with age, as follows: 95 percent of 17 to 24-year-olds, 92 percent of 25 to 44-year-olds, and 81 percent of 45 to 64-year-olds. Among male sales personnel, who are perhaps more restricted from working because of health limitations than office personnel because of the nature of their work, the age differences were greater: 91 percent of 17 to 24-year-olds, 82 percent of 25 to 44-year-olds, and 69 percent of 45 to 64-year-olds returned to work within three months (Variation in duration of disability among Metropolitan employees, 1981).

The significance of the Metropolitan Life Insurance Company statistics stems, first, from the fact that they are drawn from a specific and occupationally homogeneous population, since the effects of health on job performance vary widely among different occupations. Secondly, office and sales personnel would be expected to be much less seriously restricted from performing their jobs for reasons related to health than employees in more physically demanding jobs, and these data would thus be expected to suggest a conservative estimate of the effects of age on health-related absences.

National Health Interview Survey data also show an increase with age (up to age 65) of work-loss days due to illness or injury per year (Table 2).

**TABLE 2. Work-loss Days Due to Illness or Injury Per Year, 1981.**

| AGE | MALE | FEMALE |
|---|---|---|
| 17–24 | 3.5 | 4.8 |
| 25–44 | 4.4 | 5.4 |
| 45–64 | 5.6 | 5.9 |
| 65+ | 4.4 | 3.8 |

Source: Derived from data in U.S. Public Health Service (1982).

The above discussion of the effects of aging on health and job performance has focused on the under-65 age group. Only 18 percent of men 65 and over and 8 percent of women 65 and over are in the labor force, and together they make up only 3 percent of the labor force (Morrison, 1983). Nevertheless, there are important personnel policy decisions that need to be made concerning these oldest employees, and knowledge about their health and productivity is central to such decisions.

The problem in making generalizations, on the basis of population data, about the effects of aging on the health and job performance of this distinct minority of older persons 65 and over who work is even greater than has been noted for the under-65 work force. There is a wide range of individual differences in health status in the older population, and employed persons 65 and older could be presumed to be among the healthiest of their age group. There is one measure available for comparing working persons aged 65 and over with working persons 55 to 64, namely the number of days lost from work because of illness. Persons aged 65 and over actually report fewer days lost from work because of illness than persons 45 to 64 (Table 2).

Data on incidence and duration of illness absences provide evidence of reduced job performance of older workers (up to age 65) to the extent that absence from the job reduces overall job performance over a period of time. On the other hand, the effects of absence from the job due to illness may be counterbalanced by other performance attributes of older workers, such as experience, effort, and a lower rate of *avoidable* absences (Doering, Rhodes, and Schuster, 1983).

### Other Factors Affecting Job Performance

There are, of course, other age-related factors that may affect job performance as well as changes in health. Some factors in job performance can be related to age because they are related to a closely associated factor, tenure on the job, or because they reflect cohort differences. Age-related factors affecting job performance include obsolescence and cohort differences in education and training, discussed in Chapter 7 of this volume. Other age-related factors are life stage and cohort differences in motivation and attitudes toward work (Rhodes, 1983; Sonnenfeld, 1978), cognitive functioning (Salthouse, 1982), age discrimination (Haber, 1970; Rosen and Jerdee, 1977), and the structure and environment of the work place (see Chapter 7).

### Age and Job Performance

If age-related health changes, as well as other age-related factors, do in fact have an impact on job performance, then we should find research evidence of an association between age and job performance. Work site research on age differences in job performance has been inadequate for drawing useful generalizations, however; reviews of the limited empirical literature on age and productivity include those by Baugher (1978), Kelleher and Quirk (1973), Meier and Kerr (1976), Rhodes (1983), and Robinson (1983).

In general, variability in performance measures within age groups far outweighs differences among age groups, but age differences can be observed more readily in some occupations than in others. Although there are age differences that are measurable in some aspects of functioning (e.g., vision), most jobs do not demand performance at the level of maximum capacity. Jobs demanding physical strength and a rapid work pace result in the greatest declines in performance with age whereas in some jobs, which require experience or the building of a clientele, the more mature worker is at an advantage. Tenure and seniority, which tend to be associated with age, sometimes place the older worker in less physically demanding jobs. The processes of self-selection and termination tend to reduce age differences in performance in the surviving work force. In the future, industrial trends away from heavy manufacturing and toward the service and knowledge sectors can be expected to reduce the impact of age on job performance.

## WORK-PLACE INTERVENTIONS TO REDUCE THE IMPACT OF AGING ON HEALTH

Health and functioning do not inevitably decline in the middle and later working years. Furthermore, there are certain interventions in the work place that can prevent or reduce health decrements. Examples of such interventions are the reduction of work hazards and health promotion.

### Reducing Work Hazards

Declines in health and functioning that sometimes occur over the work life of the individual may be attributable not so much to aging as to the effects of the work environment itself. Hazards to health in the work environment include toxic elements and other unsafe conditions; sedentary patterns of work; noise; stress; and frustrating and discouraging aspects of work (Cooper, 1984; Donoghue, 1977; Shephard, 1984; Social Security Administration, 1983; Stellman and Daum, 1973; see also Chapters 2 and 3, this volume). Reduced vitality and illnesses such as chronic lung disease, cancer, and degenerative diseases may be the effects of these work conditions, but most workers are unprotected from work site risks (U.S. Public Health Service, 1979). Older workers are in general more vulnerable to accidental injury and to highly stressful work conditions, although age differences in vulnerability to work-place hazards have not been systematically studied. The effects may be cumulative throughout the career span, and may not begin to manifest themselves until after a period of latency, as in recent revelations about the serious effects of asbestos. The reduction of work-place hazards is one intervention that can prevent some of the illnesses and functional declines observable in the middle and later years.

### Health Promotion in the Work Place

It is conceivable that individuals can actually become healthier and can function at higher levels of performance as they grow older, if there are significant improvements in their health-related behavior and their environment. It is certain that many of the health decrements associated with aging can be reduced or prevented by exercise, proper diet, weight control, and not smoking.

The work place itself is a reasonable site for health promotion because employees spend such a high proportion of their time at work and because employers have a vested interest in the health of their employees. Declines in health and functioning associated with aging can be prevented or forestalled through the multifaceted health promotion programs which are becoming increasingly common in large companies (Allen, 1984; Karson, 1982; Robinson, 1984). Work-site health promotion efforts include various combinations of programs such as aerobic exercise, smoking cessation, hypertension screening and control, weight management, nutrition education, and stress management. Recent developments in work-site health promotion programs focus on the identification of health risk factors and appropriate referral and follow-up procedures. The potential for the improvement of the health status and job performance of middle-aged and older workers in the future is a key factor in the consideration of work-place intervention strategies.

Evaluation of the effectiveness of these programs is especially difficult to measure (Brennan, 1982; Fielding, 1984). The most impressive results to date have come from hypertension screening and control efforts (Kristein, 1977; 1982). Hypertension is a disease of the middle and later years and is one of the major risk factors in cardiovascular accidents (Roemer, 1984); cardiovascular disease, in turn, is the largest category of chronic conditions causing work disability in 45 to 54-year-old men, and one of the top categories in other older age groups of men and women. Work-site hypertension screening and control programs have reported up to a 90 percent success rate in the control of hypertension among the hypertensives identified (Kiefaber, 1983; Rocella, 1982).

## WORK-PLACE INTERVENTIONS TO REDUCE THE IMPACT OF AGE-RELATED HEALTH DECLINES ON JOB PERFORMANCE

One strategy to reduce age-related health decrements and their effects on job performance is to intervene to prevent or mitigate age-related health decrements per se, as discussed above. Another strategy involves work-place interventions designed to minimize the effects of given health decrements on job performance. This strategy involves practices to circumvent and compensate for limitations through assessment, work-place accommodations, and retraining.

### Assessment

Fitting, and continually refitting, the right individual to the right job is a key strategy in dealing with middle-aged and older employees. Since chronological age is not a useful criterion in making personnel decisions (and is prohibited by law in many circumstances), the accurate assessment of changes in employees' job-related capabilities and limitations is required for appropriate placement and subsequent accommodations and retraining. The technology of assessment for complex jobs has unfortunately lagged behind the need. Performance appraisal—i.e., the evaluation at regular intervals of the employee's actual performance of the job—is also essential for fitting employees to appropriate jobs in face of individual employee aging (Walker and Lazer, 1978). Assessment that reveals reduced capabilities can be followed by altering the nature of the job or by retraining the employee for a different job, as constructive approaches in lieu of termination.

### Work-place Accommodations

A number of strategies have been widely discussed as methods to promote the retention of older workers in the face of possible health limitations. The most frequently recommended set of methods falls under the broad category of alternative work arrangements, such as providing the option of part-time work or job sharing (McConnell, 1981). These options make possible the continued employment of older workers whose health and vigor may not be adequate for full-time work.

The redesign of jobs has been used successfully to accommodate specific limitations of older workers, such as difficulty in lifting, climbing, or prolonged standing (Barkin, 1970; Laufer and Fowler, 1971; U.S. Department of Labor, 1967). The modification of jobs because of older worker limitations is usually carried out informally and is often undertaken on behalf of a single worker. Job redesign can involve mechanization to reduce physical effort, and improvements in equipment and work station; it can also involve changing the content of the job by redistributing certain tasks, such as lifting, to other jobs.

Recent technological advances have made possible increased substitution of mechanical and electronic systems for physical exertion, and have been used to make productive job performance possible for handicapped employees, in particular in compensating for vision and hearing losses. These same advances can be applied in the case of middle-aged and older employees who experience age-related limitations (Robinson, Livingston, and Birren, 1984).

### Retraining

Whereas work-place accommodations are designed to alter the structural arrangements of the job, it is also possible to alter the employee's ability to work in spite of health limitations. One approach is to provide retraining for other kinds of work tasks when health limitations prevent performance on the current job. (See Chapter 6 of this volume for a discussion of retraining.) Sometimes transfer to a different job is possible without retraining.

## DISCUSSION

One of the problems associated with age-related declines in health and their subsequent effects on job performance is the lack of awareness on the part of most business-sector decision makers of the research findings that have been discussed in this chapter, namely, the relatively low proportion of older workers (below age 65) who experience substantial limitations in their ability to work productively; the high degree of variability in health and functioning among workers within the same age range; and the potential within the work place for interventions to reduce the impact of aging on health and job performance.

A second problem is the lack of published data on the health and job performance of employees in their middle and later years, data that would be useful in business decisions and that are in fact available within many companies on their own employees. This chapter has also pointed out the deficits that exist in national data bases and in the research literature on the health of the middle-aged and older *working* population, age differences in job performance, and the relationship between age-related health changes and job performance. In addition, further study is needed of work-place interventions to reduce the impact of aging on health. For example, to what extent is age a factor in vulnerability to work-place hazards? In health promotion programs, what age differences need to be taken into account in appropriateness of various types of programs, in utilization rates, and in effectiveness?

Although this chapter has focused on age-related health *decrements* and the *adverse* effects of aging on job performance, it could also be argued that aging can be accompanied by health gains and thus result in positive effects on job performance. There are two possible ways that this might occur. First, individuals, or a cohort of individuals, may engage in health-promoting behavior that makes them healthier in middle age and old age than they were as young adults. Second, environmental conditions may improve over time, with the result that a given cohort experiences improved health in the middle and later years. Neither of these is likely to be a substantially important trend. Although improvements in health and functioning as a result of the aging process itself are difficult to conceptualize, aging is nevertheless often accompanied by experience and improved attitudes and judgment which can more than compensate for age-related losses.

The effects on job performance of age-related health decrements depend on the kind of work performed and the conditions of the work environment. Employment in the service and knowledge industries places fewer physical demands on employees in their middle and later years than does strenuous physical labor or assembly line production, and although older workers are now concentrated in the latter kinds of jobs, the trend in employment is clearly away from manufacturing and toward the service and knowledge sectors. The health and functioning of older workers in the future may therefore be increasingly adequate for continued employment.

## CONCLUSION

Aging and accompanying health decrements eventually take their toll in reduced job performance for some workers, but jobs vary in their demands on physical performance, individuals of the same age vary greatly in their level of functioning, and most individuals are not significantly affected by health losses until advanced age and well after their retirement. Not all age-related health limitations affecting job performance are inevitable or impossible to circumscribe, but more information on these limitations is needed, and business practices need to be directed to reducing and accommodating age-related health limitations. Even with the limited data available on aging, health, and job performance, the implications for business are clearly evident: policies of reducing health hazards, promoting good health, assessing changing capabilities, providing alternative working arrangements, redesigning jobs, and retraining are needed.

### *REFERENCES*


ALLEN, R. F. (1984). Corporate demonstrations of support help employees maintain healthy life styles. *Business and Health,* December, 40.

ANDRISANI, P. (1977). Effects of health problems on the work experience of middle-aged men. *Industrial Gerontology,* Spring, 97–112.

BARKIN, S. (1970). Retraining and job redesign: Positive approaches to the continued employment of older persons. In H. L. Sheppard, (Ed.), *Toward an industrial gerontology*. Cambridge, Mass.: Schenckman.

BAUGHER, D. (1978). Is the older worker inherently incompetent? *Aging and Work, 1,* 243–250.

BIRREN, J. E., BUTLER, R. N., GREENHOUSE, S. W., SOKOLOFF, L., and YARROW, M. R. (1971). *Human aging: A biological and behavioral study.* Washington, D.C.: U.S. GPO.

BRENNAN, A. J. (1982). Health promotion: What's in it for business and industry? *Health Education Quarterly, 9,* 9–19.

COOPER, C. L. (1984). Sources of occupational stress among older workers. In P. K. Robinson, J. Livingston, and J. E. Birren (Eds.), *Aging and technological advances.* New York: Plenum.

Disability among Metropolitan employees in 1980–81. (1983). Metropolitan Life Insurance Company *Statistical Bulletin,* January–June, 17–19.

DOERING, M., RHODES, S. R., and SCHUSTER, M. (1983). *The aging worker.* Beverly Hills: Sage.

DONOGHUE, S. (1977). The correlation between physical fitness, absenteeism, and work performance. *Canadian Journal of Public Health, 68,* May/June, 201–203.

FIELDING, J. E. (1984). Evaluation of worksite health promotion: Some unresolved issues and opportunities. *Corporate Commentary, 1,* 9–15.

FOX, H. (1951). Utilization of older manpower. *Harvard Business Review, 29,* 40–54.

HABER, L. D. (1970). Age and capacity devaluation. *Journal of Health and Social Behavior, 11,* 167–181.

KARSON, S. G. (1982). New emphasis on health promotion: The insurance business. *Health Education Quarterly, 9,* 42–48.

KELLEHER, C. H., and QUIRK, D. A. (1973). Age, physical capacity and work: An annotated bibliography. *Industrial Gerontology, 19,* 80–98.

KIEFABER, A. (1983). Wellness at the workplace. *Generations,* Spring, 38–40, 62.

KRISTEIN, M. M. (1977). Economic issues in prevention. *Preventive Medicine, 6,* 252–264.

KRISTEIN, M. M. (1982). The economics of health promotion at the worksite. *Health Education Quarterly, 9,* 27–91.

LANDO, M. E., CUTLER, R. R., and GAMBER, E., (1982). *1978 survey of disability and work: Data book.* Washington, D.C.: U.S. GPO.

LAUFER, A. C., and FOWLER, W. M., JR. (1971). Work potential of the aging. *Personnel Administration,* March–April, 20–25.

McCONNELL, S. R. (1981). Alternative work options for older workers: Part II—the manager's view. *Aging and Work, 4,* 81–87.

MEIER, E. L., and KERR, E. A. (1976). Capabilities of middle-aged and older workers. A survey of the literature. *Industrial Gerontology, 3,* 147–156.

MORRISON, M. H. (1983). The aging of the U.S. population: Human resource implications. *Monthly Labor Review,* May, 13–19.

NEWQUIST, D., and ROBINSON, P. K. (1983). Health and extended worklife. Paper prepared for the Administration on Aging by the National Policy Center on Employment and Retirement, University of Southern California Andrus Gerontology Center.

PALMORE, E. (Ed.). (1970). *Normal aging: Report from the Duke longitudinal study, 1955–1969.* Durham: Duke University Press.

PALMORE, E. (Ed.). (1974). *Normal aging II: Reports from the Duke longitudinal study, 1970–1973.* Durham: Duke University Press.

RHODES, S. R. (1983). Age-related differences in work attitudes and behavior: A review and conceptual analysis. *Psychological Bulletin, 93* (2), 328–367.

ROBINSON, P. K. (1983). *Organizational strategies for older workers.* New York: Pergamon Press.

ROBINSON, P. K. (1984). Facing up to health care costs of retirees. *Business and Health*, June, 23–26.

ROBINSON, P. K., COBERLY, S., and PAUL, C. E. (1985). Work and retirement. In R. Binstock and E. Shanas (Eds.), *Handbook of aging and the social sciences*, 2nd edition. New York: Van Nostrand Reinhold.

ROBINSON, P. K., LIVINGSTON, J., and BIRREN, J. E. (Eds.). (1984). *Aging and technological advances*. New York: Plenum.

ROCELLA, E. J. (1982). Selected roles of the federal government and health promotion/disease prevention focus on the worksetting. *Health Education Quarterly, 9*, 83–91.

ROEMER, M. I. (1984). The value of medical care for health promotion. *American Journal of Public Health, 74*, 243–248.

ROSEN, B., and JERDEE, T. H. (1977). Too old or not too old. *Harvard Business Review, 55*, 97–106.

SALTHOUSE, T. A. (1982). *Adult cognition: An experimental psychology of adult cognition*. New York: Springer Verlag.

SHEPHARD, R. J. (1969). The working capacity of the older employee. *Archives of Environmental Health, 18*, 982–986.

SHEPHARD, R. J. (1983). Equal opportunity for a geriatric labor force: Some observations on marine surveying. *Journal of Occupational Medicine, 25*, 211–214.

SHEPHARD, R. J. (1984). Technological change and the aging of work capacity. In P. K. Robinson, J. Livingston, and J. E. Birren, (Eds.), *Aging and technological advances*. New York: Plenum.

SOCIAL SECURITY ADMINISTRATION. (1982). *1978 survey of disability and work*. Washington, D.C.: U.S. DHHS.

SOCIAL SECURITY ADMINISTRATION. (1983). *Some aspects of the work environment and subsequent disability among working-age men*. Washington, D.C.: U.S. GPO.

SOLOMON, D. (1984). Age, health and productivity: Effects of aging on health and cognitive function. In J. Livingston and P. K. Robinson, *Age, Health and Productivity*. Report to the Administration on Aging. Mimeo.

SONNENFELD, J. (1978). Dealing with the aging workforce. *Harvard Business Review, 56*, 81–92.

STELLMAN, J. M., and DAUM, S. M. (1973). *Work is dangerous to your health*. New York: Pantheon Books.

SVANBORG, A., LANDAHL, S., and MELLSTROM, D. (1982). Basic issues of health care. In H. Thomae and G. L. Maddox (Eds.), *New perspectives on old age*. New York: Springer.

U.S. DEPARTMENT OF LABOR. (1967). *Job redesign for older workers—ten case studies*. BLS Bulletin 1523. Washington, D.C.: Bureau of Labor Statistics.

U.S. PUBLIC HEALTH SERVICE. (1979). *Healthy people: The Surgeon General's report on health promotion and disease protection*. DHEW (PHS) Pub. No. 79-55071. Washington, D.C.: U.S. GPO.

U.S. PUBLIC HEALTH SERVICE. (1981). *Current estimates from the National Health Interview Survey: United States, 1979*. Series 10, No. 136, DHHS Pub. No. (PHS) 81-1564.

U.S. PUBLIC HEALTH SERVICE. (1982). *Current estimates from the National Health Interview Survey: United States, 1981*, Series 10, Number 141, DHHS Pub. No. (PHS) 83-1569.

U.S. PUBLIC HEALTH SERVICE. (1984). *Health characteristics of persons 45 years and older*. NCHS. Working Paper Series No. 19.

Variation in duration of disability among Metropolitan employees. (1981). *Statistical Bulletin,* July–September, 8–10.

WALKER, J. W., and LAZER, H. L. (1978). *The end of mandatory retirement: Implications for management.* New York: John Wiley.

WEG, R. B. (1975). Changing physiology of aging: Normal and pathological. In D. S. Woodruff and J. E. Birren (Eds.), *Aging: Scientific perspectives and social issues.* New York: Van Nostrand.

WELFORD, A. T. (1976). Thirty years of psychological research on age and work. *Journal of Occupational Psychology, 49,* 129–138.

WEN, C. P., TSAI, S. P., and GIBSON, R. L. (1983). Anatomy of the healthy worker effect: A critical review. *Journal of Occupational Medicine, 25,* 283–289.

5

# FUNCTIONAL AGE
## *Examination of a Concept*

Timothy A. Salthouse

It has long been argued that people differ in the rate at which they manifest characteristics of aging, and many researchers have attempted to find a better index than years since birth to reflect an individual's susceptibility to processes of aging. The term ***functional age*** has been used as a descriptive label for many of these research efforts, in that it has been suggested that functional capabilities are likely to be more meaningful than mere chronological age for characterizing the status of an individual. Although the goal of monitoring a person's capacity for functioning is certainly commendable, the concept of functional age has generated such controversy and confusion that the time may now be ripe to review the various foundations of this concept and the logic behind each of its multiple usages.

Before attempting to examine the functional age concept, it is useful to consider how earlier authors have defined functional age, and its related concepts of working capacity, effective age, psychological age, biological age, and physiological age. Some researchers have adopted a very broad interpretation, as reflected in the statement by Birren and Renner (1977) that "functional age is an individual's level of capacities relative to others of his age for functioning in society" (p. 5). Others, however, have felt that functional age is more limited, as indicated by McFarland's (1973, 2) claim that functional age is the ". . . ability to perform efficiently the tasks involved in specific jobs." What appears to be a still different interpretation of the functional age concept has been proposed by several biologically oriented researchers who have suggested that functional or biological age should ". . . designate the position of the individual along his life span" (Birren, 1959, 18), or the person's "... nearness to death" (Nuttall, 1972, 149). Perhaps the only common theme across these various efforts is the belief that the tremendous variability among individuals of the same chronological age makes it imperative that some alternative index be developed that is more sensitive to individual differences.

The point about the variation among individuals of the same age can be illustrated with the aid of a fictitious, but generally realistic, example presented in Figure 5–1. The ordinate of this diagram is unlabeled to allow applicability to several dependent variables, but in all cases a higher score represents better performance on the relevant dimension. Notice that while there is a tendency for the average scores to decline with increased age, there is considerable variability at each age. In particular, individuals can be identified who have scores above the mean value for the age group (A), and who have scores below the age group mean (B). Categorizing these people together simply because they share the same chronological age is clearly an extremely crude, and often misleading, basis for classification. As a first step toward improving classification, functional age researchers have sometimes proposed that an individual should be categorized according to the age at which the average score is equivalent to the individual's score. In terms of Figure 5–1, the person represented as A would be designated functionally younger than his or her age, while the person represented as B would be considered functionally older than the chronological age would indicate.

Although the logic of Figure 5–1 appears straightforward, the ordinate has

**FIGURE 5-1** **Illustration of logic behind the functional age concept. The ordinate represents increasingly better performance on some variable, while the abscissa portrays chronological age. The individual labeled (A) would be considered functionally young, while the individual labeled (B) would be considered functionally old.**

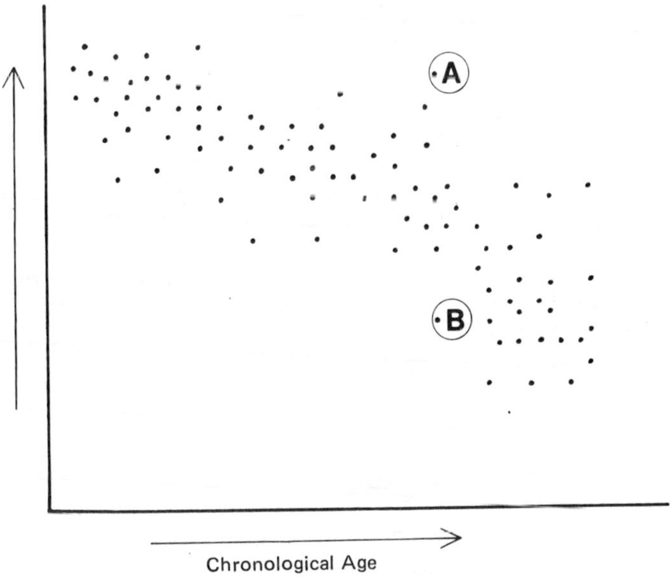

deliberately been left unlabeled, and much of the confusion concerning the functional age concept may be due to the acceptance of different criteria or dependent variables against which the functional age measures are to be assessed and validated. Birren (1969) has suggested that possible criteria include survival of the organism, capability of independent living, presence of disease, work output, training capacity, accident-proneness, and even self-concept of age. If various research efforts focus on different criteria, then it is not surprising that the field of functional age research is in disarray. The rationale for the research, the specific measures examined, and the prognosis for the ultimate value of the concept will all vary, given the existence of such diverse criteria that could be used for evaluating the validity of functional age.

Another likely factor contributing to confusion associated with the notion of functional age is the many different meanings of the terms *function* or *functional*. In fact, it appears that most of the major functional age research can be placed into three categories according to the particular connotation of *function* implicitly guiding the research efforts. One synonym for *functional* is *effective,* in the sense that something that is functional is effective in accomplishing its goals. Research designed to assess an individual's competency in a particular occupation appears to be based on this conceptualization of *functional,* and will be called *occupational functional age.* The assessment of effectiveness need not be restricted to paid employment, however, and could be applied in the measurement of proficiency at any specific activity.

A second connotation of *function* is *purpose* or *utility toward a higher action.* It is in this context that biomedical researchers refer to the functioning of bodily systems and organs in contributing to the continued survival of the organism. This type of functional age will therefore be referred to as *biomedical functional age.*

Still another definition of *function* is the mathematical one in which function indicates a specific relationship among two or more variables. Researchers attempting to determine the interrelationship of behavioral and biological characteristics across the adult life span can be considered to be investigating this type of *structural organization of human functioning.*

The present classification system is by no means exhaustive nor mutually exclusive, and clearly omits several of the possible criteria mentioned by Birren (1969). Nevertheless, the occupational, biomedical, and structural categories appear to encompass the major usages of the functional age concept in the research literature, and therefore they can serve to organize and classify the discussion of functional age. Table 1 outlines the major characteristics of each functional age category and highlights the important differences among the various usages of functional age. A major theme of the current chapter is that while the different versions of functional age are superficially similar, they actually have very little in common, and to interchange their meaning and purpose only exacerbates the chaotic status of the functional age concept.

## OCCUPATIONAL FUNCTIONAL AGE

The term *functional age* was apparently first introduced into the scientific literature by McFarland (1943) as a proposed substitute for chronological age in characterizing the proficiency of older workers. McFarland argued that it was unreasonable to

**TABLE 1**

| Category | Purpose | Variable Selection Procedure | Validation Criterion | Role of Age |
|---|---|---|---|---|
| Occupational | Predict competence in specific class of activity | Behavioral representa-tiveness in relevant class of activity | Job performance | Largely irrelevant |
| Biomedical | Assess relative health status | Importance for life maintenance | Survival | Surrogate for nearness to death |
| Structural | Determine interrelation-ship of human characteristics | Age sensitivity, theoretical predilection | Theoretical understanding | Continuum along which structural change is monitored |

judge a worker's ability to perform a specific job simply on the basis of his/her chronological age, as is the case when arbitrary ages are used to dictate job placement, training, reassignment, and retirement. A better basis for making occupational decisions was said to be information about the individual's actual capability for functioning in his or her job. This perspective has gained wide acceptance and has since been represented in legal decisions ("I believe strongly that functional capacity and not chronological age ought to be the most important factor as to whether or not an individual can do a job safely," Judge Parsons in Greyhound Bus Discrimination Case, cited in McFarland, 1973) and in popular slogans ("Don't judge a man's worth by his date of birth").

It is unfortunate that the word *age* has been used in this occupational context, because the basic idea was simply to replace arbitrary chronological age cutoffs with actual assessments of job performance in making personnel decisions. Less confusion and controversy would probably have resulted had terms like ***functional capacity, functional competence,*** or ***functional ability*** been used rather than ***functional age.*** Interchangeability of ***age*** with terms like ***ability, competence,*** or ***capacity*** could only be justified if a well-established, and widely recognized, relationship existed between age and competence. However, at the present time very few well-documented age-competence relationships are available in the scientific literature, and folklore stereotypes are too unreliable to provide a rational basis for personnel decisions.

As indicated by the earlier quote from McFarland (1973), the initial occupational version of functional age was closely tied to the work activities of the individual, and was primarily concerned with the assessment of job proficiency or competence. The job-specific nature of McFarland's proposal was evidently too limiting for many later researchers, and much of the subsequent emphasis has been upon the development of a battery of abstract measures that could have relevance for a variety of different occupations. This shift from the measurement of actual job competence to the attempt to assess general suitability for work has led to many problems, however, and there is considerable doubt that any general assessment instrument will have much utility in actual employment situations. Among the most important objections to this ***universal occupational competence*** ideal are that job requirements differ so greatly from one job to another that no single set of measures would be relevant for more than a very small number of occupations, and that years or decades of experience performing a job may have led to the acquisition of different modes of performance that are not reflected in abstract job-independent measures.

Although some gerontological researchers seem to believe that a single index of functional age might be possible and desirable (e.g., Shock, 1981), nearly all vocational guidance counselors recognize that the great diversity of possible jobs requires that many different skills and aptitudes be assessed to determine suitability for various occupations. Actually, the necessity of obtaining measurements on a variety of factors rather than attempting to derive a unitary index was pointed out by Heron and Chown (1967), who advocated the development of functional age profiles. Birren (1969), Costa and McCrae (1980), and Salthouse (1982) have also made similar arguments against the feasibility of a unitary index. Moreover, simply expanding the number of different functional ages to be considered also fails to solve the basic problems, as revealed by the following discussion.

One example of a relatively sophisticated personnel selection instrument is the General Aptitude Test Battery (GATB) and its companion set of Occupational Aptitude Patterns (OAPs). The GATB consists of 12 subtests which are combined to provide scores on the following nine aptitudes: Intelligence, Verbal Aptitude, Numerical Aptitude, Spatial Aptitude, Form Perception, Clerical Perception, Motor Coordination, Finger Dexterity, and Manual Dexterity. An individual's profile across the different aptitudes is then compared with configurations of aptitude scores considered optimal for various families of occupations. Thirty-six major Occupational Aptitude Patterns have been identified, although the requirements of nearly any specific job could be individually defined in terms of a particular configuration of the nine aptitude scores.

Several large-scale studies have been conducted analyzing the effects of age on GATB performance (e.g., Droege, Crambert, and Henkin, 1963; Fozard and Nuttall, 1971; Hirt, 1959; Stein, 1962), and all have reported that increased age is associated with lower average performances on most of the aptitude scales. The declines are not large with several aptitudes (e.g., Verbal Aptitude), but statistically significant differences between 20 and 60 years of age have been found with each aptitude in at least one major study. These results have, in turn, led to dramatic age-related reductions in the number of occupations for which the individual is qualified according to the match of aptitude profiles with Occupational Aptitude Patterns. In fact, some estimates indicate that the average 60-year-old would be suitable for less than half of the 36 occupational families.

Because older workers are prevalent, and usually performing satisfactorily, in nearly all occupations in society, one should be somewhat skeptical about the application of aptitude measures such as these to the assessment of experienced older workers. While aptitude tests are frequently useful for purposes of selection, they may be meaningless when evaluating the proficiency of individuals performing a job they have held for some time. Over years or decades of experience a worker might be expected to develop efficient modes of performance that could not be easily predicted from abstract aptitude tests. The continued performance of specific activities could lead to the preservation of abilities that would otherwise deteriorate, or might allow for the compensation of abilities that are declining with age (e.g., Dirken, 1972; McFarland, 1943; Murrell and Griew, 1965; Welford, 1965). In either case, the results of selection procedures will frequently not be useful for assessing the performance of workers continuing on an old and familiar job.

Personnel decisions concerned with retention also differ fundamentally from those dealing with selection because the opportunity to observe actual job performance eliminates problems of low validity of predictor variables, and also allows consideration of such difficult-to-test characteristics as motivation, perseverance, responsiblity, and compatibility with colleagues. Furthermore, objective and accurate performance appraisal is necessary for meaningful and legally defensible (e.g., Walker and Lupton, 1978) personnel decisions, and the age of the individual being evaluated should therefore be as irrelevant as his or her sex, race, or ethnic background. There may be some resistance to the implementation of such prescribed performance appraisal systems, but a procedure of this type now seems to be dictated both by legal precedents and concern for the rights of the individual worker.

A second problem associated with the use of occupational functional age to predict work competence is that the introduction of age into the prediction situation appears to be an unnecessary, and largely irrelevant, complication. If the goal is to predict how successfully an individual will perform in a specific job context, the standard procedure is to evaluate the level of performance on a set of predictor variables of known validity. A variety of different decision rules can be used to relate predictor performance to personnel policies (e.g., hire the applicant with the highest score among current applicants, hire anyone above the minimum score, etc.), but in all cases it is the individual's performance on the predictor variables rather than his or her age that should be the most important determinant of the applicant's ability to handle the requirements of the job. To do as some functional age advocates seem to imply and convert scores on the predictor variables to a functional age index merely adds an extraneous complication because the functional age scale is not directly related to job performance.

Consider what would happen if an individual's scores on the GATB were to be used to develop a functional age profile. Norms are available describing the age relationships for each aptitude scale, and thus it would be a simple matter to express the person's score on each aptitude in terms of the age at which that score was the mean value. In other words, a set of nine "ages" could be derived to represent the person's functional level in each of the nine aptitudes. But where does this leave us? The functional ages are themselves useless for the purpose of prediction because all the validation with job performance was carried out with the original aptitude scores. In order to retain the correspondence with likelihood of occupational success, the functional age scores must be reconverted back to the original aptitude values from which they were derived. Translation to functional age in this case is, therefore, an unnecessary complication, confusing rather than clarifying the relationship between an individual's actual job performance and his or her scores on a set of predictor variables.

It may be argued that it is important to retain some temporal dimension in the assessment of occupational proficiency in order to represent dynamic changes in competence. While it is often desirable to be able to measure rates of change in proficiency, it is questionable whether chronological age rather than job tenure or career age is the more meaningful index. In many occupations the contribution of on-the-job experience is so great that chronological age adds very little predictive power, and in most others there is likely an interaction between amount of relevant experience and chronological age. Without considerably more information, therefore, it is rather naive to think that progressive changes in proficiency on a job are related in a simple fashion to chronological age.

In view of the preceding discussion, the prognosis for the occupational concept of functional age is decidedly poor. Even if abstract measures could be devised that had general applicability and were as valid for experienced workers as for beginning workers, there seems to be no gain by referring to functional age rather than merely functional competence. Occupational functional age, therefore, appears to have little relevance to the three "ires" of personnel managers–whom to hire, should one fire, and when to retire. The first concern is best addressed by aptitude tests with known validity, and the latter two decisions should always be based on thorough and accurate performance appraisals.

It is true that knowledge of the average age of a pool of applicants may be helpful in predicting the proportion of applicants achieving a criterion score on the relevant predictor variables, but this information is no more useful at the individual level than comparable information about the racial or ethnic composition of the applicants. A fixed age for retirement has been convenient for purposes of social policy, and the high costs of health-care plans and pensions in combination with low potential return on the investment in training programs often bias decisions against older workers, but these considerations should not be confused with issues of competency. Furthermore, the failure to place an older individual into a suitable occupation because of low aptitude scores does not mean that he or she is to be abandoned, any more than would be the case for other "disadvantaged" members of the population. Vocational counseling and training, skill-development programs, and even job redesign are some of the alternatives that are often pursued after initial attempts at job placement are unsuccessful.

It is sometimes argued (e.g., Arvey and Mussio, 1973) that knowledge of a job applicant's age could be important if selection variables are found to have differential validity for different age groups. While this possibility cannot be unequivocally dismissed, there is little evidence of differential validity across age groups at the current time, and some research has actually indicated that validity coefficients are virtually unchanged after adjusting for applicant age (e.g., Droege, Crambert and Henkin, 1963). Moreover, even if such differential validity evidence were available, one must be careful in the evaluation of validity coefficients obtained from subsets of the population because restriction of the range of a variable (as would be done by focusing only on low-performing individuals, for example) almost always attenuates the value of a correlation involving that variable. In other words, if there is an age relationship with the predictor variables, it is likely that the validity coefficients obtained from a single age group will be lower than that of the entire population because of a restricted range of variation. This would lead to a spuriously small validity coefficient based on the data from a subsample of the larger population, even if the true validity remained the same.

There is one exception to the irrelevancy of age in occupational competency decisions, namely in occupations in which a sudden incapacitation can endanger lives. For example, airline pilots, air traffic controllers, bus drivers, and others in commercial transportation and related fields must continuously maintain a high level of performance in order to ensure passenger safety. In these types of occupations an unexpected stroke or heart attack could prove disastrous, and thus all possible precautions are taken to minimize the likelihood of such an occurrence. Unfortunately, current medical procedures are still too imprecise to make accurate predictions about the immediate likelihood of a stroke or heart attack in a given individual, and consequently there has been a reliance upon chronological age for determining occupational suitability because of the probabilistic relationship between age and cerebrovascular accident or cardiovascular disease. Health-related considerations are best viewed in the context of biomedical variables, however, and it is to this topic that we now turn.

## BIOMEDICAL FUNCTIONAL AGE

A different tradition for functional age research has concentrated on the goal of attempting to measure rate of biological aging. Here the focus has been upon determining the relative rates of aging of different organ systems within the individual. Phrases such as "He has the lungs of a 20-year-old" or "His arteries are those of an 80-year-old" reflect the emphasis upon establishing separate age scales for the functional capacity of different organs. The presumption is that some weighted aggregate of the scaled age of each organ system would reflect the composite functional age of the individual. This biomedical conception of functional age, therefore, seems to be based upon the idea that because the deterioration of body parts is correlated with increased age, the amount of deterioration can be scaled in years of age. A major purpose of biomedical functional age is to predict a person's time until death, or in the words of Benjamin (1947), to develop for ". . . the individual what our actuaries and biostatisticians have figured out so ingeniously for groups" (p. 226).

Actually, there appear to be at least three distinct criteria to which this type of functional age might be applied, all relating to the individual's biomedical status. One criterion, certainly the least ambiguous, is the person's remaining life span or residual longevity. Here the various measures are combined in order to predict the number of years until the individual can expect to die from natural (i.e., other than accident, homicide, or suicide) causes. A second criterion is the current health status or vitality level relative to some population-defined optimum. Although it is not clear how such an optimum level of physiological functioning could be defined, deviations from that optimum level might provide a meaningful index of aging in the living organism. The third criterion is the rate of biological change of the organism, measured against some previous level of performance. Because there is only a finite amount of decremental change that any organism can tolerate, this criterion is related to both the remaining life span and the relative health status criteria.

The recognized difficulties in establishing an appropriate criterion (e.g., Birren, 1969; Costa and McCrae, 1980; Damon, 1972; Dempster, 1972; Dirken, 1972; Jalavisto, 1965; Jalavisto and Makkonen, 1963; Shock, 1981; Tobin, 1981) have hampered investigation of biomedical functional age in the past. Indeed, one of the earliest suggestions for the derivation of a biomedical functional age did not even specify a criterion against which the index was to be validated, and instead proposed relying on clinical impressions of arbitrarily selected factors to obtain the global index (Benjamin, 1947). Perhaps not surprisingly, this initial proposal did not generate any serious research related to the concept of functional age.

The most popular approach for investigating biomedical functional age has been to use a multiple-regression equation to predict chronological age on the basis of measurement of a number of biomedical variables. A multidimensional perspective toward biomedical health status is generally assumed, although the number of predicted ages can vary from one for each variable to a single aggregate measure derived from all variables. Of course, the purpose of these analyses was not really to predict the individual's age, because it would obviously have been much simpler to ask the person directly about his or her age. Instead, chronological age appears to have been used as a surrogate for the true variable of interest—nearness to death. In other words, because older age is associated with a general increase in vulnerability of the organism to a wide assortment of diseases, years from birth is used as a convenient substitute for years until death. The predicted age derived from the regression equation then serves as the individual's functional age, with people having a predicted age greater than their chronological age considered functionally old, and people having a predicted age less than their chronological age considered functionally young.

Although plausible as an initial step in the investigation of biomedical functional age, Costa and McCrae (1980) have pointed out several major problems with this approach. One problem concerns the assumption that "... the difference between chronological age and functional age may be attributed to a difference in the rate of aging" (Webster and Logie, 1976, 549). The difficulty here is that it is extremely unlikely that all of the variation around the mean of an age group is attributable to different rates of aging. This is clearly an unreasonable assumption at young ages, and its likelihood is only slightly greater at older ages because of the confounding of aging rates with all other sources of individual differences (e.g., genetic background, nutrition and exercise habits, exposure to toxic environmental conditions, etc.). A much more reasonable, although still not infallible, assessment of functional aging rate might be possible by focusing on the amount of change in performance across two or more time periods. In this manner the absolute level of performance is factored out, and only the difference across various times of measurement is important. There is still no assurance that the change observed over past time periods will be similar to that in future time periods, but a longitudinal approach of this type seems the best available at the current time.

Costa and McCrae (1980) also mentioned the logical paradox confronting the multiple regression approach to the measurement of functional age in which the multiple regression equation can be too good to be useful. This occurs because the goal of the regression procedure is to maximize the correlation with the criterion variable, in this case chronological age; but if the correlation were perfect, predicted age would be the same as chronological age and there would be nothing gained from the regression procedure. The problem of ensuring that the variables are related to aging but not simply a more complicated index of chronological age was considered by Dirken (1972) and Jalavisto and Makkonen (1963), but has not yet been satisfactorily resolved.

Another problem discussed by Costa and McCrae (1980) was that there still has not been any convincing evidence that the measures investigated thus far are actually valid indicators of functional age by any of the criteria mentioned earlier. Some relevant research has been conducted, but the results are not yet conclusive. One attempt, reported by Costa and McCrae (1980) themselves, examined the hypothesis that "the functionally older would age more rapidly, and thus show greater changes . . . over 5-and 10-year periods" (p. 33). Little support was found for this hypothesis since chronological age proved to be equivalent or superior to the functional age measures for predicting change. However, it is not clear why one should expect those who are functionally old to necessarily exhibit more functional change over a given period than those who are functionally young, and thus this particular test of validity can be questioned on theoretical grounds.

An intuitively more reasonable approach has been pursued by Furukawa, Inoue, Kajiya, Inada, Takasugi, Fukui, Takeda, and Abe (1975) and Webster and Logie (1976), who reported that their less healthy subjects (defined either by elevated blood pressure or subjective evaluation) had higher predicted (functional) ages than their healthy counterparts. These findings are therefore consistent with the suggestion that the healthy groups had slower rates of aging. However, true validation (at least for time until death as the criterion) will require repeated measurements until all subjects have died, and then carrying out retrospective analyses of the relationship between assorted variables and the time until death. Some relevant research has been reported (e.g., Birren, 1965; Borken and Norris, 1980; Jarvik and Falek, 1963; Tobin, 1981), but all either had very small samples or only a few measures available for comparison. Large-scale longitudinal studies of this type will be necessary to establish the predictive validity of biomedical functional age measures, with remaining life span or rate of change as the criterion. The use of relative health status as the criterion may not require longitudinal designs, but large-scale studies will still be necessary to provide the norms against which the individual's functional status can be compared.

Although there are definite problems with the notion of biomedical functional age, none seem irresolvable and the construct has enough potential value to warrant further investigation. One benefit of a valid measure of rate of aging is to provide a more efficient method than longevity analyses to assess the impact of environmental factors such as work conditions, chemical pollutants, nutritional habits, etc. As it currently stands, most adverse influences are detected only by noting an abnormally high death rate, and it would certainly be more humane if these factors could be identified before the death of the relevant population. An initial step in this type of research might be to compare populations known to differ in their age-specific mortality rates, under the assumption that the population with the higher death rate has an accelerated set of aging processes (e.g., Jalavisto and Makkonnen, 1963; Walthana-Kasetr and Spiers, 1973). The factors responsible for the above-normal death rates may not be reflected in the biomedical functional age measures, but such an approach appears to be more efficient than waiting until large numbers of a thoroughly measured population have died.

A second advantage of valid measures of the rate of aging concerns the possibility for intervention if detrimental factors can be detected before their influence has resulted in the death of the organism. If it is determined that a group of individuals is aging at an accelerated rate, special action might be taken to remedy the relevant conditions before it is too late for action. The possibility of intervention to alter the rate of aging leads to the intriguing implication that steps taken to increase life expectancy might add years to one's life and actually make the patient "grow younger" in a biomedical sense.

Still a third advantage of a biomedical functional age is potentially greater clarification of age relationships in that groups of individuals might be identified who are equivalent in a physiologically meaningful fashion. This could have relevance in certain occupations, although as discussed in the preceding section, actual job competency should be the most important determinant of most occupational decisions. Another useful application of biomedically equivalent cohorts would be in gerontological research. Much of the variability found across individuals within the same chronological age range might be reduced, and maturational trends more clearly revealed, if the subjects were known to be comparable in important biomedical dimensions.

In contrast to the situation with the occupational usage of functional age, the prognosis for a biomedical functional age can be fairly optimistic. Only very primitive research efforts have yet been pursued, and thus the empirical support for this conceptualization is still quite weak. There are also important problems that must be resolved before further progress can be made, including that of determining the specific criterion to be employed—remaining life span, relative health status, or rate of change in health. Nevertheless, the potential benefits of an accurate index of biomedical functional age are large enough that it is likely this issue will continue to receive the active attention of many researchers.

## STRUCTURAL ORGANIZATION OF HUMAN FUNCTIONING

The third major category of use for functional age measures has been to determine the interrelationship of biological and behavioral characteristics across the adult life span. This emphasis has evolved in part as a by-product of the data obtained from the previous two categories of research. The availability of measures from an assortment of variables on individuals of different age ranges has allowed the examination of patterns of correlations (i.e., structural organizations) and possible changes in the correlational pattern or organizational structure across ages. The fundamental question from this perspective is whether the various characteristics that are age-related are themselves interrelated.

Research directed at discovering functional relationships between chronological age and a variety of biological and behavioral variables is important if for no other reason than to help establish the true nature of aging. Without an *a priori* definition of the concomitants of aging, investigators are forced to define it empirically by identifying the variables that exhibit a correlation with chronological age. That is, the essence of aging might be considered to be that assortment of anthropometric, biological, behavioral, and perhaps even social variables that exhibit consistent correlations with chronological age across different historical periods and different physical and cultural environments. Moreover, only if a phenomenon is clearly described by determining the interrelationships of major variables can one begin to explain it adequately. The goal of identifying the variables that are a function of age is therefore important as an initial step in the investigation of any process of aging.

Theoretical issues are also addressed by means of this correlational approach. For example, the distinction between one or many processes of aging might be investigated by examining the correlation of change scores across different variables. A single aging factor would be revealed if the assorted variables were highly correlated with one another, while alternative correlational patterns would indicate the existence of more than one process of aging. The evidence on this issue is currently ambiguous, as some researchers have discovered only a single aging factor (e.g., Clark, 1960; Jalavisto, 1965) while others have reported several factors with large age weightings (e.g., Birren and Spieth, 1962; Heron and Chown, 1967). The various studies have employed many different dependent measures, however, and it is not yet clear whether they should truly be considered contradictory.

Another important issue that could be addressed by means of this correlational approach concerns the nature of what is assumed to be the primary aging factor. One of the few general processes that has been proposed as a possible fundamental behavioral aging mechanism is the slowing of nearly all behavioral activities with increased age (Birren, 1965, 1974; Salthouse, 1982, 1985), and Jalavisto has summarized the reasoning behind a correlational approach for the investigation of this hypothesis:

> The assumption that there is a common process affecting speed of behavior implies that all tests which require speed should be intercorrelated. However, because they are all age-dependent, crude correlation coefficients are not informative. One could, naturally, calculate the partial correlation coefficients with elimination of the age dimension, but the factorial approach is probably more efficient. In factor analysis, intercorrelation if genuine, would manifest itself in a speed factor (Jalavisto, 1965, 355).

Indeed, the evidence from four relatively large (i.e., samples greater than 100) factor analytic studies indicates that speeded variables are consistently included within the aging factor, apparently regardless of the composition of the other variables in the analysis (e.g., Clark, 1960; Dirken, 1972; Heron and Chown, 1967; Jalavisto, 1965). Chown (1961) reported an additional factor analytic study which revealed that:

> The speed tests formed their own unique factor in the young group, maintained this to a lesser extent in the middle group, and were loaded most highly on the nonverbal intelligence factor in the old group. Thus among old people, but not among the young, these speed tests became a measure of intellectual capability and of the extent of the preservation of this function (Chown, 1961, 361).

Birren, Riegel, and Morrison (1962) reached a very similar conclusion in a later study of this type. A next step in the examination of this hypothesis might be to systematically vary the nature of additional biomedical or psychological variables and to determine the composition of the speed factor at different ages.

The advantage of this type of correlational approach to the investigation of theoretical issues is that unlike univariate approaches, data could be obtained that are relevant to both causes and consequences of what is suspected to be a fundamental aging mechanism. Causal factors could be inferred by examining the cluster of physiological variables found to be closely linked with indices of the suspected fundamental mechanism. Higher-order processes that are influenced by the primary mechanism might be identified by determining the behavioral variables that are related to the fundamental mechanism. Evidence such as this could not be considered conclusive, but it is a rich source of hypotheses about the nature of age differences.

An optimum procedure for determining the structural interrelationships of variables might consist of the following four steps: (1) assemble as many relevant measures as possible (where relevance is determined by theory and domain of interest); (2) determine the values of these measures for many individuals of a given age; (3) identify the interrelationships or structural connections among variables; and (4) repeat steps (2) and (3) at different ages. Chronological age will then emerge as a dimension or continuum for examining possible changes in structural relationships among variables. The interpretation of the relationships will likely be dictated by theory—either one specified in advance of the data, or one inferred from the pattern of results obtained. Evaluation of the adequacy of the theory is based on the resulting degree of understanding of the mechanisms responsible for dynamic changes in relationships among variables.

It is important to point out that while the structural conceptualization of functional age has some aspects in common with the occupational and biomedical functional ages, the interrelationship of age-related characteristics need not be related to job performance or to residual life span. As an example, a discovery that visual and auditory changes are correlated across the adult life span would be interesting from the structural perspective, but would probably be irrelevant for the prediction of either job performance or future life expectancy.

While there has been little research directly aimed at discovering the structural relationships among biological and behavioral variables across the adult age range, it is likely that this topic will emerge as a distinct and separate area of research in the future. The complexity of the human organism seems to dictate a multidimensional and multidisciplinary interpretation of biological and behavioral development during adulthood. Therefore, the prognosis for this conceptualization of functional age appears favorable, at least until such time that sufficient research is available to reveal any unforeseen difficulties with this approach.

## SUMMARY

Although chronological age is an extremely powerful index for characterizing average trends in performance, it is much less useful for making predictions about a specific individual. Concepts like functional age have been developed in an attempt to extend knowledge about group trends to the level of the individual. Among the particular questions one might like to have answered are: Can this person handle this job? How much longer can this person be expected to live? And what is responsible for the changes that have occurred to this person over his or her lifetime?

It has been suggested that the preceding three questions exemplify the major categories of research conducted under the rubric of functional age. The categories can be easily distinguished (see Table 1 for a summary of their major characteristics), but the failure to do so in the past seems to have led to much confusion and lack of real progress. Future research in this area should recognize, and consider separately, the multiple definitions of functional age. At the present time, the occupational concept of functional age does not appear useful, but both the biomedical and structural conceptualizations are promising and should be pursued in further research.

## *REFERENCES*

ARVEY, R. D., and MUSSIO, S. J. (1973). Test discrimination, job performance and age. *Industrial Gerontology,* (Winter), 22-29.

BENJAMIN, H. (1947). Biologic versus chronologic age. *Journal of Gerontology, 2,* 217-227.

BIRREN, J. E. (1959). Principles of research on aging. In J. E. Birren (Ed.), *Handbook of aging and the individual.* Chicago: University of Chicago Press.

BIRREN, J. E. (1965). Age changes in speed of behavior: Its central nature and physiological correlates. In A. T. Welford and J. E. Birren (Eds.), *Behavior, aging, and the nervous system.* Springfield, IL: Charles C. Thomas.

BIRREN, J. E. (1969). The concept of functional age: Theoretical background. *Human Development, 12,* 214-215.

BIRREN, J. E. (1974). Translations in Gerontology—From lab to life: psychophysiology and speed of response. *American Psychologist, 29,* 808-815.

BIRREN, J. E. and RENNER, V. J. (1977). Research on the psychology of aging. In J. E. Birren and K. W. Schaie (Eds.), *Handbook of the psychology of aging,* New York: Van Nostrand Reinhold.

BIRREN, J. E., RIEGEL, K. F., and MORRISON, D. F. (1962). Age differences in response speed as a function of controlled variations in stimulus conditions: Evidence of a general speed factor. *Gerontologia, 6,* 1-18.

BIRREN, J. E., and SPIETH, W. (1962). Age, response speed and cardiovascular functions. *Journal of Gerontology, 17,* 390-391.

BORKAN, G. A., and NORRIS, A. H. (1980). Assessment of biological age using a profile of physical parameters. *Journal of Gerontology, 35,* 177-184.

CHOWN, S. M. (1961). Age and the rigidities. *Journal of Gerontology, 16,* 353-362.

CLARK, J. W. (1960). The aging dimension: A factorial analysis of individual differences with age on psychological and physiological measurements. *Journal of Gerontology, 15,* 183-187.

COSTA, P. T., and McCRAE, R. R. (1980). Functional age: A conceptual and empirical critique. In S. S. Haynes and M. Feinleib (Eds.), *Epidemiology of Aging,* Bethesda, MD: National Institutes of Health.

DAMON, A. (1972). Predicting age from body measurements and observations. *Aging and Human Development, 3,* 169-173.

DEMPSTER, A. P. (1972). Functional age and age-related measures. *Aging and Human Development, 3,* 195-196.

DIRKEN, J. M. (1972). *Functional age of industrial workers.* Groningen, Netherlands: Wolters-Noordhof.

DROEGE, R. C., CRAMBERT, A. C., and HENKIN, J. B. (1963). Relationship between G.A.T.B. Aptitude scores and age for adults. *Personnel Guidance Journal, 42,* 502-508.

FOZARD, J. L., and NUTTALL, R. L. (1971). General Aptitude Test Battery scores for men differing in age and socioeconomic status. *Journal of Applied Psychology, 55,* 372-379.

FURUKAWA, T., INOUE, M., KAJIYA, F., INADA, H., TAKASUGI, S., FUKUI, S., TAKEDA, H., and ABE, H. (1975). Assessment of biological age by multiple regression analysis. *Journal of Gerontology, 30,* 422-434.

HERON, A., and CHOWN, S. (1967). *Age and function.* Boston: Little, Brown and Co.

HIRT, M. (1959). Use of the General Aptitude Test Battery to determine aptitude changes with age and to predict job performance. *Journal of Applied Psychology, 43,* 36–39.

JALAVISTO, E. (1965). The role of simple tests measuring speed of performance in the assessment of biological vigour: A factorial study in elderly women. In A. T. Welford and J. E. Birren (Eds.), *Behavior, aging and the nervous system.* Springfield, IL: Charles C. Thomas.

JALAVISTO, E., and MAKKONEN, T. (1963). On the assessment of biological age: I. A factor analysis of physiological measurements in old and young women. *Annales Academiae Scientiarium Fennicae,* Helsinki, 1–38.

JARVIK, L. F., and FALEK, A. (1963). Intellectual stability and survival in the aged. *Journal of Gerontology, 18,* 173–176.

McFARLAND, R. (1943). The older worker in industry. *Harvard Business Review,* (Summer), 505–520.

McFARLAND, R. (1973). The need for functional age measurements in industrial gerontology. *Industrial Gerontology, 19,* 1–19.

MURRELL, K. F. H., and GRIEW, S. (1965). Age, experience and speed of response. In A. T. Welford and J. E. Birren (Eds.), *Behavior, aging and the nervous system.* Springfield, IL: Charles C. Thomas.

NUTTALL, R. L. (1972). The strategy of functional age research. *Aging and Human Development, 3,* 149–152.

SALTHOUSE, T. A. (1982). *Adult cognition: An experimental psychology of human aging.* New York: Springer-Verlag.

SALTHOUSE, T. A. (1985). Speed of behavior and its implications for cognition. In J. E. Birren and K. W. Schaie (Eds.), *Handbook of the Psychology of Aging,* (Second Edition). New York: Van Nostrand Reinhold.

SHOCK, N. W. (1981). Indices of functional age. In D. Danon, N. W. Shock, and N. Marois (Eds.), *Aging: A challenge to science and society, volume 1: Biology.* Oxford, England: Oxford University Press.

STEIN, C. T. (1962). The G.A.T.B.: The effect of age on intersample variation. *Personnel Guidance Journal, 60,* 779–785.

TOBIN, J. D. (1981). Physiological indices of aging. In D. Danon, N. W. Shock, and N. Marois (Eds.), *Aging: A challenge to science and society, volume 1: Biology.* Oxford, England: Oxford University Press.

WALKER, J. W., and LUPTON, D. E. (1978). Performance appraisal programs and age discrimination law. *Aging and Work, 1,* 73–83.

WALTHANA-KASETR, S., and SPIERS, P. S. (1973). Geographic mortality rates and rates of aging—a possible relationship? *Journal of Gerontology, 28,* 374–379.

WEBSTER, I. W., and LOGIE, A. R. (1976). A relationship between functional age and health status in female subjects. *Journal of Gerontology, 31,* 545–550.

WELFORD, A. T. (1965). Performance, biological mechanisms and age: A theoretical sketch. In A. T. Welford and J. E. Birren (Eds.), *Behavior, aging and the nervous system.* Springfield, IL: Charles C. Thomas.

6

# TRAINING AND RETRAINING ADULT AND OLDER ADULT WORKERS

Harvey L. Sterns

## INTRODUCTION

The changing individual in a changing environment has been a major theme of life-span development. Nowhere is this becoming more evident than in the work place. Decisions to change jobs or careers or decisions to engage in career development activities may come about as a result of changes within the individual, the environment, or an interaction of both. Adult and older adult workers are imbedded in professional and job roles that may be changing rapidly due to economic, societal, and technological forces.

The Age Discrimination in Employment Acts of 1976 and 1978 define older workers as individuals in the age range of 40 to 70. Thus, a major portion of adult workers fall into this category. Throughout this paper the term *older adult worker* will be used to describe individuals 40 and above.

A primary purpose of this chapter is to examine issues, theory, and research in personal growth, career development, training, and retraining opportunities for adult and older workers. Selected areas of adult developmental psychology, industrial/organizational psychology, and industrial gerontology that influence the individual and the organization are reviewed.

Individuals can engage in career development through self-directed learning, participation in organizational training and retraining programs, formal credit education and degree programs, as well as continuing education. Organizations can promote training and retraining through a formal company process and encourage formal education by providing support in release time and/or financial support (Cross, 1981; Peterson, 1983). Issues in training and retraining will be considered within a life-span context.

The orientation of a life-span approach first emphasizes that behavior change processes can occur at any point in the life course. No special state of maturity is assumed as a general principle. Development is seen as a lifelong process. The task is to identify the form and course of these behavioral changes as they occur at various points in the life course (Baltes, Reese, and Lipsitt, 1980).

One line of research has focused on the existence of cohort (generational) differences in the nature of life-span development. Cohort serves as an index for the environmental influences that affect attitudes and behaviors for a given group of individuals born at a particular point in time. Both workers and organizations are influenced by such forces. A second line of concern focuses on intergenerational constancy and change; and a third concern is with pluralistic conceptions of development.

Three sets of influences impact adults and older adults in the work place. Normative age-graded (ontogenetic) influences are defined as the biological and environmental determinants that have a strong relationship to chronological age. Examples are biological maturation, age-graded socialization events which include many aspects of education, occupation, and the family life cycle. Age-graded events are normative if they tend to occur in highly similar ways for all individuals in a given culture or subculture.

Normative history-graded (evolutionary) influences are environmental determinants associated with historical time and historical contexts related to cohort. They are normative if they occur to most members of a given cohort (generation) in similar ways. These are events influencing different age-cohorts living at the same time. Impacts such as major changes in the economy, technological change, and social policy change would be work-related examples.

Non-normative life events refer to biological and environmental determinants that do not occur in any normative age-graded or history-graded manner for most individuals. Examples relevant to the work place would include antecedent patterns associated with career changes, such as promotion, layoffs, firings, accidents, health changes, divorce, or death of a significant other.

These three types of influences which impact on the individual may result in regularities common to many individuals and also point to the enormous possibilities regarding individual differences both within and between cohorts.

Much of the aging and work literature of the past has often focused on general statements regarding older workers, rather than on a careful analysis of these three dimensions.

Industrial gerontology in Great Britain began over three decades ago to address issues in aging and work (Welford, 1976). In the United States, the National Council on Aging has stimulated consideration of issues surrounding middle-aged and older workers with conferences, reports, and curriculum materials, e.g., *Proceedings National Conference on Manpower Training and the Older Worker* (1966); *Industrial Gerontology: Curriculum Materials* (1968); and most recently, *Significant Segment–Handbook I–Employment and Training of the Mature Worker: A Resource Manual* (Bauer, Barocas, and Ferber-Cahill, 1982); *Handbook II–Employment and Training of the Mature Worker: A Training Design* (Barocas, 1982); as well as books (e.g., Shatto, 1972).

More recent works dealing with general issues of aging, work, and retirement would include: *Work Decisions in the 1980's* (Ginsberg, Mills, Owen, Sheppard, and Wachter, 1982) and *The Graying of Working America* (Sheppard and Rix, 1977).

Important recent works emphasize new policies and approaches. Examples of successful innovative approaches focusing on adult and older workers include: *The Future of Older Workers in America: New Options for an Extended Working Life* (1980); *Young Programs for Older Workers* (Jacobson, 1980); and *Management and the Older Workforce* (Humple and Lyons, 1983). Two major reviews of selected areas of research on aging workers have recently appeared (Doering, Rhodes, and Shuster, 1983; Rhodes, 1983) which are valuable as background resources.

A common theme for multiple decades, and still a major concern, is the negative stereotype of the older worker. The social impact of this stereotype is greatest when held by an employer, and is even more problematic when held by older persons themselves (Stagner, 1971).

The primary aim of education and training should be the optimization of individual development across the life span. As individuals continue to learn and change, educational intervention is a viable mechanism for facilitating development at all periods in life (Schaie and Willis, 1978; Sterns and Mitchell, 1979; Willis, 1985). The need to integrate work and learning continues to be a major challenge (Cross, 1981; O'Toole, 1978; Peterson, 1983).

> Lifelong learning includes, but is not limited to adult basic education, continuing education, independent study, agricultural education, business education and labor education, occupational and job training programs, and education for older and retired people; remedial education, special educational programs for groups and individuals with special needs; and also, educational activities designed to upgrade occupational and professional skills; to assist business, public agencies and other organizations in the use of innovation and research results; and to serve family needs and personal development (Higher Education Act of 1965, Title I, Part B, Section 132).

This definition includes all the activities that would be considered a part of training programs in industry. Traditionally, the industrial psychology literature has had more specific definitions regarding personnel training activities.

"Training is here defined as a planned effort by an organization to facilitate the learning of job-related behavior on the part of its employees. The term 'behavior' is used in the broad sense to include any knowledge and skills acquired by an employee through practice" (Wexley, 1984, 519-520). Cascio (1982) indicates that training and development activities lead to changes in skill, knowledge, attitude, and social behavior.

A major issue in the training of older workers is assuring equitable access to training opportunities. Training policies and practices may reflect informal age restrictions, standards, and assumptions that may exclude older employees. In an era of extended work life, training and retraining provide older workers with opportunities to strengthen their knowledge and skills (*The Future of Older Workers in America,* 1980).

The Age Discrimination in Employment Acts of 1976 and 1978 define older workers as individuals in the age range of 40 to 70. By law, workers age 40 to 70 cannot be limited, segregated, or classified in any way that would restrict their

-nployment opportunities or otherwise adversely affect their status as employees. Thus, adult and older workers should not be deprived of the opportunity to participate in training programs because of their age (Edlemen and Siegler, 1978).

A major finding in industrial settings is that employers remain reluctant to hire persons over 40 and offer training, or to train or retrain those already employed (Rosen and Jardee, 1977; Sonnenfeld, 1978). Older workers have developed fine records indicating that they are healthy, dependable, have low accident rates, and are productive; however, beliefs about aging lead to employers not taking advantage of good available workers who happen to be older (Meier and Kerr, 1976).

Older workers themselves also contribute to this situation because they are often reluctant to volunteer for training or retraining. This may be due to feelings of inadequacy about being able to do well in a training program, fear of competition with younger individuals, or the expectation that supervisors would encourage them if they felt it was appropriate.

Highly productive older workers run the risk of not being included in training opportunities as well. Their involvement in important ongoing projects makes supervisors reluctant to spare workers for training and retraining. The problem faced by workers of any age is that if they do not engage in retraining they grow further and further out of touch with new information, technology, and processes (*The Future of Older Workers in America,* 1980).

Lifetime retraining and/or self-education is necessary so that one can continue to build on previous knowledge and experience. The notion that one must inevitably become obsolete is obsolete thinking. Rapid technological changes create obsolescence of knowledge among all age groups. Middle-aged and older workers may need updating, but today the need for retraining is shared by people in their twenties, thirties, forties, fifties, sixties, seventies, and beyond.

## GENERAL ISSUES IN EDUCATION AND TRAINING

The development of educational approaches for older adults has been eloquently discussed by H. R. Moody (1976). He presents four stages of development in approaches to the education of older adults. These four stages of educational development have been further discussed by Sterns and Sanders (1980) in relation to education of adults and older adults. The central issue here is how attitudes about aging permeate decision making by and for adults and older adults in terms of education, training, and retraining.

Stage I, *rejection,* is a product of the negative attitudes about aging prevalent in our society. Old age is seen as representing the antithesis of prevailing values of modern life. Old age is a reminder of our mortality. Education is *not* seen as justified since it makes little sense on economic grounds; education is for the future, and there is little payoff with older adults.

Extensions of this level of thinking to the cognitive realm are discussions of inevitable decrements and beliefs that nothing can be done to improve functioning in older adulthood. The question "What do you expect for someone your age?" is indicative of this level of thought. This stage is exemplified by the belief that there are declines in cognitive functioning at all levels, on all dimensions, for everyone.

The rejection stage is evident when it is believed that cognitive ability declines with age, so why bother to train older workers. Even though older workers are likely to be healthy, have low levels of accident involvement, and are productive, employers remain reluctant to hire persons over 40 and to train or retrain those already employed. One reason is that employers continue to believe the myths and stereotypes regarding older workers. Likewise, older workers are reluctant to volunteer for retraining because they often have feelings of inadequacy about their ability to complete the training program successfully.

Stage II, *social services,* embodies the assumption of the welfare state and interest group liberalism, and describes education for adults and older adults as a "leisure time" activity. This assumes, at least for older adults, their prior disengagement from major educational involvement.

The characteristic educational level of Stage II can be described as separate education and training programs. The emphasis is on less serious educational activities—as a consumer, not as a producer; in the mode of leisure, not in the mode of work. There is an assumption of passivity and segregation. Older people are seen as *not* engaging in serious and meaningful educational activity.

An extension of this mode of thinking to the cognitive realm leads us to such concepts as age credit on intelligence tests, and suggestions of bigger print and more light. Ability-extraneous issues may be relevant here, the idea being that older adults can function, but cannot function as well as younger people. The approach is to adapt the educational environment to fit the person as he or she is believed to be at this period of life.

This stage emphasizes developing training and intervention imposed on the worker. This is a passive recipient model. The older worker is not seen as performing as well as the younger worker, but can improve with assistance. Changes are made in the physical environment and/or the task to accommodate the older worker. Change in job or redesigning the job may be recommended; however, the older worker may not be part of the decision-making process. Input from experienced workers may be of great value, but is not sought.

In many firms, the average age in certain occupations may be in the fifties and rising. Yet company studies of in-service skills-upgrading programs show that younger workers are more likely to be enrolled. Lower participation of senior workers may be due to their heavy commitment to important work projects and the reluctance of managers to spare them for training. Older workers are not directly involved in decisions about their careers. The result is that large numbers of older workers grow further and further out of touch with new technologies and processes in an unnecessary waste of knowledge and experience.

Although rapid technological change creates more obsolescence of knowledge among middle-aged and older workers than among younger workers, incentives for updating and upgrading skills have been scanty. Long-service employees have seen little point, therefore, in putting energy and time into upgrading their knowledge.

Stage III, *participation,* emphasizes that self-directed study, education, and training can serve as preparation for new active roles or as a political challenge to stereotypes of old age. The goal of this level is to enable older people, as far as possible, to live their lives in contact with the mainstream of society and to pursue the activities associated with a normal life in that society. The answer is not to expand special situations for older adults, but to change practices and policies that have contributed to the problem.

Participation suggests that meaningful, carefully selected activity is the fundamental criterion of successful aging. It suggests that the passivity inherent in the social services model is inappropriate for the majority of the older worker population.

One very important concept that is often missing in discussions of adult and older adult learning is the important role that self-initiated and self-directed learning can play in the development of new skills (Cross, 1981).

Education and training should be designed to offer a supportive environment and the opportunity to continue and further develop one's career, to pursue a second career or personal interests, and should not focus on disengagement. The mode here is integration rather than segregation; older workers remain involved in their present jobs or initiate second careers. A key point is consciousness raising that allows older workers a positive attitude toward themselves and their situation. Older workers accept many negative stereotypes about aging, but each sees himself or herself as the exception. Stage III is the cutting edge of social reform: right to work, continued opportunity for promotion, and growth—opportunity to live in the mainstream of society. The extension to the cognitive domain would be represented in the notion that there is plasticity in behavior during the older adult period. The notion here is that alleviation and prevention (Baltes and Schaie, 1973; Birren and Woodruff, 1973) are possible. Here we have the notion that special training approaches can be used to improve, compensate, or maintain levels of functioning. This is not to deny biological change, but to understand how to compensate for, or improve existing levels of functioning. This is an active response.

The participation stage assumes that meaningful, carefully selected activity is the fundamental criterion for successful aging. The importance of older workers' participation in choosing the activity is emphasized. Training approaches are implemented to improve, compensate, or maintain specific levels of functioning.

Retraining and continuing education emulate the participation approach. This approach emphasizes the ability of the older worker to learn new tasks, different jobs, or to update current skills. The emphasis is placed upon the individual variability of older adult performance rather than homogeneity (Baltes and Danish, 1980).

Stage IV, *self-actualization,* describes adulthood and older adulthood as a period of potential psychological growth. This represents the mature years as a special period (integrity vs. despair, according to Erickson). There must be something uniquely possible in older adulthood that is available only at this point in the life cycle. Issues of self-growth and personal satisfaction are paramount here. Disengagement or reorganization may be required, but only for the sake of more meaningful activity. The older worker may be liberated from roles and involvement demanded by earlier work and child-rearing responsibilities. For training, the challenge rests with the development of educational and training approaches that nourish psychological growth and allow older learners to bring a lifetime of experience to their studies.

In the cognitive domain, we are perhaps addressing the unique differences present in individuals regardless of age, and the continuing capacity for creativity among older adults. Research concerning wisdom and knowledge in older adulthood would be an example.

Self-actualization assumes that adulthood is a period of potential growth that the older worker can utilize to his and to the company's best interests, if given the right opportunity. For older workers, this translates as a period of evolution—when skills, abilities, or interests acquired during their life span are utilized. This may mean an abrupt career change from a lifelong interest to a new area. Examples of Stage IV, *self-actualization,* are found in *The Ulyssean Adult* (McLeish, 1976), which emphasizes the issue of creativity in the middle and later years. Self-actualization for the older worker can be extremely beneficial to the organization if appropriate selection procedures are developed that detect, develop, and encourage exploration into new roles and responsibilities.

## TRAINING AND RETRAINING ADULT AND OLDER ADULT WORKERS

Job change, promotion, prevention of obsolescence, and personal growth can be facilitated through well-designed training programs. Training programs for workers are designed to: (a) improve self-awareness regarding one's role and responsibility in an organization, (b) increase job-related knowledge and skill, and (c) enhance motivation to perform the job well. Training is an important way to achieve productivity, job satisfaction, and organization revitalization (Bass and Barrett, 1981; Wexley and Latham, 1981).

A number of recent reviews emphasize the important role that training has in response to technological change (Dooling and Klemmer, 1982; Goldstein, 1982; Nickerson, 1982; Sterns and Patchett, 1984; Wexley, 1984). However, as Hoos (1967) has so eloquently stated in discussing retraining programs, "despite general acceptance of the idea that retraining will provide a means to more effective labor force participation, there has been only limited substantive research to ascertain what kinds of programs are in operation at present, and what sectors of the population can be reasonably expected to benefit from them" (p. 255). Unfortunately, this statement still applies to the situation today. In fact, many of today's adult and older workers who are in need of training are casualties of a failure over the last two decades of industry to carry out appropriate responses to future training needs. Routine consistent updating through in-service programs could keep workers current. Apathy and resistance on the part of the work force is also responsible. Few companies try to overcome the barriers to training and retraining unless there is a serious shortage of workers (Hoos, 1967).

The issues of training and retraining the older adult worker are embedded in a whole set of issues surrounding personnel training in industrial psychology (Cascio, 1982; Wexley, 1984; Wexley and Latham, 1981). Wexley (1984) states that the push for training and retraining is just beginning, requiring employed and displaced workers to continually acquire new knowledge and skills. Good evaluative training research, with or without special concerns regarding older adult workers, is still not really available. Recommendations for such research are clearly presented (Cascio, 1982; Goldstein, 1982; Wexley, 1984; Wexley and Latham, 1981).

The ability of individuals to learn and benefit from training and education at all points in the life span is increasingly emphasized in contemporary adult learning literature. (Cross, 1981; Peterson, 1983; Sterns and Sanders, 1980; Willis, 1985). Previous educational experience and highest educational level, as well as the opportunity for continued growth as part of the work experience, are important predictors of future training or retraining success (Peterson, 1983; Willis, in press). For many individuals the work place is an important mechanism for continued learning, either vicariously on the job or by more formal training programs. The largest provider of adult education in middle and older adulthood is industry, not higher educational institutions (Cross, 1981).

### Training Approaches

Valasek and Sterns (1981) recommend training principles enumerated by authors such as Goldstein (1974). They suggest that any training program might be successful if properly developed and that careful development of the entire training program is the most important parameter for successful training of the older adult worker, irrespective of the actual training technique used. Task analysis is an important component of training programs for older individuals performing complex tasks in both experimental and applied settings. Sterns and Sanders (1980), for example, highlight the central importance of task analysis in age-comparison research which examines cognitive functioning deficits in older groups. Proper task and job analyses become particularly important when hierarchical learning procedures are incorporated in a training program.

Sheppard (1976) suggests that training of the older worker may require changes in traditional training methods in order to accommodate special needs and limitations. Barkin (1970) identifies traditional training methods as those based on exposition and presentation of theory, followed later by practical applications. He believes that such traditional methods are more suited to younger people who must recall material for written examinations.

Several training techniques directed to the special needs of the older worker will be presented. Belbin (1965, 1970) and Belbin and Belbin (1972) have used a number of training approaches: the discovery method, activity learning, and programmed instruction.

The discovery method attempts to increase motivation of the older worker by allowing the trainee to progress through the learning program, discovering for himself how things work and why. Tasks are graded in difficulty and are presented in appropriate order as the trainee progresses through the program. The trainer's role is to observe trainee errors and regulate presentation of training material contingent on trainee performance. The trainee determines the rate of the presentation of the material. The discovery method is designed to facilitate learning by the adult or older individual by taking into consideration decreased memory abilities for learning verbal material, interference from irrelevant events in the learning environment, and lack of a meaningful context for learning tasks.

The activity learning method is a technique in which the learner actively manipulates or processes the material to be learned, rather than listening to, observing, or repeating it passively. It is believed that activity learning is successful when it stimulates creative thinking rather than merely a series of mechanical responses.

Belbin and Downs (1964) concluded that whereas physical activity encouraged mental activity and involvement in the task, activity learning led to the greatest gains in comparison to memorization, and produced the greatest recall. Belbin and Downs (1966) trained post office manual sorters and found that activity learning that incorporated a self-learning deduction technique was superior to learning from written lists, a progressive part method, and programmed instruction.

Programmed instruction systematically presents material, graded in difficulty, to the learner through a display such as a book, computer, or mechanical apparatus. An important advantage of programmed instruction is immediate feedback and positive reinforcement of correct responses, combined with a branching process designed to correct mistakes. Neale, Toye, and Belbin (1968) examined the effectiveness of programmed instruction for training bus conductors and found no difference in the effectiveness of programmed and more standard classroom techniques for the older trainees. However, a younger group of trainees performed in a superior manner when given programmed instruction. A second study demonstrated that session length for different age groups had a crucial effect on relative effectiveness of programmed instruction. It was found that medium-length sessions of one hour each were most effective for the older trainees. Self-pacing and sequential presentation of small bits of material graded in difficulty were important attributes of the programmed instruction technique.

A more recent investigation of programmed instruction, with individuals aged 16 to 32 and aged 67 to 84, was carried out by Siemen (1976). Using programmed material, he studied age-related differences in learning basic concepts of anatomy and physiology. There was significant improvement in pretest and posttest performances by the younger and older groups. There were no significant differences in mastery of the material between the two age groups using programmed instruction. This program was self-paced; however, older subjects took more than twice as long to complete the modules than did the younger group. The training sessions were designed to reduce anxiety in the older subjects by making the learning situation as nonthreatening as possible.

Downs and Roberts (1977) have developed what they call the CRAMP technique of training. The CRAMP training method divides learning into five distinct types: *comprehension,* which requires an understanding of the subject matter; *reflex,* which requires skilled movement and perception; *attitude,* which requires a change in attitude on the part of the trainee; *memory,* which requires retention of subject matter; and *procedure,* which requires knowing what to do in a given situation although the information need not be recognized. This approach takes into account the characteristics of the trainee as well as the type of learning involved. The component tasks identified through task analysis are keyed into appropriate training methods via the five learning types.

The CRAMP technique was used to train underground train guards and the resultant training methods included guided-discovery learning, discrimination learning, "cumulative-whole" learning, and role playing. Trainees were permitted to work on their own material at their own pace. It was concluded that use of the CRAMP technique produced a greater pass rate of adult men (older than 30 years of age) and also reduced resignations during training—compared to a conventional training program utilizing lectures and dictation of notes—by using question-and-answer techniques and demonstrations (Downs and Roberts, 1977).

One of the best studies demonstrating the efficiency of retraining programs is the Aer Lingus (Irish airlines) study by Mullan and Gorman (1972). It incorporates many of the principles already discussed. Mullan and Gorman emphasized the importance of participation, communication, and active-discovery learning in the overall design for effective management of change. The study documents the steps taken to transform a cargo warehouse to a semiautomatic facility with electronically controlled storage and retrieval of freight and an associated computerized storage documentation system. A first phase emphasized orientation to the change to take place. The second phase involved a description of the system and discussion about it. The third phase involved workers learning to operate the system using the discovery method. The training-program design and outcome was successful with the workers mastering the new computerized system and successfully carrying out their new work roles. What makes this such a fine example is the active role the workers played in the process.

### Training and Retraining Program Design

The adult and older adult training and retraining literature has documented a number of dimensions for successful training programs. Many of the recommendations in this section are principles of learning that apply to well-designed training at any age. However, special sensitivity may be needed in specific situations involving older adults. Five major areas emerge that should be considered when designing training programs. These include: motivation, structure, familiarity, organization, and time (Valasek and Sterns, 1981).

*Motivation.* The issue of motivation in any training situation is not new, however, the concerns are slightly different for the older trainee. For all trainees, the desire to participate and learn is important, but for the older trainee, the desire may be masked by a fear of failure or the fear of an inability to compete against younger, better-educated trainees. The trainer must encourage the older worker to set aside past negative feelings developed in previous educational experiences. For those who have been out of school for many years and/or who had little formal education, the motivational and self-concept aspects can influence participation in a program and the results (Belbin, 1965; Belbin and Belbin, 1972).

Recent discussion of the adult and older adult in an education and training role draws upon Bandura's (1977, 1981, 1982) self-efficacy theory (Rebok and Offermann, 1983). Much of the very sensitive early work on adult and older adult training and retraining supports the importance of self-efficacy in education and training situations. Self-efficacy is based on an individual's judgment about how well one can organize and execute courses of action required to deal with prospective situations—mainly ambiguous, unpredictable, and often stressful elements. Although initially conceived to deal with clinical situations, it appears that self-efficacy theory may provide important sensitivity in behavioral functioning of older adult trainees.

Once the trainee has been motivated to enroll in training or retraining, he/she should be continually encouraged to continue and complete the training program. The trainee should be informed of progress via positive feedback and receive assistance in understanding the criterion behavior that he/she is working to accomplish. As for all training programs, attention should be given to the physical setting for maximum learning enhancement, taking into consideration the human-factor design issues (lighting, noise, temperature, seating, rest periods, etc.).

*Structure.* The training situation should be structured so that the material appears relevant, gives positive feedback, and encourages the self-confidence of the trainee. This should aid in eliminating the fear of failure (Belbin, 1970; Belbin and Downs, 1964, 1966; Griew, 1964). The actual training material should be based on a job analysis (Goldstein, 1974, 1980, 1982; Wexley, 1984; Wexley and Latham, 1981).

It has been found that an effective training procedure is to arrange the training sequence according to increasing complexity. This must be based on very careful (task) analysis. The task or material to be learned is then carefully introduced. Easier aspects should be presented first. After mastery of the basic skills, more difficult aspects are then introduced until the task or material is mastered (Gagné and Briggs, 1974; Gagné, Mayor, and Paradise, 1962).

Past work on training intervention has concluded that older adult learning can be improved. The use of a task-analysis approach appears to be a strong predictor of the success of the training program, especially for complex tasks. A critical feature for training is the assurance of task mastery of each component prior to the introduction of the next one. This allows the trainee to build self-confidence in his/her ability to complete the training. The program structure should allow for the varying amount of time needed for individual trainees. The elimination of paced or time-pressured situations is beneficial to the older worker (Sterns and Sanders, 1980). All these suggestions would facilitate learning by younger workers as well. However, these approaches maximize the opportunity for older adults to be successful. Younger workers may not need the same level of structure to be successful.

*Familiarity.* It is important to use familiar elements in the training program. Industrial training efforts should emphasize the use of former skills on the new task when appropriate. The training program should be built on past knowledge and abilities, whenever possible using relevant, meaningful material from the perspective of the trainee. If the material must be abstract, explain to trainees the rationale so that it becomes meaningful to them. Emphasize the transferability of previous training and experience to the learning of the new material (Johnson and White, 1980; McGhee and Thayer, 1961; Mullan and Gorman, 1972; Welford, 1959).

*Organization.* Previous industrial training has found that many older workers have difficulty organizing information adequately (Belbin, 1965; Belbin and Belbin, 1972). At a different level, research on memory has examined organizational processes in depth and has found that older adults can improve performance by the use of appropriate learning strategies and the organization of material on memory tasks (Hulicka and Grossman, 1967; Hultsch, 1971, 1975; Schmidt, Murphy, and Sanders, 1981; Treat and Reese, 1974).

The implication is that information within the training program should be organized so that the knowledge can be built upon at each step in the program; however, this organized structure should also assure comprehension and retention. The older adult trainee must be trained in the use of the organized information and in the use of memory techniques (Blum and Naylor, 1968; Czaja and Drury, 1981).

*Time.* Older workers often take longer than younger workers to learn a new task; however, when given sufficient time, older workers perform as well as younger workers. Older adults may need a slower presentation rate and longer periods of study as well as instructions on the efficient use of this time. The longer training time may be tied to the need for organization and memory strategy training. At a physical level, the older adult may also show slower reaction time for new tasks, although well-practiced tasks may not show this decrement.

The training program should be designed to allow for variability in the time needed to complete the training segment. Longer training times are not effective if the older worker has not been trained in efficient use of that time. Strategies for retention, recall, and application of the information are an important part of any training program for the older worker (Belbin, 1965; Belbin and Belbin, 1972).

## CAREER DEVELOPMENT IN MIDDLE AND LATER ADULTHOOD: IMPLICATIONS FOR TRAINING AND RETRAINING

A life-span approach to career development would emphasize the fact that behavior change processes can occur at any point in the life course. Also, older adult workers have developed a knowledge base and abilities that continue to grow.

Older adult workers have experience-related strengths that can guide their own self-training. Depending on the level of work and worker, in the absence of stagnation and burnout, individuals can be continually developing and improving their work performance. Recent research and discussions of aging and expert cognition emphasize that individuals may show no decline in aspects of cognition that are fundamental to areas of lifetime specialization (Hoyer, 1984).

According to Walker (1978), career planning is "the personal process of planning one's life work, which entails evaluating abilities and interests, considering alternative career opportunities, establishing career goals and planning practical developmental activities" (p. 2). In the past, career-planning activities were largely left up to the individual. In more recent years, however, organizations have begun to recognize that career-planning programs fill an integral space in the human resource system (Von Glinow, Driver, Brousseau, and Prince, 1983; Wexley and Latham, 1981). For example, such programs may aid in reducing turnover among entry-level personnel by clarifying career paths within the organization (Wexley and Latham, 1981).

In reviewing the career development literature, Patchett and Sterns (1984) have emphasized the following: Theorists such as Levinson, Darrow, Klein, Levinson, and McKee (1978); Vaillant (1977); and Super (1980) envision career development as one aspect of life-span development intimately intertwined with other aspects of the life cycle. For example, Super's 1980 update of his 1957 theory describes nine major roles people play in life—including that of child, student, leisureite, citizen, worker, spouse, homemaker, parent, and pensioner. The role of worker may include both the unemployed worker and nonworker. Super recognizes that at different stages of life some roles may be more important or more appropriate than others, and that a person may emphasize one role at one point in life while playing several simultaneous roles at other times.

A rather fixed sequence of career stages was originally proposed by Super in 1957. He theorizes that children from birth to age 14 (the stage of growth) develop certain interests and abilities by role-playing activities. Between ages 15 and 24 people are in a stage of exploration, i.e., involved in making tentative choices and entering the labor market. From ages 25 to 44 comes the establishment stage in which occupational changes sometimes occur and an effort is made to stabilize a career. By ages 45 to 65 people are expected to hold on to what they have in the so-called maintenance stage. Finally, from age 65 on, the person enters into a stage of decline, where the pace is slowed and retirement occurs. In his 1980 theory update, Super retains these age-stage categories as a *general* description of lifelong career progression. However, he also notes that career growth, exploration, maintenance, and decline may occur at any or at many points in the life span. Thus, Super's work may be categorized as one example of what Sonnenfeld and Kotter (1982) term life-cycle theories–i.e., those theories that recognize career development as one aspect of life-span development.

Theorists such as Katz (1980) emphasize career development as it occurs after a person has entered an organizational setting. In a model of job longevity, Katz describes three successive stages: socialization, innovation, and adaptation. Stage I, *socialization,* occurs during the first few months on the job. During this stage, one tries to establish a situational identity, decipher situational norms, learn role expectations, build social relationships, and prove oneself as an important contributing member of the organization. Stage II, *innovation,* is characterized by a transition in employee job concerns. Occuring approximately between the sixth month and the third year of job longevity, the major concern is on achievement and accomplishment. Attempts are made to improve special skills, enlarge the scope of one's contributions, enhance visibility and promotional potential, and influence the organizational surroundings. Gradually, however, if promotion or movement does not occur, tasks become less challenging and more routine, and the person enters into Stage III, *adaptation.* In this stage, the individual must adapt to the job or leave the organization. If the individual adapts to the job, extrinsic motivators of the job and outside social life tend to take on greater meaning and importance, while efforts are made to protect one's autonomy and minimize vulnerability. If the organization is left, then the socialization phase of job longevity is reentered. Katz views socialization as a process that can occur throughout the span of the career. Life-cycle and stage theories have been criticized for using male workers as the basis for the development. It is becoming increasingly evident that career progressions of women may be quite different from those of men, as the former juggle the roles of student, housewife, paid worker, mother, etc. Life-cycle and stage approaches have also been criticized for failure to test propositions adequately. Particularly lacking is longitudinal research using subjects over age 50. A criticism of stage and within-job theories is that they tend to ignore the interaction of work and nonwork aspects of life (Sonnenfeld and Kotter, 1982).

A question that may apply to all the theories is: How cohort-specific are they? Super's original theory has been revised to consider career changes in middle and older adulthood, but is this because of an increased sensitivity to issues of adulthood and aging or because of certain cultural or historical changes that may have occurred?

Finally, as Cross (1981) and O'Toole (1978) point out, most theories of career progression follow the "linear life plan," i.e., the life pattern in which education is a task for the young, work is for the middle-aged, and leisure is for the elderly. The criticism of using the linear life plan as a basis for theory is that it perpetuates the notion that these are *the* appropriate tasks for each life stage, discouraging intermixing all three tasks across the life span. Sterns and Patchett (1983) and Patchett and Sterns (1984) have attempted to develop a model of adult and older adult career development that is non-age specific. The model assumes that transitions in work life may occur many times throughout a career (see Figure 6-1).

Looking at the model, the decision to change jobs or careers or to exit the system is directly influenced by attitudes toward mobility and success or failure in previous career-development activities. Numerous factors are hypothesized to affect mobility attitudes, such as employment, tenure or stage in career, growth, need, fear of stagnation, marketability perceptions, job-market conditions, and chance encounters. The decision to change jobs or careers also may affect one's attitudes toward entering or reentering the work force. Any of these variables also could be mediated by the effects of various personality variables.

The model incorporates Hall's model of career growth (1971), which conceptualizes career planning from a goal-setting perspective. Once a career-goal decision —such as the decision to engage in training or retraining—is made, then goal attainment should lead to identity growth and enhanced self-esteem. Such enhanced self-esteem may then lead to greater commitment to future career-developmental

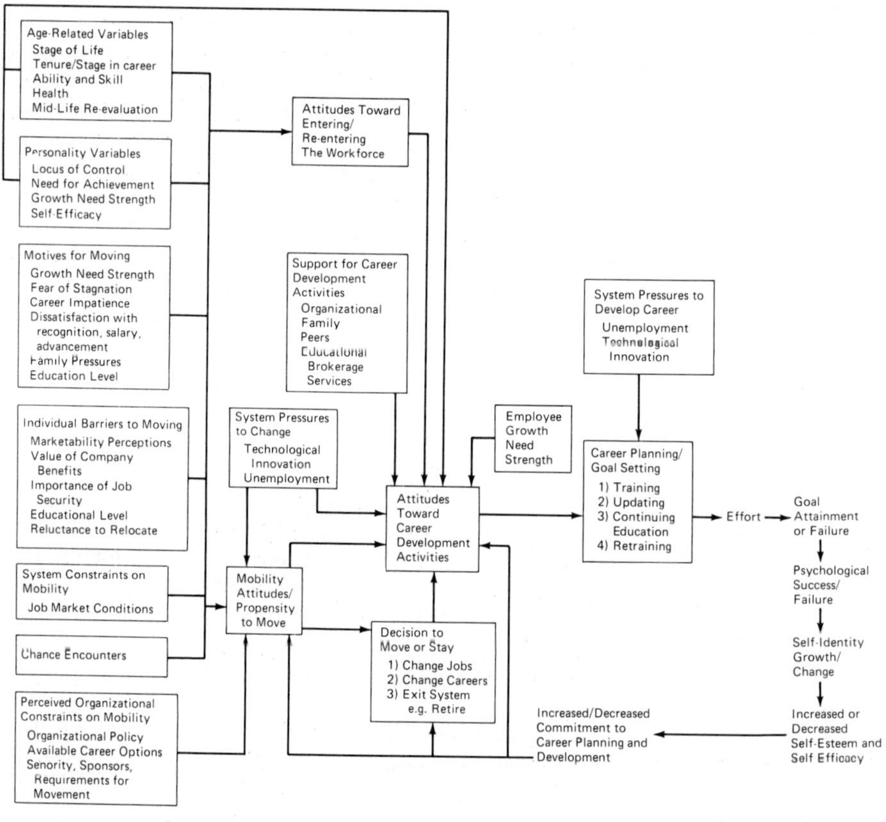


**FIGURE 6-1. Career Progression in Middle and Later Adulthood. From Patchett and Sterns (1984).**

goals. Goal attainment enhances self-esteem, which may increase perceptions of self-efficacy and future commitment to career-development activities. Note that for an older adult with doubts about his/her abilities to perform well in training and/or retraining situations, successes early in the program may be crucial. Not only would successes enhance feelings of self-efficacy, but decisions to engage in future retraining may be enhanced as well. Failure could easily result in a decision to drop out of the retraining program as well as future programs, jeopardizing future career-growth opportunities and decisions.

Sterns and Patchett (1983) advance that a person seeking mobility within the organization or between organizations most likely would hold a positive attitude regarding a career-development program.

Age or life stage is an important determinant of behavior. Numerous models suggest that the mobility rates of younger persons (up to around age 30) are much higher than those of older persons (Hall and Nougiam, 1968; Super, 1957; Veiga, 1973) as the younger generations move about seeking their niche in life and the older ones maintain theirs as they plan for retirement. Research on actual mobility rates seem to bear out these hypotheses (Byrne, 1975; Saben, 1967; Sommers and Eck, 1977; Veiga, 1983). Veiga (1983) also found that age correlated significantly and negatively with propensity to move. With regard to career development, Gould (1979) predicted that career planning would be highest during Super's *stabilization period* (age 31 to 44), when there is stable growth as the person attempts to secure his/her place within the occupation. Research support has not been found for this hypothesis.

Along similar lines, tenure (seniority) or stage in one's career has been a variable of interest in the mobility literature. Schein (1971) describes three stages in a career: socialization, performance, and obsolescence versus the development of new skills. In the third stage, the obsolete person may be retained as "deadwood," with no options for mobility, or he/she may be retrained, transferred into a lateral position, or forced into early retirement. Although career development could be helpful to the employee in all three stages, it seems likely that the person who would most strongly desire such help would be in a third stage of Schein's model. In terms of actual research, "mobility in the earliest stage of one's career bears an unequivocal relationship with one's later career" (Rosenbaum, 1979, 220; Veiga, 1981, 1983). Thus, the person who is mobile early on is most likely to favor career development programs later in his/her career. Such individuals most likely will be mobile in the latter career stages.

The "individual barriers to moving" bear some relationship to these issues of age and seniority. As Veiga (1983) suggests, perceptions of one's own marketability may strongly influence one's efforts to explore alternative career opportunities, either within one's own organization or in an outside firm. Holding a particular position within the same organization for an extended period of time may only reinforce one's feelings of specialization and/or obsolescence rather than one's feelings of marketability potential. Similarly, the longer a person remains with a company and the older that person gets, the more likely he/she will be to think twice about risking any benefits accrued through the years in order to move to a new organization. The same may be true for the person who strongly values job security, regardless of age. Mobility implies a certain degree of risk to one's job security; in which case career-development programs may be seen as a waste of time if there is little motivation to move.

Veiga (1983) also identified five motives for moving which significantly influenced propensity to leave: fear of stagnation; career impatience; and dissatisfactions with one's salary, recognition, and/or advancement. Again we assume that people expressing a desire to move will react positively to the initiation of a career-development program which could conceivably help them on their way.

Additional personality variables are hypothesized to affect mobility and career development attitudes: need for achievement and locus of control. Neapolitan (1980) investigated occupational changes in midcareer and found that people who changed regardless of great obstacles tended to reflect an internal locus of control. A comparison group of people dissatisfied with their careers who did *not* change tended to perceive great risk beyond their control which would doom any efforts to change. According to Greenhause and Sklarew (1981), exploration "is a proactive attempt to understand and influence one's life" (p. 2). Thus, we might expect internals to engage in greater career-planning activity then externals. Research by Gould (1979) tends to support this hypothesis. Beehr, Taber, and Walsh (1980) looked at locus of control and perceived channels of mobility. They found that employees who had not had a recent opportunity to change jobs were more likely to see mobility opportunities as controlled by external forces such as luck or favoritism, whereas employees with recent change opportunities tended to perceive mobility as contingent upon performance (an internally controlled factor). We may conclude that persons believing that mobility opportunities are controlled by forces beyond their control (an external locus of control) would be less likely to view a career development program as beneficial to them and, hence, be less likely to participate in one.

A similar argument could be made for other perceived constraints on mobility. Mobility within an organization often depends on the size and structure of the organization (Vardi, 1980).

Patchett and Sterns (1984) emphasize three factors regarding their career-development model. First, decisions to change jobs or careers, or decisions to engage in career development activities may come about as a result of changes within the individual, the environment, or a combination of both. Other models, however, have a tendency to concentrate on either the individual alone as a source of decision making (an organismic perspective) or on environmental factors that change and cause the individual to make career decisions (a mechanistic perspective). The Patchett and Sterns model can accommodate both a mechanistic and organismic perspective, but tends to emphasize the changing individual in a changing world, and thus views career decisions as a result of the interaction between these two factors.

Another important emphasis is the recognition that adults make multiple career transitions throughout the life span. Patchett and Sterns believe that there are people who are 60 to 70 years old and older who are still interested in working, changing jobs, and further developing their careers. Unfortunately, past gerontological discussions have almost exclusively focused on the decision to retire; not enough attention has been given to multiple career transitions which may occur within a normal working life.

Finally, previous models have tended to emphasize the "usual" career progressions of middle-aged and older adults, often assuming fairly stable careers—particularly for white-collar workers. This model allows for the non-normative career events, which affect the working individual, such as unemployment and technological obsolescence, as well as for the normative events such as promotions, lateral moves, etc.

## CONCLUSION

The adult and older adult worker of today is faced with the continuing need to retrain and update skills. Education and training in organizations and in formal educational settings should emphasize the optimization of individual development for continued career growth.

Managers and supervisors need to be sensitive to the individual needs, aspirations, and career goals of older workers. At the same time, older adult workers need to take advantage of training and retraining opportunities in order to continue to maintain a current knowledge base and to be competitive with workers of all ages. Displaced workers will need extremely supportive recruitment, training, and placement programs for reentry into the work role.

Training and retraining methods have been explored over the last three decades. There are some fine examples of training and retraining programs that have been carried out with adult and older adult workers. However, there has not been the level of research and demonstration needed to meet the current and future needs of our adult and older adult workers. Major attempts to stimulate interest in aging and training in the 1960s led to a period of minimal activity throughout most of the 1970s. The issue of today is whether we will begin to apply the information we now have in major training and retraining efforts for older adult workers with appropriate evaluation and follow-up. The growing demands over the next two decades require an immediate response.

### *REFERENCES*

BALTES, P. B., and DANISH, S. J. (1980). Intervention in life-span development and aging: Issues and concepts. In R. E. Turner and H. W. Reese (Eds.), *Life-span developmental psychology: Intervention.* New York: Academic Press.

BALTES, P. B., REESE, H. W., and LIPSITT, L. P. (1980). Life-span developmental psychology. *Annual Review of Psychology, 31,* 65–110.

BALTES, P. B., and SCHAIE, K. W. (Eds.). (1973). *Life-span developmental psychology: Personality and socialization.* New York: Academic Press.

BANDURA, A. (1977). Self-efficacy: Toward a unifying theory of behavioral change. *Psychological Review, 84,* 191–215.

BANDURA, A. (1981). Self-referent thought: A developmental analysis of self-efficacy. In J. H. Flavell and L. Ross (Eds.), *Social cognitive development: Frontiers and possible futures.* Cambridge, England: Cambridge University Press.

BANDURA, A. (1982). Self-efficacy mechanisms in human agency. *American Psychologist, 37,* 122–147.

BARKIN, S. (1970). Retraining and job redesign: Positive approaches to the continued employment of older persons. In H. L. Sheppard (Ed.), *Toward an industrial gerontology.* Cambridge, MA: Schenkman Publishing Company.

BAROCAS, V. S. (1982). *Handbook II–Employment and training of the mature worker: A training design.* Washington, D. C.: The National Council on the Aging, Inc.

BASS, B. M., and BARRETT, G. V. (1981). *People, work and organizations.* Boston: Allyn and Bacon, Inc.

BAUER, D., BAROCAS, V. S., FERBER-CAHILL, P. (Eds.) (1982). *Significant segment–Handbook I–Employment and training of the mature worker:*

*resource manual.* Washington, D. C.: The National Council on the Aging, Inc.

BEEHR, T. A., TABER, T. D., and WALSH, J. T. (1980). Perceived mobility channels: Criteria for intraorganizational job mobility. *Organizational Behavior and Human Performance, 26,* 250–264.

BELBIN, E., and BELBIN, R. I. (1972). *Problems in adult retraining.* London, England: Heineman Publishing Company.

BELBIN, E., and DOWNS, S. M. (1964). Activity learning and the older worker. *Ergonomics, 7,* 429–437.

BELBIN, E., and DOWNS, S. M. (1966). Teaching paired associates: The problem of age. *Occupational Psychology, 40,* 67–74.

BELBIN, R. M. (1965). *Training methods for older workers.* Paris: Organization for Economic Co-operation and Development.

BELBIN, R. M. (1970). *The discovery method in training older workers.* In H. L. Sheppard (Ed.), *Toward an industrial gerontology.* Cambridge, MA: Schenkman Publishing Company.

BIRREN, J. E., and WOODRUFF, D. S. (1973). Human development over the lifespan through education. In P. B. Baltes and K. W. Schaie (Eds.), *Life-span developmental psychology: Personality and socialization.* New York: Academic Press.

BLUM, M. L., and NAYLOR, J. C. (1968). *Industrial psychology.* New York: Harper and Row.

BYRNE, J. J. (1975). Occupational mobility of workers. Washington, D.C.: U.S. Bureau of Labor Statistics, Special Labor Force, Report No. 176.

CASCIO, W. F. (1982). *Applied psychology in personnel management.* Second edition. Reston, VA: Reston Publishing Company, Inc.

CROSS, K. P. (1981). *Adults as learners: Increasing participation and facilitating learning.* San Francisco, CA: Jossey-Bass.

CZAJA, S. J., and DRURY, C. G. (1981). Aging and pretraining in industrial inspection. *Human Factors, 23,* 485–494.

DOERING, M., RHODES, S. R., and SHUSTER, M. (1983). *The aging worker: Research and recommendations.* Beverly Hills, CA: Sage Publications.

DOOLING, D. J., and KLEMMER, E. T. (1982). New technology for business telephone users: Some findings from human factors. In R. A. Kasschau, R. Lachman, and K. R. Laughery (Eds.), *Information technology and psychology: Prospects for the future.* New York: Praeger.

DOWNS, S., and ROBERTS, A. (1977). The training of underground train guards: A case study with a field experiment. *Journal of Occupational Psychology, 50,* 111–120.

EDLEMAN, C. D., and SIEGLER, I. C. (1978). *Federal age discrimination in employment law: Slowing down the gold watch.* Charlottesville, VA: The Michie Company.

GAGNÉ, R. M., and BRIGGS, L. I. (1974). *Principles of instructional design.* New York: Holt, Rinehart and Winston.

GAGNÉ, R. M., MAYOR, J. R., and PARADISE, N. E. (1962). Factors in acquiring knowledge of a mathematical task. *Psychological Monographs, 76,* whole no. 526.

GINSBERG, E., MILLS, D. Q., OWEN, J. D., SHEPPARD, H. L., and WACHTER, M. L. (1982). *Work decisions in the 1980s.* Boston, MA: Auburn House Publishing Company.

GOLDSTEIN, I. I. (1974). *Training: program development and evaluation.* Monterey, CA: Brooks/Cole Publishing Co.

GOLDSTEIN, I. I. (1980). Training in work organizations. *Annual Review of Psychology.* Palo Alto, CA: Annual Reviews, Inc.

GOLDSTEIN, I. I. (1982). Training in the 1970's: A view toward the 1980's. In R. A. Kasschau, R. Lachman, and K. R. Laughery (Eds.), *Information technology and psychology: Prospects for the future.* New York: Praeger.

GOULD, S. (1979). Characteristics of career planners in upwardly mobile occupations. *Academy of Management Journal, 22,* 539–550.

GREENHAUSE, J. H., and SKLAREW, N. D. (1981). Some sources and consequences of career exploration. *Journal of Vocational Behavior, 18,* 1–12.

GRIEW, S. (1964). *Job redesign: The application of biological data on aging to the design of equipment and the organization of work.* Paris: Organization for Economic Co-operation and Development.

HALL, D. T. (1971). Potential for career growth. *Personnel Administration, 34,* 18–30.

HALL, D. T., and NOUGAIM, K. (1968). An examination of Maslow's need hierarchy in an organizational setting. *Organizational Behavior and Human Performance, 3,* 12–35.

HOOS, I. R. (1967). *Retraining the workforce: An analysis of current experience.* Berkeley, CA: University of California Press.

HOYER, W. J. (1984). Aging and the development of expert cognition. In T. M. Schlecter and M. P. Toglia (Eds.), *New Directions in Cognitive Science.* Norwood, N.J.: Ablex.

HULICKA, I. M., and GROSSMAN, J. L. (1967). Age group comparison for the use of mediators in paired-associate learning. *Journal of Gerontology, 22,* 46–51.

HULTSCH, D. F. (1975). Adult age differences in retrieval: Trace-dependent and cue-dependent forgetting. *Developmental Psychology, 11,* 197–201.

HUMPLE, C. S., and LYONS, M. (1983). *Management and the older workforce: Policies and programs.* New York: American Management Association.

JACOBSON, B. (1980). *Young programs for older workers.* New York: Van Nostrand Reinhold Company.

JOHNSON, D. F., and WHITE, C. B. (1980). Effects of training on computerized test performance in the elderly. *Journal of Applied Psychology, 65,* 357-358.

KATZ, R. (1980). The influence of job longevity on employee reactions to task characteristics. *Human Relations, 31,* 703–725.

LEVINSON, D. J., DARROW, C., KLEIN, E., LEVINSON, M., and MCKEE, B. (1978). *The seasons of a man's life.* New York: Knopf.

MCGHEE, W., and THAYER, P. W. (1961). *Training in business and industry.* New York: Wiley and Sons.

MCLEISH, J. A. B. (1976). *The Ulyssean adult: Creativity in the middle and later years.* Toronto, Canada: McGraw-Hill Ryerson Limited.

MEIER, E. L., and KERR, E. A. (1976). Capabilities of middle aged and older workers: A survey of the literature. *Industrial Gerontology, 3,* 147–156.

MOODY, H. R. (1976). Philosophical presuppositions of education for old age. *Educational Gerontology, 1,* 1–16.

MULLEN, C., and GORMAN, L. (1972). Facilitating adaptation to change: A case study in retraining middle-aged and older workers at Aer Lingus. *Industrial Psychology, 15,* 23–29.

NATIONAL INSTITUTE ON INDUSTRIAL GERONTOLOGY. (1968). *Industrial gerontology: Curriculum materials.* New York: National Council on Aging.

NEALE, J. G., TOYE, M. N., and BELBIN, E. (1968). Adult training: The use of programmed instruction. *Occupational Psychology, 42,* 23–31.

NEAPOLITAN, J. (1980). Occupational change in mid-career: An exploratory investigation. *Journal of Vocational Behavior, 16,* 212–225.

NICKERSON, R. S. (1982). Foreword: Information technology and psychology—

an invitation for speculation. In R. A. Kasschau, R. Lachman, and K. R. Laughery (Eds.), *Information Technology and Psychology: Prospects for the Future.* New York: Praeger.

O'TOOLE, J. (1978). Work, learning and the American future. San Francisco: Jossey-Bass Publishers.

PATCHETT, M. B., and STERNS, H. L. (1984). Career progression in middle and later adulthood. Paper presented as part of the symposium "Industrial Gerontological Psychology: Current Issues for the Curriculum and Research," at Tenth Annual Meeting of the Association for Gerontology in Higher Education, February, Indianapolis.

PETERSON, D. A. (1983). *Facilitationg education for older learners.* San Francisco: Jossey-Bass Publishers.

*Proceeding national conference on manpower training and the older worker.* (1966). Washington, D. C.: The National Council on the Aging.

REBOK, G. W., and OFFERMAN, L. R. (1983). Behavioral competencies of older college students: A self-efficacy approach. *Journal of Gerontology, 23,* 428–432.

RHODES, S. R. (1983). Age-related differences in work attitudes and behavior: A review and conceptual analysis. *Psychological Bulletin, 93*(2), 328–367.

ROSEN, B., and JARDEE, T. H. (1977). Too old or not too old. *Harvard Business Review, 55,* 97–106.

ROSENBAUM, J. E. (1979). Tournament mobility: Career patterns in a corporation. *Administrative Science Quarterly, 24,* 220–241.

SABEN, S. (1967) Occupational mobility of employed workers. Washington, D.C.: U.S. Bureau of Labor Statistics, Special Labor Force Report No. 84.

SCHAIE, K. W., and WILLIS, S. L. (1978). Life-span development: Implications for education. *Review of Research in Education, 6,* 120–156.

SCHEIN, E. H. (1971). The individual, the organization, and the career: A conceptual scheme. *Journal of Applied Behavioral Science, 7,* 401–426.

SCHMIDT, F. A., MURPHY, M. D., and SANDERS, R. E. (1981). Training older adults free recall rehearsal strategies. *Journal of Gerontology, 36,* 329–337.

SHATTO, G. M. (Ed.). (1972). *Employment of the middle-aged.* Springfield, IL: Charles C. Thomas.

SHEPPARD, H. L. (1976). Work and retirement. In R. H. Binstock and E. Shanas (Eds.), *Handbook of aging and the Social Sciences.* New York: Van Nostrand Reinhold Co.

SHEPPARD, H. L., and RIX, S. E. (1977). *The graying of working America: The coming crises in retirement-age policy.* New York: The Free Press.

SIEMEN, J. R. (1976). Programmed material as a training tool for older persons. *Industrial Gerontology, 3,* 183–190.

SOMMERS, D., and ECK, A. (1977). Occupational mobility in the American labor force. *Monthly Labor Review, 100,* 3–19.

SONNENFELD, J. (1978). Dealing with the aging work force. *Harvard Business Review, 56,* 80–90.

SONNENFELD, J., and KOTTER, J. P. (1982). The maturation of career theory. *Human Relations, 35,* 19–46.

STAGNER, R. (1971). An industrial psychologist looks at individual gerontology. *Aging and Human Development, 2,* 29–37.

STERNS, H. L., and MITCHELL, S. (1979). Personal and cognitive development across the life-span. In H. L. Sterns, E. F. Ansello, B. M. Sprouse, and R. Layfield-Faux (Eds.), *Gerontology in higher education: Developing institutional and community strength.* Belmont, CA: Wadsworth Publishing.

STERNS, H. L., and PATCHETT, M. (1984). Technology and the aging adult:

Career development and training. In P. K. Robinson, J. E. Livingston, and J. E. Birren (Eds.), *Aging and Technological Advances.* New York: Plenum Press.

STERNS, H. L., and PATCHETT, M. Technology and the aging adult: Career development and training. In P. K. Robinson, J. E. Livingston, and J. E. Birren (Eds.), *Aging and Technical Advances.* New York: Plenum Press.

STERNS, H. L., and SANDERS, R. E. (1980). Training and education in the elderly. In R. R. Turner and H. W. Reese (Eds.), *Life-span Developmental Psychology: Intervention.* New York: Academic Press, 370–330.

SUPER, D. E. (1957). *The psychology of careers.* New York: Harper and Row.

SUPER, D. E. (1980). A life-span, life-space approach to career development. *Journal of Vocational Behavior, 16,* 282–298.

*The future of older workers in America: New options for an extended working life.* (1980). New York: Work in America Institution, Inc.

TREAT, N. J., and REESE, H. W. (1976). Age imagery and pacing in paired-associate learning. *Developmental Psychology, 12,* 119–124.

VAILLANT, G. E. (1977). *Adaptation to life.* Boston: Little Brown.

VALASEK, D. L., and STERNS, H. L. (1981). Task analysis and training: Applications from lab to the field. Paper presented as part of the "Symposium on Industrial Gerontological Psychology: Why Survive?" 34th Annual Scientific Meeting of The Gerontological Society of America, November, Toronto, Ontario, Canada.

VARDI, Y. (1980). Organizational career mobility: An integrative model. *Academy of Management Review, 5,* 341–355.

VEIGA, J. F. (1973). The mobile manager at mid-career. *Harvard Business Review, 51,* 115–119.

VEIGA, J. F. (1981). Plateaued versus non-plateaued managers: Career patterns, attitudes, and path potential. *Academy of Management Journal, 24,* 566–578.

VEIGA, J. F. (1983). Mobility influences during managerial career stages. *Academy of Management Journal, 26*(1), 64–85.

VON GLINOW, M. A., DRIVER, M. J., BROUSSEAU, K., and PRINCE, J. B. (1983). The design of a career-oriented human resource system. *Academy of Management Review, 8,* 23–32.

WALKER, J. W. (1978). Does career planning rock the boat? *Human Resources Management, 17,* 2–7.

WELFORD, A. T. (1959). Psycho-motor performance. In J. E. Birren (Ed.), *Handbook of aging and the individual.* Chicago, IL: University of Chicago Press, 562–613.

WELFORD, A. T. (1976). Thirty years of psychological research on age and work. *Journal of Occupational Psychology,* 49, 129–138.

WEXLEY, K. N. (1984). Personnel training. *Annual Review of Psychology, 35,* 519–551.

WEXLEY, K. N., and LATHAM, G. P. (1981). *Developing and training human resources in organizations.* Glenview, IL: Scott, Foresman and Co.

WILLIS, S. L. (1985). Toward an educational psychology of the older adult learner: Intellectual and cognitive bases. In J. E. Birren and K. W. Schaie (Eds.), *Handbook of the psychology of aging.* New York: Van Nostrand Reinhold Company.

# 7

# LABOR MARKETS, AGING, AND HEALTH

Shelby Stewman*

## LABOR MARKETS—AN EXPANDED CLASS OF MODELS

Perhaps the best way to begin pointing out the need for an expanded class of labor market models is to suggest a few questions having policy significance that can be addressed by such an expansion. Then we will pursue the theoretical significance of such an expansion across several disciplines—demography, economics, psychology, and sociology. To begin the discussion, consider the following questions:

1. What are the relative job opportunities for middle-aged and older workers? In terms of the relative number of such workers making a major occupational change or reentering the labor market over a five-year period, does one third seem high for U.S. workers? For workers in Europe? In Japan?

2. What are the impacts from retirement on current workers, unemployed workers, and new entrants? What are the effects of changes in retirement rates? How important are disabling health processes in the retirement decision? Is 25 percent a bottom figure? Are retirement preferences and plans as to the timing of the decision to retire only realized in half the population?

*I particularly thank Judy Treas for making available the age-specific labor market data book from the 1970 U.S. Census and Judy Stryckman for interpreting Alfred Sauvy's *La Machine et Le Chomage: Le Progress Technique et L'Employ* for my use. This research was in part supported by a grant from the National Science Foundation (SES 80-17884).

**3.** What are the implications to employers and employees of increasing or decreasing growth rates of new jobs or of relative declines in the number of already-existing jobs in various industrial sectors or in different occupations? If on the growth side, where are an employer's best chances for filling such jobs? If on the decline side, where are the best chances for workers getting a job?

**4.** If, for example, one million job vacancies initially enter the labor market from worker exits and/or growth of new jobs, how many job opportunities are generated? Are there possibly two million job opportunities arising due to a chain reaction effect? To whom do these job opportunities go? How does the job vacancy chain reaction process filter through the occupational, sex, and age distributions? What proportion of job vacancies is filled from inside the labor market (current work force) versus from the outside (new hires, reentrants)?

**5.** How rapidly are the age and sex distributions in the job structure changing, and what are the processes generating these changes?

What the above questions have in common is that each involves a population of *both* workers *and* jobs. It is new theoretical development pertaining to populations of jobs, in conjunction with the already-existing theoretical development on populations of persons (workers, in this case) that necessitates an expanded class of labor market models or theory. To be more specific, models are needed that can treat worker exits, growth and/or decline in jobs, employer hiring and staffing practice, the distribution of jobs and their relative redistribution, the interrelationships of job moves (including exits which trigger the chain reaction), and the relative attributes of labor supply (e.g., age, sex, work experience, education, etc.) as part of one process. In particular, labor demand processes–such as growth, occupation redistributions from differential demand and/or technological change, employer hiring/staffing decisions, and job vacancy chains–need to be brought into the modeling of labor markets. In turn, the modeling of labor markets needs to be brought into the study of employment and aging.

Demographic, economic, psychological, and sociological theories of labor supply (see Blau and Duncan, 1967; Hauser and Featherman, 1974; Heckman, 1981; Heckman and MaCurdy, 1981; March and Simon, 1958; Mincer, 1974; and Schoen and Woodrow, 1980) would be greatly enhanced by theoretical development of demand processes and of work at the interface between populations of jobs and of persons, particularly in terms of treating entrance and exit behavior. For instance, organizational psychologists are well aware of the motivational importance of promotion chances, yet where is the model of job opportunities? In brief, the expected behavior from such motivational theories is conditional on job opportunities, but organizational psychology has advanced no such model of the opportunity structure to activate the motivational processes dynamically over time. Similarly, in economics Heckman and his associates (Flinn and Heckman, 1982; Heckman, 1981; Heckman and MaCurdy, 1981; Heckman and Singer, 1982) make extraordinarily provocative probes into supply behavior, population heterogeneity, and duration dependence, but generally assume convenient mathematical functions for labor demand. However, where are the comparable specifications of demand side structures or what might be considered features of the underlying process generally taken as "external" conditions or as conditional assumptions by supply-side theorists in the fields of demography, economics, psychology, and sociology?

As for new developments, organizational design treating the work environment has begun to play an important role in organizational psychology, while in economics, an important theoretical divergence from neoclassical theory has been offered by Doeringer and Piore's (1971) work on internal labor markets; that is on internally administered labor markets within organizations. Additionally, new theoretical developments in organizational demography by Keyfitz (1973), Stewman and Konda (1983), and White (1970) point to important demand-side processes in demography and sociology. Hence, due to the common organizational tie and the new emphasis on the neglected side of labor theory–labor demand–there is potential for considerable theoretical advancement and convergence of labor theory in demography, economics, psychology, and sociology. Not only is the organization the common meeting ground, but the joint decision making by both worker and employer is explicit, conveying the potential for theoretical equivalence between populations of workers and jobs.

In addition to the population of jobs, another neglected but extremely important feature of labor markets is their propensity to change. Consider two basic elements that are changing: the distribution of workers by age and sex, and the distribution of jobs by industry and occupation. Perhaps it will be easier to first visualize these components statically–at different points in time, say, t1 and t2. Then we may ask about the processes that generate the change from t1 to t2. On the supply side of labor markets we observe exits, entrants, and internal movement. At issue are their relative size and the differences across job types. Similarly, on the demand side we are interested in job vacancies, triggered by supply-side exits and by new growth, and in employer hiring practice.

Since the usual focus of analysis has been largely labor-supply-oriented, there has been insufficient attention to the interface of the populations of jobs and of persons as an empirical process unfolding over time. Hence, out of theoretical statics, as well as empirical ignorance, we sometimes find discussions about the inflexibility of older workers to change jobs or employers and the use of erroneous assumptions from supply-side statics that ignore the magnitude of labor market change and its internal dynamics–in both employer and worker behavior *and* job and job vacancy behavior. With respect to the latter point, the private-sector studies at MIT have found that the job loss (abolishment) rate is about 8 percent per year in the United States (time period for these data: 1969-76). Hence, in a five-year period about 40 percent of the private-sector jobs in a city, state, region, or nation have disappeared through business deaths, contractions, and relocation (Greene, 1982).[1] This holds for the fast-growing South and West as well as for the Northeast and North Central regions. What differentiates them, of course, is the extent and nature of job replacement and growth processes.

Similarly, on the labor supply front, over a five-year period (1965-70) ap-

[1]At the national level, if relocations are not outside the country, then the 40 percent figure will be dampened. More importantly, if "new" jobs and "old" jobs have different life expectancies, then the 8 percent figure above may reflect a higher rate of job loss for "new" jobs in new firms and a lower rate for "old" or "new" jobs in "older" firms. However, the distribution of loss rate by age of jobs is not known. No doubt the 8 percent figure contains losses by both "old" and "new" jobs and hence to the extent that "new" jobs' loss rate is greater than 8 percent, the 40 percent figure for the initializing job population will be high. However, if it is off, by how much? Even if it were off by one half the magnitude would remain surprising.

proximately one third of the U.S. workers had changed occupations within each of the 35-44, 45-64, and 65+ age groups, and approximately 20 percent within each of these same age groups had made major occupational shifts (e.g., sales to managerial; clerical to professional; operative to craft, etc.). If we consider not only those who stayed in the labor market, but also those who entered or reentered the labor market, then the worker renewal or change rate[2] over a five-year period is around 40 percent for males and 50 percent for females (see Sommers and Eck, 1977). The sheer size of such staffing change is surprising. The fact that it holds across *all* aging cohorts is yet another surprise. Both of these 40 percent figures (job-loss rate and employee renewal rate) attest to the importance of an expanded class of theoretical models treating both populations of jobs and job vacancies and populations of workers and aging, and to the importance of viewing the underlying processes generating the matching of these two types of populations over time.

The plan for the remainder of the chapter is as follows. The next section reviews the shifts in populations of persons by age and in populations of jobs by occupation and industry from the late 1800s through this century and beyond, where forecasts are available. Additionally, a model is suggested for linking the two types of populations over time and thereby beginning to address labor market dynamics and the behavior of workers as integrally related to and embedded in such market processes. In the third section, five labor market structures or processes from this model are presented to further delineate one example of the expanded class of models discussed above. The five structures pertain to employer hiring practice, chain reactions of job vacancies, job ratios, multiple job-worker ratios, and cohort size. Empirical examples illustrating each structure are provided, primarily using U.S. national labor market data. Two main types of trigger mechanisms prompt these labor market structures into action—exit rates of workers and relative growth or decline rates of jobs. The fourth section then focuses on one of these trigger mechanisms, exit rates, with a discussion of five types of exit rates: mortality, disability, unemployment, preretirement withdrawal from the labor force, and retirement. The health of a worker is a particularly important factor affecting exit behavior, namely in its impact on retirement, as well as through death and disability. In short, the next section provides an orientation to thinking about populations of jobs as well as persons; the third section then discusses five labor market structures involving basic underlying distributions or dynamics of these labor market populations; and the fourth section discusses one of two primary triggering mechanisms activating such labor market structures.

## POPULATIONS OF PERSONS AND POPULATIONS OF JOBS

### Populations of Persons Over Time: 1870-2025

The age structure of the U.S. population holds an important place (explicit or implicit) in gerontological research since the changing age distribution over the last 100 years, and that expected over the next 40 to 50 years, speaks to the numerical significance of aging research it will become increasingly important. Table 1

[2] Based on the destination population; in other words, a demand-side view of the population "hired."

**TABLE 1a. Population Distributions by Age for the United States: 1880–2025 (in thousands)**

| YEAR | < 5 | | 5–24 | | 25–44 | | 45–64 | | 65+ | | TOTAL |
|---|---|---|---|---|---|---|---|---|---|---|---|
| 1870 | 5,515 | 14% | 17,390 | 45% | 9,893 | 26% | 4,603 | 12% | 1,154 | 3% | 38,558 |
| 1880 | 6,915 | 14% | 22,294 | 44% | 12,919 | 26% | 6,305 | 13% | 1,723 | 3% | 50,156 |
| 1890 | | 12 | | 44 | | 27 | | 13 | | 4 | |
| 1900 | 9,181 | 12% | 31,917 | 42% | 21,434 | 28% | 10,463 | 14% | 3,099 | 4% | 76,094 |
| 1910 | | 12 | | 40 | | 29 | | 15 | | 4 | |
| 1920 | 11,631 | 11% | 40,979 | 39% | 31,798 | 30% | 17,124 | 16% | 4,929 | 5% | 106,461 |
| 1930 | | 9 | | 38 | | 30 | | 18 | | 5 | |
| 1940 | 10,579 | 8% | 46,396 | 35% | 39,868 | 30% | 26,249 | 20% | 9,031 | 7% | 132,122 |
| 1950 | | 11 | | 31 | | 30 | | 20 | | 8 | |
| 1960 | 20,341 | 11% | 60,311 | 33% | 47,140 | 26% | 36,203 | 20% | 16,675 | 9% | 180,670 |
| 1970 | 17,156 | 8% | 77,229 | 38% | 48,435 | 24% | 41,974 | 20% | 20,085 | 10% | 204,879 |
| 1980 | 16,344 | 7% | 77,413 | 33% | 62,707 | 28% | 44,497 | 20% | 25,545 | 11% | 226,506 |
| 1990 | 19,200 | 8% | 70,900 | 28% | 81,351 | 33% | 46,481 | 19% | 31,799 | 13% | 249,731 |
| 2000 | 17,624 | 7% | 74,352 | 28% | 80,105 | 30% | 60,873 | 23% | 35,036 | 13% | 267,990 |
| 2025 | 17,949 | 6% | 73,850 | 25% | 78,253 | 26% | 72,334 | 24% | 58,363 | 20% | 301,022 |

Data Sources for Table 1a:
1870 to 1890: Series A119–134, ***Historical Statistics of the United States, Colonial Times to 1970 (HSUS),*** U.S. Bureau of the Census, 1975;
1900 to 1970: Series A29-42, ***HSUS***;
1980: Table No. 31, ***Statistical Abstract of the United States 1982-83 (SAUS)***, U.S. Bureau of the Census, 1982;
1990 to 2025: Table No. 6, ***SAUS.***

**TABLE 1b. Population Change by Age Group and Period for the United States: 1880–2025 (in millions)**

| | AGE | | | | | | | | |
|---|---|---|---|---|---|---|---|---|---|
| PERIOD | < 5 | 5–24 | 25–44 | 45–64 | 65+ | < 44 | > 45 | TOTAL | % CHANGE > 45 |
| 1880–1900 | 2.3 | 9.6 | 8.5 | 4.2 | 1.4 | 20.4 | 5.6 | 25.9 | 22% |
| 1900–1920 | 2.5 | 9.1 | 10.4 | 6.7 | 1.8 | 22.0 | 8.5 | 30.5 | 28% |
| 1920–1940 | - 1.1 | 5.4 | 8.1 | 9.1 | 4.1 | 12.4 | 13.2 | 25.6 | 52% |
| 1940–1960 | 9.8 | 13.9 | 7.3 | 10.0 | 7.6 | 31.0 | 17.6 | 48.6 | 36% |
| 1960–1980 | - 4.0 | 17.1 | 15.6 | 8.3 | 8.9 | 28.7 | 17.2 | 45.9 | 37% |
| 1980–2000 | 1.3 | - 3.1 | 17.4 | 16.4 | 9.5 | 15.6 | 25.9 | 41.5 | 62% |
| 2000–2025 | 0.3 | - 0.5 | - 1.9 | 11.5 | 23.6 | - 2.1 | 35.1 | 33.0 | 106% |
| | | | | | | | | | |
| 1870–1970 | 11.6 | 59.8 | 38.5 | 37.4 | 18.9 | | 56.3 | 166.3 | 34% |
| 1970–1990 | 2.0 | - 6.3 | 32.9 | 4.5 | 11.7 | | 16.2 | 44.9 | 36% |
| 1990–2025 | - 1.3 | 3.0 | - 3.1 | 25.9 | 26.8 | - 1.4 | 52.7 | 51.3 | 103% |

shows past as well as projected future age distributions, from 1870 to 2025. The upper part of the table provides both the number of persons per age group and the associated percentages. The under-five age groups decreased by one half, from 14 percent of the population in 1870 and 1880 to 7 percent in 1980. Likewise, the 5–24 age group decreased by one fourth, from 44 percent in 1880 to 33 percent in 1980. The "baby boom" cohorts, which are first noticeable in the 5–24 age group in 1960 and are quite visible in 1970 when they are fully within this age band, constitute the exception to a fairly continuous decline. Moreover, by 2025 this age group will also be almost one half of its relative size in 1880. As for the 25-44 age group, there was little shift between 1870 and 1980; by 2025 it is at 26 percent, exactly its relative size in 1870 and 1880. Of course, the major shifts from the under-5 and 5-24 age groups must therefore go to persons over 45 years old. In the 45-64 age group, we observe an increase from 12 percent in 1870 to 20 percent in 1940; then stability at 19 or 20 percent through 1990, followed by an increase to 23 percent by 2000 and 24 percent by 2025, a doubling of its relative size in 1870. Finally, the population of persons 65 years old and over steadily increases from a very small 3 percent in 1870 and 1880 to 13 percent by 1990 and 2000 and then to 20 percent by 2025, when the "baby boom" cohorts enter this age group. Overall, between 1870 and 2025 we observe a halving of the population under age 25 (from 59 percent to 31 percent) and a corresponding increase of almost 30 percent, representing a tripling of the population 45 years old and over (from 15 percent to 44 percent).

To better grasp the above changes, observe the bottom half of Table 1, indicating the net change in each age group. The period containing the Great Depression clearly shows the effect of decreased birth rates and is an exception for the century 1880–1980, while the 1980–2025 period reverses the past dominance of youth and, in part due to increased longevity in conjunction with the aging of the "baby boom," indicates a major break with the past. For instance, from 1980 to the year 2000 the increase by 25.9 million persons in the "over 45" population is an increment larger than the entire 1980 California population (23.7 million). In fact, the *increase* in persons 65 years old and over between 2000 and 2025 almost exactly equals the 1980 California population (23.6 to 23.7 million), and the increment in persons over age 44 is expected to be 35.1 million for this time period, equivalent to the complete 1980 populations of both the states of California and Illinois, the first and fifth most populous states in the United States. Figure 7-1 provides a more readily grasped image of the nature of these changes.

### Populations of Jobs Over Time: 1900–1990

The Social Security debates in Congress in 1982 and 1983, among other things, demonstrate a current awareness that there will be major increases in older persons in the United States. Moreover, with the recent economic difficulties in the U.S. economy highlighting more basic underlying structural changes already underway in the population of jobs in the national labor market, there is also an increasing awareness of the possibility that our job population may be experiencing a major break with the past. Or is it a major break? Let us first look more closely at the long and near-term shifts in the U.S. job distribution.

Table 2 presents the U.S. job population by occupation from 1900 to that projected in 1990. We will first look at relative job losses and then gains. Perhaps the most known job change is that directly related to farming. Farmers and farm workers, constituting almost 40 percent of the U.S. jobs in 1900, were but 3 percent by 1980. Laborers, who once held 13 percent of the jobs (1900), were by 1980 one half that (6 percent). And, of course, paid private household jobs, at 5 percent in 1900 and again in 1940, toward the end of the Great Depression, decreased to 1 percent by 1980. Overall, farm-related jobs, laborers, and paid private household jobs, which were 56 percent of the U.S. labor market in 1900, were only 10 percent of the 1980 national labor market, a rather massive shift in relative size.

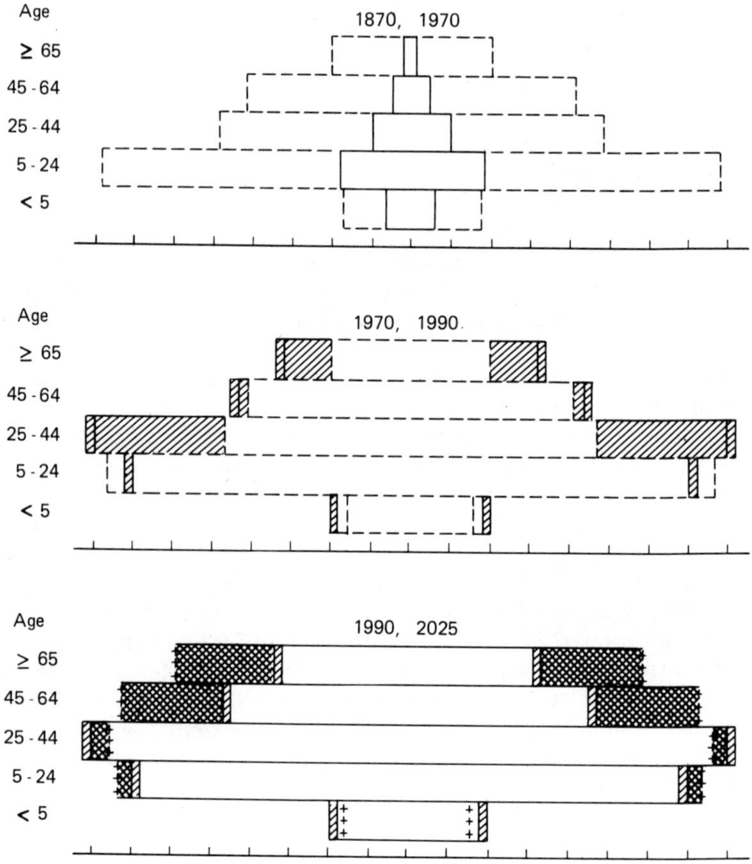


**FIGURE 7-1. Age Distribution of U.S. Population.**

**TOP.** Comparison of 1870 and 1970 Distributions —
1870: Distribution with Solid Lines
1970: Distribution with Dashed Lines

**MIDDLE.** Comparison of 1970 and Projected 1990 Distributions —
1970: (See TOP)
1990: Distribution Having Double Vertical Lines and also Hatched If Beyond That of 1970.

**BOTTOM.** Comparison of Projected 1990 and 2025 Distributions —
1990: (See MIDDLE)
2025: Distribution Having Dashed and Crossed Vertical Lines (‡) and Cross Hatched if Beyond That of 1990.

**TABLE 2. Job Distribution by Occupation for the United States 1900–1990 (in thousands)**

| | YEAR | | | | | | | | | | | | | | | | | | |
|---|---|---|---|---|---|---|---|---|---|---|---|---|---|---|---|---|---|---|---|
| OCCUPATIONS | 1900[a] | | 1920[a] | | 1940[a] | | 1960 | | | | 1970 | | 1980 | | | | 1990 | | |
| Professional | 1,234 | 4% | 2,283 | 5% | 3,879 | 7% | 7,336 | 11% | 7,469 | 11% | 11,149 | 14% | 15,968 | 16% | 16,395 | 16% | 19,700– | 20,700 | 17%–16% |
| Managerial | 1,697 | 6% | 2,803 | 7% | 3,770 | 7% | 5,489 | 9% | 7,067 | 11% | 8,295 | 11% | 11,138 | 11% | 9,355 | 9% | 10,600– | 11,300 | 9%– 9% |
| Sales | 1,307 | 5% | 2,058 | 5% | 3,450 | 7% | 4,801 | 7% | 4,224 | 6% | 4,857 | 6% | 6,303 | 6% | 6,822 | 7% | 8,100– | 8,800 | 7%– 7% |
| Clerical | 877 | 3% | 3,385 | 8% | 4,982 | 10% | 9,617 | 15% | 9,762 | 15% | 13,723 | 17% | 18,473 | 19% | 18,864 | 19% | 22,400– | 23,900 | 19%–19% |
| Crafts | 3,062 | 11% | 5,482 | 13% | 6,203 | 12% | 9,241 | 14% | 8,554 | 13% | 10,164 | 13% | 12,787 | 13% | 12,369 | 12% | 14,600– | 15,800 | 12%–13% |
| Operatives | 3,720 | 13% | 6,587 | 16% | 9,518 | 18% | 12,846 | 20% | 11,950 | 19% | 13,916 | 18% | 14,096 | 14% | 14,207 | 14% | 16,400– | 17,600 | 14%–14% |
| Service (b) | 1,047 | 4% | 1,901 | 5% | 3,657 | 7% | 5,765 | 9% | | | | | | | | | | | |
| Service and Private hh (b+e) | | 9% | | 8% | | 12% | 7,590 | 12% | 8,023 | 12% | 9,719 | 12% | 13,228 | 13% | 15,547 | 15% | 18,100– | 19,200 | 15%–15% |
| Laborers | 3,620 | 13% | 4,905 | 12% | 4,875* | 9% | 3,530 | 6% | 3,553 | 5% | 3,728 | 5% | 4,567 | 5% | 5,860 | 6% | 6,700– | 7,100 | 6%–6% |
| Farmers (c) | 5,763 | 20% | 6,442+ | 15% | 5,362 | 10% | 2,526 | 4% | | | | | | | | | | | |
| Farm Workers (d) | 5,125 | 18% | 4,948‡ | 12% | 3,632 | 7% | 1,560 | 2% | | | | | | | | | | | |
| Farm (c+d) | | 38% | | 27% | | 17% | 4,086 | 6% | 5,176 | 8% | 3,127 | 4% | 2,741 | 3% | 2,689 | 3% | 2,400– | 2,200 | 2%– 2% |
| Private hh (e) | 1,579 | 5% | 1,411 | 3% | 2,412+ | 5% | 1,825 | 3% | | | | | | | | | | | |
| Totals | 29,031 | | 42,205 | | 51,740 | | 64,536 | | 65,778 | | 78,678 | | 99,301 | | 102,108 | | 119,000–126,600 | | |

a – 14 years old and over in 1900–1940; 16 years old and over in 1960–1990.
* – Peaked in 1930 at 5,335
+ – Peak
‡ – Peaked in 1910 at 5,370

Data Sources:
1900 to 1st 1960: Series D 182-232, *Historical Statistics of the United States, Colonial Times to 1970*, U.S. Bureau of the Census, 1975;
2nd 1960, 1970 and 1st 1980: Table No. 648, *Statistical Abstract of the United States 1982–83*, U.S. Bureau of the Census, 1982;
2nd 1980, 1990: *Occupational Projections and Training Data*, Bulletin 2202, U.S. Bureau of Labor Statistics, 1982.

In contrast, the crafts show an interesting property, remaining almost constant over this century (11 to 14 percent), while a probable hint as to the future is shown in operative jobs. At 13 percent in 1900, operatives appear to have peaked in relative size after 60 years, at 20 percent in 1960. Subsequently, in a comparatively short period of 20 years, the relative size of operatives has declined from 20 percent to 14 percent, almost the same as that in 1900. Automation, via robotics and other new technologies, is expected to have its greatest impacts on these semiskilled jobs. The greatest hiring probabilities for operatives are from other operative jobs, from skilled craft jobs, which have been stable in relative size, or from nonprivate household service jobs, which have increased from a small 4 percent in 1900 to 14 percent in 1980 and are expected to continue to increase in relative size (see Stewman, 1982).[3]

As for where the remaining growth is occurring, clearly it is in white-collar jobs—professional, managerial, sales, and clerical. In fact, it is almost entirely professional and clerical. Between 1900 and 1980, managerial jobs have increased from 6 percent to 9–11 percent, a 50 percent to 80 percent relative growth rate (RGR), while sales jobs have increased from 5 percent to 7 percent, a 40 percent RGR. On the other hand, professional jobs have increased from 4 percent to 16 percent, a 250 percent RGR; and clerical jobs have increased the fastest, from 3 percent in 1900 to 19 percent in 1980, a 533 percent RGR. (Service jobs had a 250 percent RGR). In sum, we observe the following rank ordering in relative growth rates during this century: (1) clerical, (2) service, (3) professional, (4) managerial, and (5) sales. Crafts and operatives combined have a RGR of slightly over 10 percent while farm-related work, non-farm laborers, and paid private household jobs decreased dramatically.[4]

Table 3 provides a somewhat different picture, treating only the increments and decrements in the job population. At the bottom of the table, observe that during the period 1900–1920, 50 percent of the job growth was blue-collar; in contrast, during 1960–1980 it was 21 percent, a decrease by more than one half. Farming's share of growth in 1900–1920 was 4 percent; and during the period 1960–1980 it was negative. Hence, we see a decrease in the share of job growth in blue-collar and farming jobs from 54 percent during 1900–1920 to 21 percent during 1960–1980 (–33 percent) and a corresponding increase in white-collar (+24 percent) and service (+9 percent) jobs.

A second important feature about Table 3 is the relative size of net job growth over the 80-year period. The birth of new jobs in the national labor market between 1960 and 1980 (36 million) is larger than the two prior periods combined, 1900–1920 and 1940–1960. This is clearly "baby boom" related. Note that its size, however, is even larger than the expected person population increments noted earlier for older persons due not only to the "baby boom" increment, but also to the increased labor force participation rate of women. More specifically, this 36 million job increment in the last 20 years is greater than that of the total population of the states of California and Illinois in 1980. These 36 million additional

[3]It should be pointed out that in absolute number of jobs, operatives are, in fact, growing—just not as fast as the overall job growth rate.

[4]In fact, both farm-related and paid private household jobs also declined in actual number of jobs, from 12.5 million in 1900 to 3.7 million in 1980.

jobs are equivalent to 36 percent of the jobs in the United States in 1980. If we use the net job increment (33.5 million) between 1960 and 1980, it is equivalent to 34 percent of the jobs in the United States in 1980. Certainly, in terms of the near-term job increments experienced in the United States, the 1960–1980 period was dramatic in size. Over the longer term, 1900–1980, we observe major changes in job distributions (from 38 percent to 3 percent, from 3 percent to 19 percent, etc.) and relative shifts in growth which are equally, if not more, important than the incremental change. These distributional changes also indicate that the relative shift from operatives, for example, is not a new phenomenon. Figure 7-2 depicts the changes in the three highest growth periods of this century and provides a more concrete distributional imagery for comparing the more commonly used age distribution for populations of persons.

To round off the job population discussion more fully, Table 4 presents the U.S. job distribution by industry from 1900 to 1980. These data are for nonagricultural payrolls or establishments. There are four industries losing their relative share and four others gaining a larger relative share. As before, we will first take up the relative declines and then the gains. Mining, at 4 percent in 1900, declined to 1 percent in 1960 and has remained at that level through 1980. Construction also had a relative decline of 3 percent, from 8 to 5 percent by 1960, with no change through 1980. Manufacturing comprised over one third of the nonagriculture jobs in 1900 but only slightly above one fifth in 1980, experiencing a relative decline of 5 percent (from 36 percent to 31 percent) from 1900 to 1960 and a subsequent 9 percent decline (from 31 percent to 22 percent) over the last 20 years (1960–1980). Manufacturing's peak (39 percent) was in 1920. Likewise, transportation,

**TABLE 3. Job Changes by Occupation and Period for the United States: 1900–1980 (in thousands)**

| OCCUPATION | PERIOD | | | | | | | |
|---|---|---|---|---|---|---|---|---|
| | 1900–1920 | | 1920–1940 | | 1940–1960 | | 1960–1980 | |
| Professional | 1,049 | | 1,596 | | 3,457 | | 8,499 | |
| Managerial | 1,106 | | 967 | | 1,719 | | 4,071 | |
| Sales | 751 | | 1,392 | | 1,351 | | 2,079 | |
| Clerical | 2,508 | | 1,597 | | 4,635 | | 8,711 | |
| Crafts | 2,420 | | 721 | | 3,038 | | 4,233 | |
| Operatives | 2,867 | | 2,931 | | 3,328 | | 2,146 | |
| Service (a) | 854 | | 1,756 | | 2,108 | | N/A | |
| Including | | | | | | | | |
| Private hh (b) | 686 | | 2,757 | | 1,521 | | 5,326 | |
| Laborers | 1,285 | | - 30 | | - 1,345 | | 1,014 | |
| Farm | 502 | | - 2,396 | | - 4,908 | | - 1,391 | |
| White-Collar | 5,414 | 41% | 5,552 | 47% | 11,162 | 63% | 23,360 | 65% |
| Blue-Collar | 6,572 | 50% | 3,622 | 30% | 5,021 | 28% | 7,393 | 21% |
| Service | 686 | 5% | 2,757 | 23% | 1,521 | 9% | 5,205 | 14% |
| Farm | 502 | 4% | - 2,396 | | - 4,908 | | - 2,435 | |
| Total | 13,174 | | 9,535 | | 12,796 | | 33,523 | |
| | (13,174) | | (11,931) | | (17,704) | | (35,958) | |

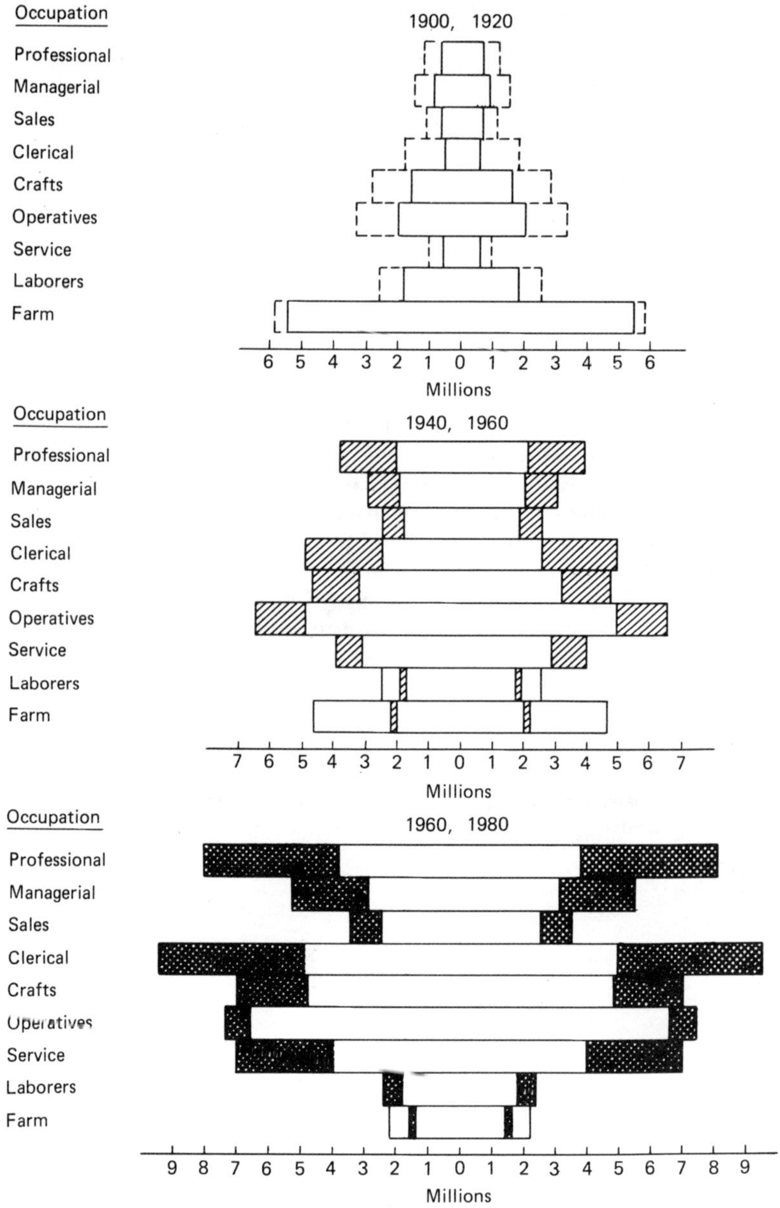


**FIGURE 7-2.** **Occupational Distribution of U.S. Labor Market.**

**TOP.** **Comparison of 1900 and 1920 Distributions —**
**1900: Inner Distribution**
**1920: Outer Distribution Having Dashed Lines**

**MIDDLE.** **Comparison of 1940 and 1960 Distributions —**
**1940: Solid Lines Without Hatching**
**1960: If Outside 1940 Lines, Hatched Area**
**If Inside 1940 Lines, Hatched Vertical Lines**

**BOTTOM.** **Comparison of 1960 and 1980 Distributions —**
**1960: Solid Lines Without Cross Hatching**
**1980: If Outside 1960 Lines, Cross Hatched Area**
**If Inside 1960 Lines, Cross Hatched Vertical Lines**

which was 15 percent in 1900, increased to 16 percent by 1920, but declined steadily thereafter until 1970, when it was 6 percent, at which level it remained. Overall, on the decline side, there was a shift from almost 63 percent of the jobs in mining, construction, manufacturing, and transportation in 1900 to 34 percent in 1980.

On the gain side, trade, sizable in 1900 at 16 percent, increased to 21 percent by 1940 and has remained about steady through 1980 (with a 1 percent gain from 1970 to 1980). Similarly, finance, at 2 percent in 1900, reached 5 percent in 1940 and remained about there through 1980 (also with a 1 percent gain from 1970 to 1980). Services, on the other hand, remained at 11 percent from 1900 through 1940 and has increased in relative size to 20 percent, almost a doubling, in the last 40 years. Government, at 7 percent in 1900, increased slowly throughout most of the 80-year period until 1970, when it reached 18 percent and remained steady through 1980.[5] In summary, the 30 percent loss in relative size noted earlier was gained by the following industries: government (+11 percent), service (+9 percent), trade (+6 percent), and finance (+4 percent). Moreover, if we take the last 40 years as a baseline, the industry growing most rapidly is services, since all of the 9 percent gain occurred in this period.

The bottom of Table 4 provides data on job increments and decrements by industry during this century. Whereas in 1900 manufacturing was 36 percent of the nonagricultural job base, between 1900 and 1920 it had 42 percent of the job growth, with transportation, trade, services, and government following far behind at 10–16 percent. Of these, manufacturing, transportation, and government increased faster than their proportional share. In the Great Depression period, 1920–1940, manufacturing growth was only 4 percent of the total growth, with trade and government having massive gains. Then, between 1940 and 1960, large job growth returned to the manufacturing and service sectors. Trade's growth was proportional to its relative size; service and government's share was again greater and manufacturing, having 34 percent of the nonagricultural jobs in 1940, had only 26 percent of the growth—less than its relative size; hence it continued to decline. In the 1960–1980 period, manufacturing accounted for only 10 percent of the job growth; trade, 25 percent; services, 29 percent; and government 22 percent. Hence,

[5] Local, state, and federal government employment increased from 1.1 million in 1900 (7 percent) to 12.5 million in 1970 (18 percent) and 16.2 million in 1980 (also 18 percent). Within government, it is important to keep in mind the relative size of state and local government to the federal branch. These data are as follows (in millions):*

| *Year* | *State and Local* | *Federal* | *Total* |
|---|---|---|---|
| 1930 | 2.6 (83%) | .5 (17%) | 3.1 |
| 1940 | 3.2 (76%) | 1.0 (24%) | 4.2 |
| 1950 | 4.1 (68%) | 1.9 (32%) | 6.0 |
| 1960 | 6.1 (73%) | 2.3 (27%) | 8.4 |
| 1970 | 9.8 (78%) | 2.7 (22%) | 12.5 |
| 1980 | 13.4 (82%) | 2.9 (18%) | 16.2 |
| 1981 | 13.3 (83%) | 2.8 (17%) | 16.0 |

The Federal share moved from 17 percent to 32 percent between 1930 and 1950, where it peaked, and has been declining for the last 30 years, reaching exactly the same relative share in 1981 as it had in 1930.

*Sources: 1930–1970 U.S. Bureau of the Census (1975), Table D127-141; 1980–81 U.S. Bureau of Labor Statistics (1980b). Table 10, p. 78.

**TABLE 4a. Job Distributions by Industry (Nonagricultural Establishments) for the United States: 1900–1980 (in thousands)**

| NONAGRICULTURE INDUSTRY[+] | YEAR 1900 | | 1920 | | 1940 | | 1960 | | 1970 | | 1980 | |
|---|---|---|---|---|---|---|---|---|---|---|---|---|
| Mining | 637 | 4% | 1,180 | 4% | 925 | 3% | 712 | 1% | 623 | 1% | 1,027 | 1% |
| Construction | 1,147 | 8% | 850 | 3% | 1,294 | 4% | 2,926 | 5% | 3,588 | 5% | 4,346 | 5% |
| Manufacturing | 5,468 | 36% | 10,702 | 39% | 10,985 | 34% | 16,796 | 31% | 19,367 | 27% | 20,285 | 22% |
| Transportation[a] | 2,282 | 15% | 4,317 | 16% | 3,038 | 9% | 4,004 | 7% | 4,515 | 6% | 5,146 | 6% |
| Trade | 2,502 | 16% | 4,012 | 15% | 6,750 | 21% | 11,391 | 21% | 15,040 | 21% | 20,310 | 22% |
| Finance[b] | 308 | 2% | 902 | 3% | 1,502 | 5% | 2,629 | 5% | 3,645 | 5% | 5,160 | 6% |
| Services | 1,740 | 11% | 3,100 | 11% | 3,681 | 11% | 7,378 | 14% | 11,548 | 16% | 17,890 | 20% |
| Government | 1,094 | 7% | 2,371 | 9% | 4,202 | 13% | 8,353 | 15% | 12,554 | 18% | 16,241 | 18% |
| Total | 15,178 | | 27,434 | | 32,377 | | 54,189 | | 70,880 | | 90,405 | |

[+]Employees on nonagricultural payrolls
[a]Transportation and public utilities
[b]Finance, insurance, and real estate

Data Sources for Table 4a:

1900, 1920, 1940: Series D127-141, ***Historical Statistics of the United States, Colonial Times to 1970***, U.S. Bureau of the Census, 1975;

1960, 1970, 1980: Table No. 659, ***Statistical Abstract of the United States 1982–83***, U.S. Bureau of the Census, 1982.

**TABLE 4b. Job Changes by Industry[+] and Period for the United States: 1900–1980**

| | PERIOD | | | | | | | |
|---|---|---|---|---|---|---|---|---|
| | 1900–1920 | | 1920–1940 | | 1940–1960 | | 1960–1980 | |
| Mining | 543 | 4% | - 255 | | - 213 | | 315 | 1% |
| Construction | - 297 | | 444 | 7% | 1,632 | 7% | 1,420 | 4% |
| Manufacturing | 5,234 | 42% | 283 | 4% | 5,811 | 26% | 3,489 | 10% |
| Transportation | 2,035 | 16% | -1,279 | | 966 | 4% | 1,142 | 3% |
| Trade | 1,510 | 12% | 2,738 | 42% | 4,641 | 21% | 8,919 | 25% |
| Finance | 594 | 5% | 600 | 9% | 1,127 | 5% | 2,531 | 7% |
| Services | 1,360 | 11% | 581 | 9% | 3,697 | 17% | 10,512 | 29% |
| Government | 1,277 | 10% | 1,831 | 28% | 4,151 | 19% | 7,888 | 22% |
| Total | 12,256<br>(12,553) | | 4,943<br>(6,477) | | 21,812<br>(22,025) | | 36,216<br>(36,216) | |

[+]Employees on nonagricultural payrolls

manufacturing has been declining in relative size over the last 60 years. Trade, finance, services, and government have, alternatively, been increasing in relative size over this 60-year period. No doubt, the nature of the U.S. economy may be experiencing new automation growth spurts, but the signs of the United States shifting to a postindustrial society (see Bell, 1973) have been evident for a very long time. Note that this last set of comparisons did not treat agriculture at all; thus, the relative shifts being discussed in these later comparisons are not a part of the decreasing farm jobs. Indeed, it seems that the nonagricultural pendulum has been swinging away from jobs in manufacturing for a very long time.[6]

### Joint Population of Persons and Jobs Over Time

The discussion has thus far pertained to populations of persons *or* populations of jobs, with comparisons of distributive changes over time within each type of population. It now seems reasonable to juxtapose these two populations at the same point in time. Figure 7-3 provides such a comparison for 1970. Two important questions left unaddressed are the following: What are the joint job-person distributions; for example, the joint-occupational age of worker distributions? And, what are the processes that generate new job-person distributions over time? The latter question begins to address labor market behavior.

To suggest that those older workers who change jobs do so primarily due to loss of a job or layoffs, by generalizing from those cases most visible from the news or from casual conversations, would be quite misleading. To know that a far greater number of older workers change occupations in response to dissatisfaction with work or the job, for health reasons, better pay, or alternative job offers in other companies, moves us yet further toward what is actually occurring in the U.S. work force. Yet individuals' motives still tell only part of the story—job dynamics and labor market structures, generally unexamined, account for at least half the remainder of the story.

[6]For an excellent discussion of some of the more profound changes at issue see Bell, 1973; Clark, 1957; Keyfitz, 1982; and Sauvy, 1969 and 1980.

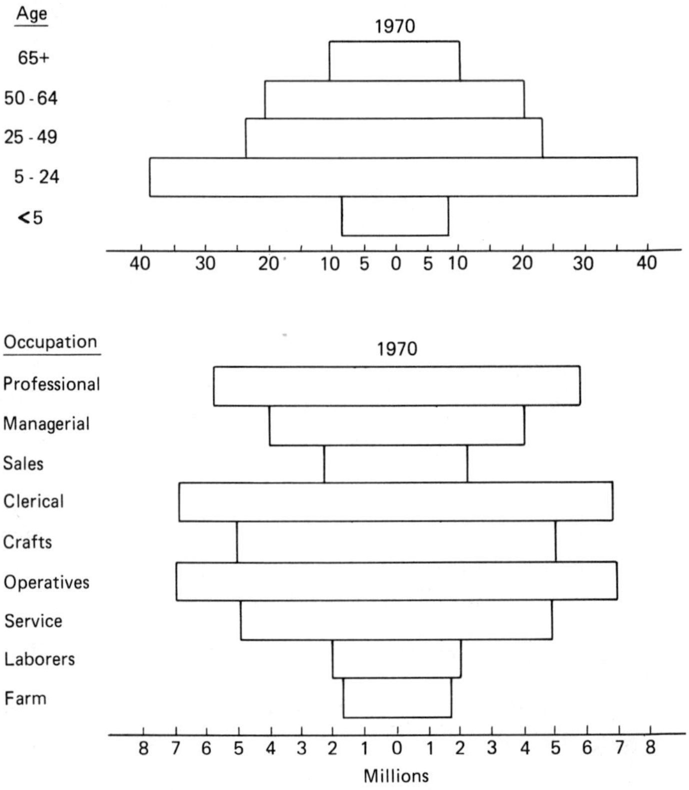


**FIGURE 7-3. U.S. Population of Persons and of Jobs (1970)**

**TOP. Age Distribution of U.S. Population of Persons**

**BOTTOM. Occupational Distribution of U.S. Population of Jobs**

Figure 7-4 provides an initial step in conceptualizing such dynamics, and a more complete story. The outside of the rectangular cylinder is a hypothetical space, the width, for instance, defined by the largest job class (occupation) and the height set arbitrarily equal to the width, but divided into levels corresponding to the number of occupations. Since job vacancies usually clear the market rather fast (compare, for instance, the life expectancy of a person and that of a job vacancy), and are at any moment a small portion of the total set of jobs, most of the jobs will be filled. Within each of the job class "plates" we may impose an age distribution. Of course, if a job becomes vacant, the job usually does not carry an age requirement and, hence, it may be allocated to the non-age-specific vacancy class where managerial hiring practice will determine the age of the job's next incumbent.

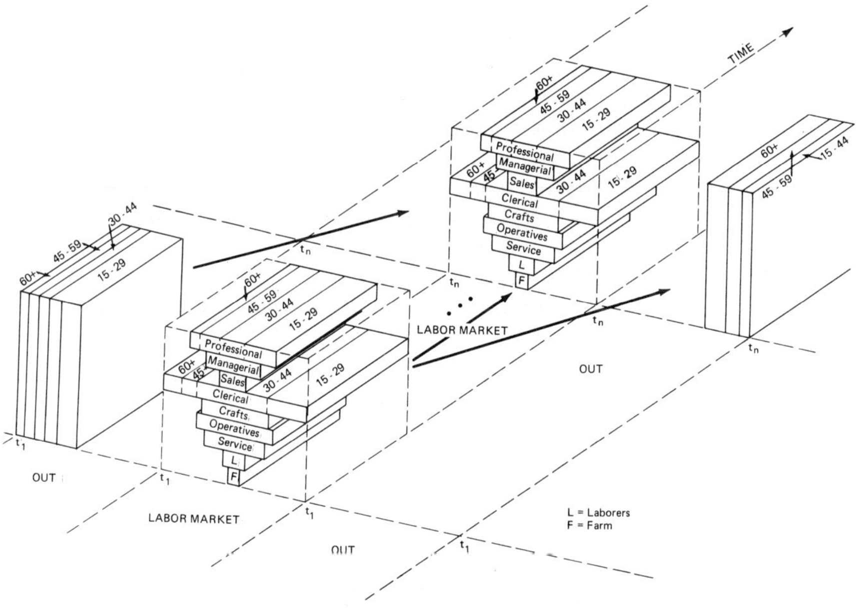


**FIGURE 7-4. Labor Market with Joint Populations of Persons and Jobs Over Time.**

Time in Figure 7-4 is represented by the length of the structure. Over time, each cell within the width-height dimensions may become vacated (e.g., via exit or layoff) or end if the job is abolished. Hence, there is a continuous movement in the number of cells—in some cases expanding, in others contracting. There are also redistributions which occur as new job cohorts are added whose distribution by occupation differs from the existing job distribution prior to their point of entry. In any event, Figure 7-4 helps to visualize the nature of this complex process mixing two simple job-person distributions over time. For instance, each occupation will possibly vary in exit and transfer rate, as well as relative growth/decline rate. Additionally, the age-specific exit and transfer rates per occupation will undoubtedly vary. At issue here is how large are these rates of exit, transfer, and growth, and how much of the age-specific labor force is new within a job distribution every year? Every five years? These are some of the initial questions that must be addressed to grasp the nature of the labor market dynamics and the consequent impacts on the workers.[7] Moreover, to begin to answer such questions we must understand the structures underlying labor markets.

[7]For the mathematical model depicting the process operative for Figure 7-4 see Stewman (1982). For a simpler model treating career mobility in organizations (private and public sector) see Stewman and Konda (1983). Somewhat similar spatial considerations, as in Figure 7-4, for social stratification and social mobility are discussed in the classic work by Sorokin (1927). Also, many of the original job vacancy ideas, including the vacancy chain reaction, which will be discussed in the following section, stem from White's (1970) work on organizations.

## FIVE LABOR MARKET STRUCTURES

This section will be organized around five national labor market structures or processes: employer hiring decisions, vacancy chain reactions, job ratios, multiple job-worker ratios, and cohort size. An empirical example illustrating each structure will be provided. The first is a choice structure operative in terms of employer hiring preferences. This structure is distributive,[8] taking into account both populations of jobs and of persons. The second is processual, transforming individual employer hiring decisions into vacancy chain reactions. The third structure pertains to job ratios arising from the job distribution. The fourth, multiple job-worker ratios, is a joint structure evolving from the combined or compound effects of all three of the aforementioned structures or processes. Finally, the fifth structure is cohort size (e.g., age cohorts) conditional on job vacancies.[9]

### Employer Hiring Decisions

Let us begin with a simple story. A job vacancy arises in organization X due either to a person leaving or a new job being created. The manager has a choice to fill the vacancy by hiring from within the labor market—for example, from within his or her own organization or from another organization (Y)—or to fill it by hiring someone not holding a job. What are the odds of the choice being internal or external? We will pursue this shortly. For now, however, let us say that the choice is internal—from within the labor market. In fact, let it also be internal to that organization, X. Again, what are the odds regarding such employer behavior? Now suppose the supervisor of the person just hired hires a replacement from firm Y which, in turn, opens yet another job vacancy, and so on until either a vacated job is abolished or filled by an outside hire. Not only do we know very little about such interorganizational hiring practice, but its relative size in comparison to hires from the unemployed population is also generally unknown. Moreover, we have yet to mention either the job class (occupation) or the ages of the persons hired, both of which are central for the task at hand.

Let us first treat the hiring-aging issue. For the 1970 employed population, there are national data to provide initial answers to some of the questions raised above and from which to begin to make estimates of both hiring practice and its associated vacancy behavior. The data contain individual employment information for both 1965 and 1970. The population working in 1970 (71.5 million) had 18.3 million hires from the outside and 12.0 million hires from within, with the latter involving a major occupational change,[10] for a total of 30.3 million hires over the

[8]For an excellent discussion of both distributive and processual forms of social structure, see Nadel (1957).

[9]The mathematical model incorporating all five of the structures is currently being tested on the U.S. Labor market by the author. Most of the interoccupational work force flows with which we are dealing in this chapter and in the tests elsewhere also pertain to interorganizational flows of staff. The model is thus applicable to macro labor markets involving interorganizational flows of staff, as in this chapter, as well as to internal labor markets of specific firms and organizations, as in Stewman and Konda (1983).

[10]The 12 major occupational classes are professional and technical, managerial (except farm), sales, clerical, skilled crafts, operatives–nontransport, operatives–transport, service workers (except private household), nonfarm laborers, farmers and farm managers, farm laborers and foremen, and private household workers. Hence a major occupational change refers to a move between one of these 12 classes.

five-year period, 1965–1970. Hence, out of the 71.5 million job-person matches, 30.3 million or over 40 percent had an age of less than five years. Further breakdowns of the five-year data by sex reveal that of the 44.7 million males working in 1970, 8.0 million were outside hires and 9.1 million were hires from within involving a major occupational change, resulting in 38 percent of the male job-person matches with an age of less than five years. The comparable female data are 26.7 million, 10.3 million, 2.9 million, and 49 percent. Not only does the probability of an outside hire vary greatly by sex (M–.26; F–.34), the probability of an internal hire does as well (M–.30; F–.09). This difference has major consequences, as will be shown below.

To help evaluate the above findings, two data points will be used. The first is that of the 1965 male workers who were also working in 1970, i.e., the population of *stayers.* For this stayer population, Table 5 indicates the amount of occupational mobility by age. Note that age throughout this section refers to age in 1965. Perhaps it is not surprising that 40 percent of the age 15–29 stayers experienced a major job change in this short five-year time period, but that an almost 20 percent figure holds for the 45–59-year-old stayers and also for the 60-year and older stayer population is quite a surprise and raises serious questions as to the concept of "the inflexibility of older workers." From what labor market population have analysts who use this concept sampled?

The second data point—that of the 1970 labor market, (i.e., the 1970 population of workers and population of jobs[11]—is shown in Table 6 for the comparable

**TABLE 5. Amount of Occupational Mobility for Males in the U.S. Labor Market in Both 1965 and 1970 by Age.***

| AGE | SAME MAJOR OCCUPATION | DIFFERENT MAJOR OCCUPATION |
|---|---|---|
| 15–29 | 60% | 40% |
| 30–44 | 79% | 21% |
| 45–59 | 83% | 17% |
| 60+ | 82% | 18% |
| TOTAL | 75% | 25% |

*Age in 1965; same or different major occupation in 1970 than in 1965.

**TABLE 6. Amount of U.S. Labor Market Renewal Rates in a Five-Year Period (1965–70) for Male Workers by Age**

| AGE | A SAME MAJOR OCCUPATION | B DIFFERENT MAJOR OCCUPATION | C OUTSIDE HIRE | JOB-WORKER RENEWAL RATE (B + C) |
|---|---|---|---|---|
| 15–29 | 38% | 25% | 37% | 62% |
| 30–44 | 73% | 20% | 8% | 27% |
| 45–59 | 78% | 16% | 7% | 22% |
| 60+ | 71% | 16% | 13% | 29% |
| Total | 61% | 21% | 18% | 39% |

[11] See Stewman (1976a,b) for further discussion. For an organizational application, see Stewman and Konda (1983).

male segment of the labor market. In terms of staff renewal, these jobs had a new incumbency rate of almost 40 percent. Per age group, the lowest rate of new incumbency is 22 percent, still a rather high figure for such a short time interval, indicative of the underlying dynamics of both job and person populations. Moreover, if such a large segment of middle-aged and older workers (45–59 and 60+ years old) are changing jobs or reentering the labor market, what is the nature of such career trajectories in later life? A statics paper by Kaufman and Spilerman (1982) suggests downward mobility, but the question can now be examined empirically and in conjunction with the labor market behavior within which it is embedded.

A pertinent feature of the brief example given for employer hiring practice was that it did not specify job type, thereby missing a key element in the process since the type of job to be filled directly affects an individual's selection chances. For simplicity, we will consider employer hiring practice for five types of job vacancies. The data are shown in Table 7. Clearly, employer preferences for internal versus external candidates vary by type of job vacancy. For instance, the external selection probabilities are .29, .47, and .73 for managerial, crafts, and professional vacancies, respectively. Additionally, as may be seen in the lower portion of the table, given an internal selection, one's selection chances vary greatly by the job type that one currently holds.

To bring initial closure to this first structural effect, note that employer hiring preferences have been shown to vary by the type of vacancy to be filled and in the following ways: (1) whether the decision preference is inside or outside the labor market (in this case meaning the job-holding labor market), (2) by the current job type of the candidates selected, and (3) by the age and sex of the candidates selected. These three features are combined into a set of conditional preferences for one type of job vacancy in Table 8 and Figure 7-5.

The vacancy in Table 8 and Figure 7-5 pertains to a managerial job; the chances of filling it externally (that is, outside the current job holders) are about 30 percent. The chances of filling it from inside the labor market are 70 percent. If an external choice is made, the chances of filling it by age are 60 percent for the 15–29 age group, 23 percent for the 30–44 age group, 13 percent for the 45–59 age group, and 3 percent for persons 60 and over. Alternatively, if the choice is from the inside, one's selection chances by age are 33 percent for those 15–29 years old, 42 percent for those 30–44 years old, 22 percent for those 45–59 years old, and 3 percent for persons 60 and over. An internal versus an external choice affects selection chances by reducing the chances for those 15–29 by almost one half while almost doubling the chances of those 30–44 and 45–59. Given an internal or external choice, selection chances are equivalent (3 percent) for persons age 60 and over. In order to calibrate such a seemingly small percentage, during this five-year period the number of managerial vacancies filled either by an external hire or by hiring a person from another major type of occupation was 2.5 million, 3 percent of which is 75,000 new hires at managerial jobs of persons age 60 and over. Adding to this 3 percent, the 18 percent of hires at ages 45–59, 21 percent of all managerial vacancies, which is 527,000—over one-half million, were filled by persons age 45 and over.

**TABLE 7. Employer Selection Probabilities in the United States (1965–70) Given a Vacancy**

| | ORIGIN OF VACANCY (DESTINATION OF PERSON) | | | | |
|---|---|---|---|---|---|
| | PROFESSIONAL | MANAGERIAL | SALES | CRAFTS | OPERATIVES NON-TRANSPORTION |
| Selection from Outside | .73 | .29 | .59 | .47 | .64 |
| Selection from Inside | .27 | .71 | .41 | .53 | .36 |
| Selections by Occupation Conditional on an Internal Selection | | | | | |
| Professional | N/A | .20 | .11 | .07 | .04 |
| Managerial | .17 | N/A | .29 | .09 | .05 |
| Sales | .12 | .23 | N/A | .05 | .06 |
| Clerical | .28 | .17 | .19 | .08 | .10 |
| Crafts | .14 | .16 | .11 | N/A | .26 |
| Operatives, Non-Transportation | .10 | .08 | .10 | .33 | N/A |
| Operatives, Transportation | .02 | .03 | .04 | .09 | .08 |
| Laborers | .05 | .05 | .05 | .15 | .16 |
| Farm | .02 | .02 | .02 | .05 | .08 |
| Service | .11 | .07 | .09 | .09 | .17 |

Data Source: ***1970 Census of Population: Occupation and Residence in 1965***, U.S. Bureau of the Census, 1973.

**TABLE 8. Employer Selection Probabilities for Filling a Managerial Job Vacancy by Position in the Labor Market, Position in the Job Distribution, Age and Sex (U.S. Labor Market, 1965–70)**

| OUTSIDE | INSIDE | TOTAL |
|---|---|---|
| .29 | .71 | 1.00 |

| | IF OUTSIDE, SEX AND AGE PREFERENCES | | | | |
|---|---|---|---|---|---|
| SEX/AGE | 15–29 | 30–44 | 45–59 | 60+ | TOTAL |
| Female | .13 | .11 | .06 | .01 | .32 |
| Male | .47 | .12 | .07 | .02 | .68 |
| Total | .60 | .23 | .13 | .03 | 1.00 |

| | | IF INSIDE, JOB TYPE (OCCUPATION), SEX AND AGE PREFERENCES | | | | |
|---|---|---|---|---|---|---|
| OCCUPATION–SEX/AGE | | 15–29 | 30–44 | 45–59 | 60+ | TOTAL |
| Professional | | .30 | .50 | .18 | .02 | .20 |
| | F | .03 | .07 | .05 | .01 | |
| | M | .27 | .43 | .13 | .01 | |
| Sales | | .27 | .43 | .25 | .04 | .23 |
| | F | .02 | .05 | .05 | .01 | |
| | M | .25 | .38 | .20 | .03 | |
| Clerical | | .39 | .38 | .21 | .02 | .17 |
| | F | .13 | .16 | .10 | .01 | |
| | M | .26 | .22 | .11 | .01 | |
| Crafts | | .30 | .45 | .23 | .02 | .16 |
| | F | .01 | .01 | .01 | .002 | |
| | M | .29 | .44 | .22 | .02 | |
| Operatives, Non-Transport | | .42 | .35 | .20 | .02 | .08 |
| | F | .03 | .05 | .03 | .003 | |
| | M | .39 | .30 | .17 | .02 | |
| Operatives, Transport | | .38 | .41 | .19 | .01 | .03 |
| | F | .004 | .01 | .01 | .0004 | |
| | M | .38 | .40 | .18 | .01 | |
| Laborer | | .48 | .31 | .19 | .02 | .05 |
| | F | .01 | .02 | .02 | .004 | |
| | M | .47 | .29 | .17 | .02 | |
| Farm | | .25 | .35 | .33 | .06 | .02 |
| | F | .01 | .02 | .01 | .01 | |
| | M | .24 | .34 | .32 | .05 | |
| Service | | .32 | .35 | .28 | .04 | .07 |
| | F | .08 | .13 | .11 | .01 | |
| | M | .24 | .22 | .17 | .03 | |
| Total | | .33 | .42 | .22 | .03 | 1.00 |
| | F | .04 | .07 | .05 | .01 | |
| | M | .29 | .35 | .17 | .02 | |

Data Source: ***1970 Census of Population: Occupation and Residence in 1965***, U.S. Bureau of the Census, 1973.

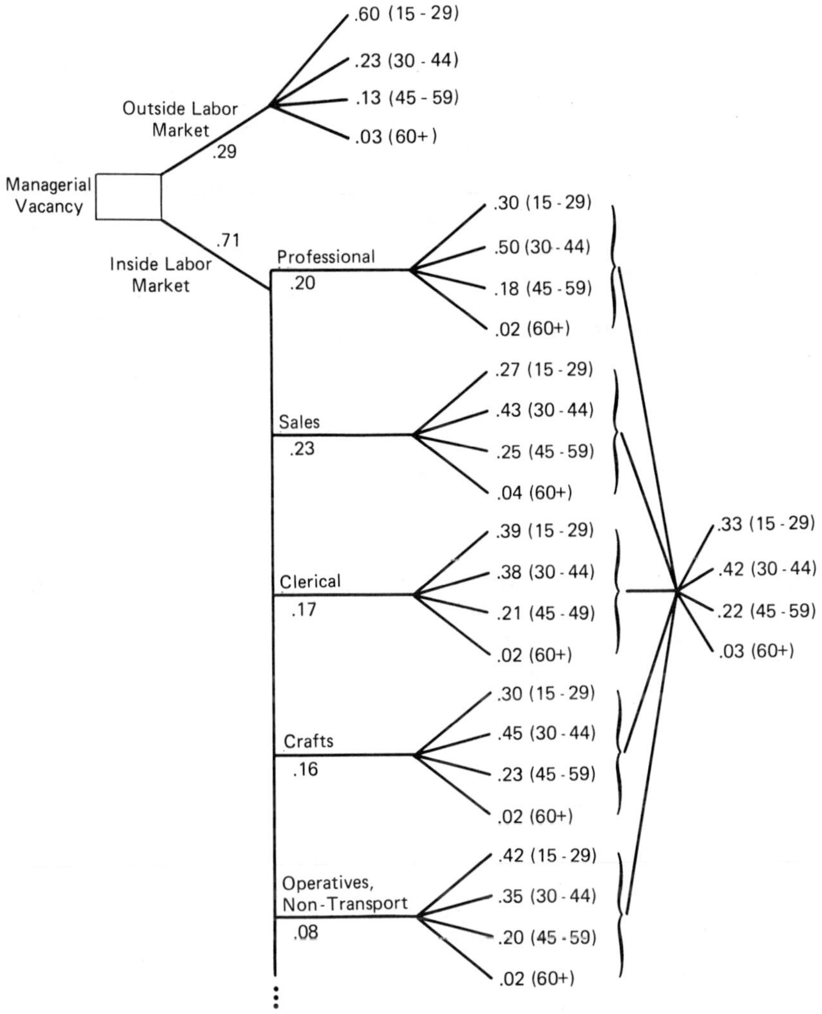


**FIGURE 7-5. Employer Selection Probabilities for Filling a Managerial Job Vacancy by Position in the Labor Market, Position in the Job Distribution and Age (1965–70).**

The second important feature of Table 8 and Figure 7-5 is that if the selection is from the inside, one's chances vary greatly depending on the type of job currently held; the greatest selection chances being those in sales (23 percent), followed by professional, clerical, and crafts (20 percent, 17 percent, and 16 percent, respectively). Selection chances from the remaining five job types total 25 percent. Perhaps the best way to treat these types of differences is by comparing them to the relative size of the job pool in which the individual is working—a feature brought out in the second section regarding job distributions. Just as relative growth in relation to the current job distribution is an important measure of the underlying process of job change, so do the relative selection chances in relation to the initial worker distribution provide a measure of selection leverage by virtue of job type held. The data in Table 9 underscore this point for this managerial vacancy example. Not only does sales have the largest selection probability, but its selection magnitude is almost 200 percent (2.88–1.0=1.88) greater than its share of the labor pool. Similarly, professionals have a 43 percent differential, and crafts, 14 percent. The other occupations are selected less than their relative share of the labor pool, with clerical and laborers at about 90 percent and 80 percent, respectively, and operatives, service, and farm around 50 percent. The differences by job type can be assessed with much greater clarity when considered in relation to the relative size of the job pools from which such selections are made.

### Vacancy Chain Reactions

Given the impact of the vacancy's location, as well as that of the candidate, an almost overlooked feature of the selection probabilities in the preceding section is that they can be linked together, thereby forming a chain reaction of job vacancies. Hence, consider the data in Table 5 to be a program for biasing the selection chances given a vacancy at the specific job type. One may think of this process stochastically or in terms of a single simulation in which a biased coin is first tossed for an inside or outside selection, and then an *n*-sided die (for *n* job types)[12] is tossed with the weights proportional to the selection probabilities. Let us take the second type of example. Start the vacancy in a managerial job and toss the coin. For brevity, let us assume that we get a series of coin tosses whose outcomes are internal selections; hence, the action will be with the die toss. Suppose the die indicates that a salesperson is selected to fill a managerial job. Again the coin toss indicates to continue with the die toss. Hence, the next outcome indicates the

**TABLE 9. Ratio of the Relative Selection Chances to Fill a Managerial Vacancy to the Relative Size of Occupation Held in the U.S. Labor Market.**

| OCCUPATION SELECTED FROM | A SELECTION PROBABILITY | B RELATIVE SIZE OF OCCUPATION* | RATIO A/B |
|---|---|---|---|
| Professional | .20 | .14 | 1.43 |
| Sales | .23 | .08 | 2.88 |
| Clerical | .17 | .18 | .94 |
| Crafts | .16 | .14 | 1.14 |
| Operatives | .11 | .21 | .52 |
| Laborers | .05 | .06 | .83 |
| Farm | .02 | .05 | .40 |
| Service | .07 | .14 | .50 |

*Renormalized without managers for comparability; that is, X′=X/(1-managerial %); 1965 occupational distribution. Source: Table A-16, Bureau of Labor Statistics, ***Employment and Earnings***, February 1966.

[12]There are actually *n* dice, as well—one for each type of vacancy. Hence, the die to be used depends on the vacancy to be filled, with each die having *n* sides.

selection of a manager, once more, to fill the sales job vacated; then the die indicates a craftsman to be selected to fill this second managerial job, and then an operative to fill the skilled crafts job, and so on. Perhaps it is useful to think of this series of events as a vacancy in a labor market distribution, ricocheting from one job type to another, in accordance with the estimated preference distribution. It continues to ricochet until the outcome of the coin toss is an external choice. The ricochet type of analogy, as shown in Figure 7-6, helps to visualize the chain reaction process. The dashed lines indicate the vacancy's path of movement and the solid lines indicate the associated worker flows. It is the chain reaction from the initial vacancy that generates these internal worker flows.

To more readily grasp the significance of this chain reaction process in terms of impacts on persons, suppose that external selection probabilities were equal, say .5, for all types of job vacancies. Then the expected vacancy multiplier or vacancy chain length would be 2.0, or a doubling of the number of initial job opportunities.[13] For the labor market data treated here (15-year-olds and over in 1965), recall that the number of internal hires was 12.0 million, external hires 18.3 million, and total hires 30.3 million. Thus, the mean chain length is 30.3/18.3 = 1.66. This 1.66 multiplier indicates that for every three initial vacancies entering the labor market there are five hires–two inside and three outside. Or, alternatively, for every 100 job vacancies there are 66 internal hires and 100 external hires. Thus, from the 18.3 million initial vacancies entering the national labor market during the period 1965–1970, 30.3 million total job opportunities were generated.

## Job Ratios

The earlier discussion pertaining to populations of jobs and the changing job distributions (occupational and industrial) over time centered on the *percentages* of jobs per job type. It is not labor market profiles in terms of such percentage distributions that are most pertinent to job and worker flows, however. Rather, it is labor market profiles in terms of the *ratios* of each job type that are more important. Perhaps this may be most easily seen if one temporarily thinks about holding

FIGURE 7-6. Vacancy Chain Reaction and Associated Person Moves.

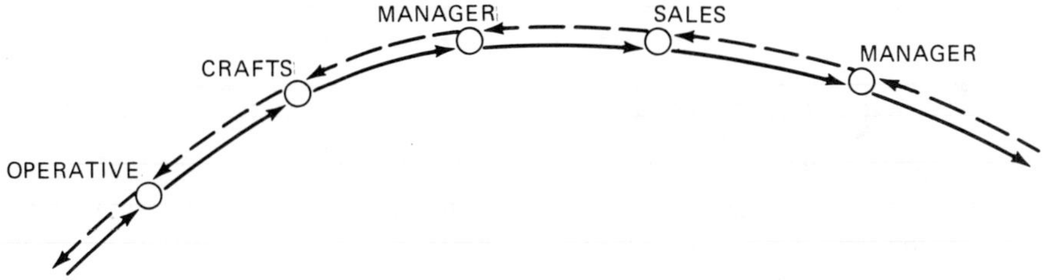


[13]The equation is 1 divided by the external selection probability. The initial job opportunities here do not include temporary layoffs. For unemployment, see the section Unemployment, under One of the Initial Trigger Mechanisms: Exit Rates of Workers.

the other structures and processes constant. Thus, for the moment, consider the following: (1) growth is proportional to the current job distribution and therefore does not generate job redistributions, (2) exit rates are equal for all job types, and (3) internal employment selection preferences are equal for all job types. The number of originating vacancies is thus proportional to the size of the job types and the joint origin-destination of these vacancies determines the job ratio at issue. In short, the ratio depicts a basic underlying structure in which each numerator pertains to vacancies and each denominator to the available labor supply in the specific job type. Hence, the ratio is in effect a job-worker ratio. Examples are provided below for the 1970 U.S. labor market:

| DESTINATION OF VACANCY | ORIGIN OF VACANCY | | | | | |
|---|---|---|---|---|---|---|
| | PROFESSIONAL | MANAGERIAL | SALES | CLERICAL | CRAFTS | OPERATIVES |
| Professional | N/A | .74 | .44 | 1.23 | .91 | 1.25 |
| Managerial | 1.34 | N/A | .59 | 1.65 | 1.23 | 1.68 |
| Sales | 2.30 | 1.71 | N/A | 2.83 | 2.09 | 2.87 |
| Clerical | .81 | .60 | .35 | N/A | .74 | 1.01 |
| Crafts | 1.10 | .82 | .48 | 1.35 | N/A | 1.37 |
| Operatives | .80 | .60 | .35 | .99 | .73 | N/A |

To view the potential impact of this ratio graphically, first observe the distributions in Figures 7-3 and 7-7, taking into account the pair of job plates at issue. Second, place the job plate referring to the job vacancy on top of the job plate referring to the job held by the worker. The examples below contrast the ratio of a vacancy in a professional job with selections from managers and sales (upper two figures) to a vacancy in a managerial job with selection from professionals and sales (lower two figures).

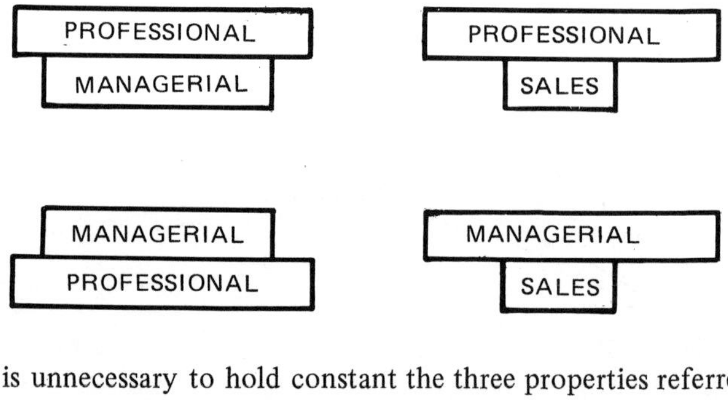


Of course, it is unnecessary to hold constant the three properties referred to above once the job-ratio concept is understood and parameterized. Growth allocation will vary, redistributing jobs; exit rates will vary per job type and in accordance with age and sex distributions; and employer hiring preferences are by no means equal, as shown in the section on Employer Hiring Decisions.

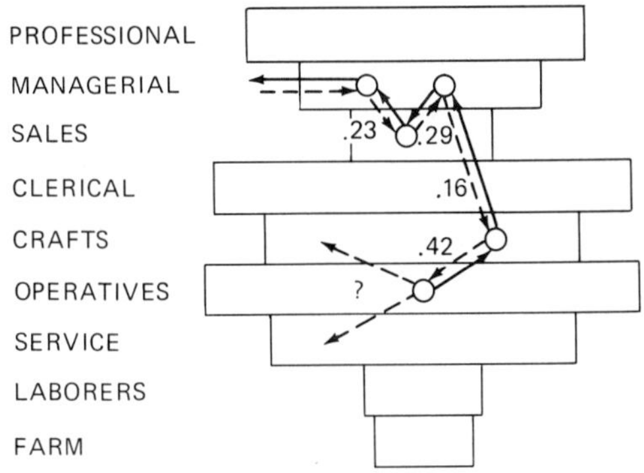


**FIGURE 7-7. Components of the U.S. National Labor Market MJR's: Employer Hiring Preferences, Vacancy Chain Reactions, Job Distribution.**

## Multiple Job-Worker Ratios

The transformation from simple job-worker ratios to multiple job-worker ratios occurs as a result of the chain reaction process. That is, the initial job vacancy, say at occupation X, activates not only a job-worker ratio between occupations X and Y, but, due to the chain reaction, also activates the ratio between occupations Y and Z, and so on. If growth allocations by job type, exit rates per job type, or employer hiring practice by joint origin-destination of the vacancy vary, then the port of origin of the vacancy will have different ripple effects on the job-worker ratios throughout the labor market. Hence, think of (1) the simple job ratios, or more accurately, the job-worker ratios as building blocks; (2) the employer hiring preferences as gatekeepers allowing a fraction of the vacancies to go from X to Y, another fraction from X to Z, etc.; and (3) the chain reaction resulting from each initial type of job vacancy as carrying an ever-truncating fraction of the initial opportunity to other job-worker ratios (e.g., X to Y, then Y to Z, etc.) where each entering vacancy's pull is further weakened as it plays itself out. In short, the simple job-worker ratios (preceding Section) are actually connected by the employer hiring preferences (Section of Employer Hiring Decisions) and the chain reaction process (Section on Vacancy Chain Reactions) into a compound structure which we call multiple job-worker ratios (MJRs). Figure 7-7 shows aspects of these three components which are parameterized in the MJR construct. The dashed arrows refer to vacancy flows (as in Figure 7-6), the probabilities to employer hiring preferences (see Table 7), and, of course, the labor market's tiers to job types, with ratios being formed between the pairs joined by the vacancy paths.[14]

In a regional labor market analysis, the following MJRs have been estimated for the western region of the United States:[15]

[14] Solid arrows moving in the opposite direction of vacancy flows indicate worker flows, which will be predicted by the five-structure model using the MJR construct.

[15] Current research by the author. Regional rather than national results are given here simply due to data accessibility on the computer—to obtain the MJRs, the full set of parameters for all variables must be available.

| DESTINATION OF VACANCY | ORIGIN OF VACANCY | | | | | |
|---|---|---|---|---|---|---|
| | PROFES-SIONAL | MANA-GERIAL | SALES | CLERICAL | CRAFTS | OPERA-TIVES |
| Professional | N/A | .19 | .06 | .10 | .09 | .05 |
| Managerial | .19 | N/A | .26 | .18 | .19 | .12 |
| Sales | .15 | .48 | N/A | .22 | .14 | .14 |
| Clerical | .17 | .17 | .10 | N/A | .08 | .08 |
| Crafts | .10 | .18 | .06 | .07 | N/A | .27 |
| Operatives | .08 | .12 | .07 | .11 | .46 | N/A |

The effect of high selection probabilities at both professional (.20) and sales (.23) jobs, when deciding to fill a managerial position, is greatly modified by the simple job-worker ratios that were shown in the section on Job Ratios. In the data above, for instance, for a managerial vacancy the MJR between managerial and professional jobs (.19) is less than half that between managerial and sales jobs (.48), indicating the importance of the size of the job-specific labor pool that an individual is in. It is the same principle as will be discussed in the next section regarding cohort size—if one's chances result from the ratio of job vacancies to labor supply, the increased chances may arise either from increased vacancies or decreased labor supply. The power of the simple ratios, described earlier, should now be much more evident.

### Cohort Size

The impact of cohort size is quite important, as shown by Easterlin (1968) Keyfitz (1973), and Stewman and Konda (1983). Summarizing the latter, four cohort size effects were specified, which will be discussed in terms of a small cohort: (1) small cohorts are advantaged at the entry point to the labor market; (2) this advantage holds throughout one's working life span, (3) exits from small cohorts add yet more advantages to those already held (i.e., equal exit rates yield a higher advantage for small cohorts), and (4) attributes stemming from the small cohort effects noted above become attached to individuals and thus a separate halo effect, exemplified as in the phrase "he/she is a 'star,' " is operative, in part and possibly greatly attributable to the cohort size phenomenon. In relative terms, the individual's acceleration and advantages are observable, while it is difficult to observe a cohort.

The above points are relevant to the task at hand in terms of age cohort effects on the total worker population and, more importantly, on job-specific populations of workers. Such cohort effects operate, of course, in conjunction with the structural effects discussed in the sections Employer Hiring Decisions, Vacancy Chain Reactions, Job Ratios, and Multiple Job-Worker Ratios. More specifically, combining employer hiring preferences by age *within* the simple job-worker ratios will produce age-specific outcomes, the results of which will incorporate cohort effects.

Perhaps the easiest example to provide at this point is the data on male stayers in Table 5: 17 percent of workers age 45 to 59 had a different major occupation, in comparison to 18 percent of workers age 60 and over. It would appear that even with much smaller selection chances for the older workers (3 percent vs.

15 percent), the exit rates (.64 vs. .22) and cohort size (4.9 vs. 14.0 million) are of a sufficient magnitude higher to produce this joint cohort size-exit rate effect among the stayers.

To be more explicit, consider the equation for the probability of changing occupations for a stayer to be as follows:

$$\frac{\text{(Total Vacancies)} \times \text{(Selection Chances for Age Group i)}}{\text{(Total Workers in Age Group i)} \times \text{(1} - \text{Exit Probability for Age Group i)}}$$

Thus we have $A = (11{,}988)(.0261)/[(4{,}851)(.3595)] = .179$ or 18 percent, and $B = (11{,}988)(.1529)/[(14{,}013)(.7758)] = .169$ or 17 percent, respectively, for the 60+ and 45-to-59 age groupings.[16] To show that both cohort size and exit rates are generating this somewhat unexpected outcome, compare the ratio of $A$ to $B$ under the following three conditions: (1) set exit probabilities equal in $A/B$ above, (2) set worker populations equal in $A/B$ above, and (3) set $A/B$, as above. When $A/B > 1$, consistency with the observed outcome, greater movement for older than for middle-aged workers, is indicated; and when $A/B < 1$ the effect is not sufficient to produce a result consistent with that observed. Condition 1 above treats cohort size alone, since vacancies and selection chances are held constant in 1, 2, and 3. Similarly, condition 2 treats exit rate alone. In condition 1, $A/B = .49$, and in condition 2, $A/B = .37$, both less than 1. Hence, neither is sufficient to solely produce the observed outcome, as in condition 3 where $A/B = 1.06$. Note that the selection ratio of .03 to .15 is about 1 to 5 (.17), the worker population ratio is about 1 to 3 (.35), and the "stay" ratio produced by exit rates is about 1 to 2 (.46). The joint worker population-stay ratio, however, is $.17 < .18$ producing 1.06. Thus we have a joint effect from cohort size and exit rates, reducing the relative stayer populations by more than the substantial selection differences.

## ONE OF THE INITIAL TRIGGER MECHANISMS: EXIT RATES OF WORKERS

Two types of processes generate initial job vacancies and hence operate as trigger mechanisms for the labor market structures discussed earlier: the exit rates of workers and the rate of growth and/or decline of jobs. The latter refers to employer allocation decisions for new and old jobs and involves the relative job distribution (new mixes); relative change in the technology-labor mixture, itself resulting in job redistributions; and increasing or decreasing the work force in a given industry or industrial segment in response to consumer demand.[17] This second type of trigger mechanism is very significant, as pointed out in the first two sections of this chap-

[16] Both vacancies and workers are here expressed in thousands (i.e., 11,988 refers to 12 million). Vacancies in this conditional probability refer to vacancies filled by workers already in the labor market, not new or reentrants. These vacancies are derived from Tables 2 and 3. *1970 Census of Population: Occupation and Residence in 1965*, U.S. Bureau of the Census, 1973. The 1965 age-specific worker population data were obtained from Table A-14, *Employment and Earnings* (February 1966), U.S. Bureau of Labor Statistics. An average of the January and December work force was used. Exit rates were then deduced, since the occupational change rates were known. These overall exit rates are consistent with those shown in the next section.

[17] These redistributional decisions may also involve the geographical movement of plants and jobs (see Birch, 1979; Bluestone, 1982).

ter. In the Section Labor Markets-An Expanded Class of Models, we noted the high degree of job dynamics in the private sector–in a five-year period about 40 percent of private sector jobs disappear from metropolitan areas, and it is such job loss and concomitant job replacement processes, in conjunction with differential job growth rates, that bring about the massive shifts in Job Distributions Over Time as seen in the period 1900–1990. Hence, for future research, this job-based triggering mechanism should receive the same amount of attention as the labor-based trigger to be discussed in this section.[18]

As a starting point, consider exit rates of workers as stemming either from exit decisions by the participants or from destructive life events such as disability or death. Exit decisions are of two general kinds in terms of initiators–voluntary decisions by the employee or involuntary exits from layoff, plant or business closing, and firing decisions by the employer. Employer decisions, for the most part, either pertain to the job-person match or to labor market conditions–the organizational labor market and/or the more macro labor market (SMSA, national, international). Voluntary exit decisions may also be labor-market-related, but the focal point has changed and, instead of the organization's interests, it is those of the individual worker–possibly a job-person mismatch, social and/or work relationships on the job, alternative job prospects, or perhaps more general life issues, such as family, health, and/or the individual's value upon and self-investment in work relative to other values and self-investments (See Faunce and Dubin, 1975). Of course, as noted earlier, there is a third type of exit behavior which generally does not arise from an individual's decision, but from destructive life events such as disability or death. In this section we will examine exit rates, with attention to five generators of such rates: three exit decisions; one life-course event, death, generally not at the individual's initiative; and one life-course event or process, disability, whose interface with work or exit from work is less certain and whose outcome is often a joint decision by employer, employee, and family. The exit rates will be covered in the following order, based on an increasing amount of decision-making latitude for the worker: death, unemployment, disability, retirement, and preretirement withdrawal from the labor market.

### Mortality

For the same five-year period examined in the sections on labor market structures, 1965 to 1970, Sommers and Eck (1977) estimate that 20 percent of the 1965 U.S. labor market population of workers exited, with 5 percent or one fourth of them via death. Hence, mortality is not a small force in the overall labor market exit rate and it is, of course, increasingly important for older workers. Table 10 reports the five-year age-sex-specific exit rates for the 1965 NLM population of workers.

Overall, exits from civilian jobs are 23 percent and withdrawal from the civilian labor market (rows 1 and 3) or death (row 4), 20 percent. Using the two primary exit modes as the base–leaving the labor market (row 1) and death (row

[18] For a specification of the effect of the redistribution of jobs, distinct of the growth effect, see Stewman, 1982. At the organizational level, this redistributional parameter is also specified in Stewman and Konda (1983); however, as yet it has still not been thoroughly investigated.

**TABLE 10. Five-Year Exit Rates for the 1965 NLM. Population of Workers by Sex, Age, and Mode of Exit**

| | AGE | | | | | | | |
|---|---|---|---|---|---|---|---|---|
| EXIT MODE | SEX | 16–19 | 20–29 | 30–39 | 40–49 | 50–59 | 60+ | TOTAL |
| Left Labor Market | F | 38.9 | 36.0 | 17.6 | 14.6 | 21.3 | 39.7 | 26.0 |
| | M | 7.7 | 2.7 | 2.3 | 3.5 | 10.9 | 35.2 | 7.9 |
| | (M+F) | | | | | | | (14.8) |
| Unemployed | F | 3.2 | 2.5 | 2.5 | 2.3 | 1.9 | 1.2 | 2.3 |
| | M | 3.9 | 2.6 | 2.1 | 2.1 | 2.2 | 1.4 | 2.3 |
| | (M+F) | | | | | | | ( 2.3) |
| Military | F | – | – | – | – | – | – | – |
| | M | 10.0 | 1.4 | .08 | .02 | – | – | 1.1 |
| | (M+F) | | | | | | | ( 0.7) |
| Death | F | 0.3 | 0.4 | 0.9 | 2.1 | 4.4 | 25.6 | 4.0 |
| | M | 0.8 | 0.9 | 1.5 | 3.6 | 8.7 | 30.3 | 6.1 |
| | (M+F) | | | | | | | ( 5.3) |
| Total | F | 42.4 | 38.9 | 21.0 | 19.0 | 27.6 | 66.5 | 32.3 |
| | M | 22.4 | 7.6 | 6.7 | 9.4 | 21.8 | 66.9 | 17.4 |
| | (M+F) | | | | | | | (23.1) |

Data Source: D. Sommers and A. Eck (1977), Table 1.

4)—we observe that death accounts for 44 percent of the five-year exit rates for males, but only 13 percent of the female exit rates. At ages 50–59, and 60+, the corresponding proportion of exit rates via death is 44 percent and 46 percent for males and 17 percent and 39 percent for females. No doubt, such ultimate health events are of major consequence for labor markets. Moreover, if we view mortality-rate increases across age cohorts (cross sectionally), we observe that the rate of increase is greater than that for labor market withdrawal up to age 50, indicative of health impacts and perhaps lending indirect support to the health data gathered from the Social Security disability surveys. At age 50 and above, the death rate statistics speak for themselves. There are major jumps in withdrawal from the labor market (row 1), but mortality effects (row 4) remain large—at 17 percent (4.4/25.7) of exit rates for females 50–59 and at 40 percent for females over 60 and for all males over 50. In terms of absolute size, almost 9 percent of the 1965 male work force age 50–59 was dead by 1970 and over 30 percent of the comparable males age 60 and over. For females these percentages are lower: 4 percent and 26 percent, respectively.

## Unemployment

Unemployment in Table 10 (2.3 percent) refers to unemployment in 1970 of the 1965 NLM worker population, and does not include unemployment of new or reentrants after 1965. In other words, it is not the unemployment rate of the 1970 NLM, which was 4.9 percent for persons 16 years and over and 3.5 percent and 4.8 percent for males and females 20 years and over, respectively. If these proportions were to hold across time, then the 5-year stayer population would have unemployment rates at about two thirds and one half that of the NLM in year five for males and females.

Further evidence supporting the above type of calculations may be found in data on the distribution of unemployed workers by mode of unemployment. Only half fit the mold of "laid off" or "fired," as may be seen below:[19]

| | REASONS FOR UNEMPLOYMENT | | | |
|---|---|---|---|---|
| YEAR | LOST JOB | LEFT JOB | NEW ENTRANT | REENTRANT |
| 1970 | 44% | 13% | 12% | 30% |
| 1975 | 55% | 10% | 10% | 24% |
| 1980 | 52% | 12% | 11% | 25% |
| 1981 | 52% | 11% | 12% | 25% |

These data are reasonably stable in distribution, with about half of the unemployed having lost their job, while the number who left their job equals the number of new entrants. Note also that the number of reentrants is over twice the number of new entrants. Thus, almost two thirds of the unemployed left or lost their jobs, while over one third are entering the labor market from the outside. Since we are dealing with exit rates, it is the "almost two thirds" of the unemployed who exit that is pertinent to this discussion. Hence, renormalizing the percentages for this portion of the unemployed, we find that about one fifth of the unemployed exit rate is due to persons leaving their jobs and thereby opening a job vacancy. The other four fifths pertains to persons who lost their job, the bulk of which, if laid off, have rights of recall to the same job; hence, for this portion of the exit rate, there is no vacancy generated, unlike the rest of the exit rates discussed in this section.

## Disability

With respect to disability and its effect on exit behavior and/or employer change, we observe the following using data from the 1978 Survey of Disability and Work (Lando, Cutler, and Gamber, 1982):

1. Of the 127 million persons aged 18–64 in the survey, 17 percent or 21.9 million identified themselves as either having a secondary (6.1 million), occupational (4.9 million), or severe (10.9 million) disability.[20]
2. Among the 21.9 million disabled persons, 31 percent were employed, compared to 60 percent of the overall population.
3. Among the severely disabled (10.7 of the 10.9 million have sufficient data for most of the following breakdowns),

   26 percent were disability insurance beneficiaries;

   14 percent were currently in the labor force;

[19] Source: Table No. 654, *Statistical Abstract of the United States 1982–83*, U.S. Bureau of the Census, 1982.

[20] The definitions are as follows: (1) severely disabled–unable to work altogether or unable to work regularly; (2) occupationally disabled–able to work regularly but unable to do the same work as before the onset of disability, or unable to work full time; (3) secondary work limitations–able to work full time, regularly and at the same work, but with limitations in the amount or kind of work performed.

26 percent had been employed during 1977 (43 percent of these intermittently);

43 percent were males and 57 percent females;

3.8 of the 4.6 million severely disabled males were employed at the onset of the disability, and 2.5 million or two thirds continued work (93 percent with the same employer);

3.2 of the 6.1 million severely disabled females were employed at the onset of the disability, and 2.2 million or two thirds continued work (91 percent with the same employer);

31–33 percent of the 7 million working at the onset of the disability stopped working; like the proverbial half-full or half-empty bucket, depending on which perspective one wishes to take, the facts are that about one third of the workers stopped working and two thirds continued working with a severe disability from their point of view;

25 percent (2.7 million) of the 10.9 million severely disabled persons reported that they were unable to work; of these, 1.9 million were males, comprising 40 percent of the 4.7 million severely disabled male population and 70 percent of the population unable to work;

70 percent of the 10.7 million severely disabled persons were over age 45, the more specific age distribution being

| 18–34 | 35–44 | 45–54 | 55–64 |
|---|---|---|---|
| 1.5(14%) | 1.6(15%) | 2.7(25%) | 5.0(47%) |

The above data are quite informative from the point of view of statics or from the point of view of having 2.8 million severely disabled individuals employed out of 99.3 million in the 1977 NLM population, about 3 percent of the labor market.

Additionally, the data indicate that the onset of a severe disability results in only a one-third chance of the worker exiting the labor market. However, equally important for our purposes, the data do not reveal the time of the disability's onset and subsequent labor market behavior. More to the point, if two thirds of the workers experiencing severe disabilities continue to work for extended time periods, why do we observe a reduction to 14 percent employed at one point in time (1978) and only 26% having been employed full time, part time, or intermittently during 1977? Somewhat masked, but possibly very important, are the *subsequent labor market experiences, in conjunction with subsequent health trajectories and one's aging.* Table 11 underscores (given the limitations of cross sectional cohort data) the increasing probability of disability incidence with age. What is needed are the concomitant labor market experiences, before and after the onset of disability. Are multiple jobs, multiple employers, multiple occurrences of unemployment, and multiple health problems involved, as well as the readjustment process to one's changed health status and the new (postdisability) job-person match?

The data in Table 11 also highlight a different kind of issue—the relative size of the disabled population of persons. Seventeen percent overall is quite large, but that 1 in 4 of the population ages 45–54 and more than 1 in 3 of the population ages 55–64 report that they are in 1 of the 3 disabled classes is a very high proportion. Also, over 10 percent of the 45–54 age group and 25 percent of the 55–64

**TABLE 11. Disability Status by Age in the United States: 1978**

| | | | DISABILITY TYPE | | |
|---|---|---|---|---|---|
| AGE | NOT DISABLED | TOTAL DISABLED | SEVERE | OCCUPATIONAL | SECONDARY |
| 18–34 | 92% | 8% | 3% | 2% | 4% |
| 35–44 | 85% | 15% | 6% | 4% | 5% |
| 45–54 | 76% | 24% | 11% | 6% | 7% |
| 55–64 | 63% | 37% | 25% | 6% | 6% |
| Total (18–64) | 83% | 17% | 9% | 4% | 5% |

Data Source: M.E. Lando, R. R. Cutler, and E. Gamber (1982), Table 2.

age group report that they are severely disabled. No wonder such self-reported data draws its critics. Are such data credible? Perhaps there is less room for readily dismissing these data as "self-serving" and "yea-saying" than has been thought. Indeed, most of the non-severely disabled persons are employed comparably to the population not disabled. Of what gain is it to these workers to report a disability? Moreover, that two thirds of the self-reported, severely disabled continued to work overwhelmingly for the same employer hardly seems to be the socially "correct" answer. That 26 percent of the severely disabled are disability insurance (DI) beneficiaries brings in yet a different type of credibility. Hence, until much more is known about the processes—near and long term—by which the onset of disability is handled by the person, the family (e.g, in the families of the 1.2 million males who stopped working at the onset of disability, 300,000 spouses began working, hardly a questionable response), the employer or employers and fellow employees, the data in Table 11, and the associated disability-employment puzzle will remain. In addition to the above needed research, we note that the job-person match is a dual process involving both employer and employee and that if, indeed, the disability survey data are valid from the respondent's perspective, whether or not the person is a DI beneficiary, then he or she may behave accordingly.[21] At issue, of course, is just what is that behavior over time with respect to work?

### Retirement

A second data set that is plausibly consistent with a static disability incidence interpretation of Table 11 is the retirement behavior of older workers—a very important exit decision in terms of generating vacancies. In this subsection and the next we will briefly treat two issues: changing labor force participation rates of older workers and changing preferences to work or retire in conjunction with health. Moreover, since considerable attention regarding retirement behavior has been given to a series of surveys in 1974, 1978 and 1981 by Louis Harris and Associates, Inc. (see Harris, 1977, 1979 and 1981, respectively) we will attempt to utilize this data on these two issues, as well as data from the much larger national samples (CPS) by the U.S. Bureau of the Census.

[21] For a provocative discussion of such individual cognition and organizational behavior, see March and Simon (1958), especially Chapters 1 and 3, and Olbrich, Chapter 3, this volume.

In *Aging in the Eighties: America in Transition (1981),* Harris states the following:

> In the seven years since 1974, a number of significant changes has occurred in the work habits of Americans 55 and over. First, the number of individuals now employed full or part time, retired or not, has grown in the 55-64 age group (55%, up from 48% in 1974) and is also up somewhat among the public 65 to 69 (21%, up from 18% in 1974). The greatest growth has occurred in the full-time category—from 38% to 46% among individuals 55 to 64, and from 4% to 8% among the 65 and over group (here: 65-69). No change is seen among individuals 70 to 79 (11%) or 80 and over (4%) (p. 40).

Two elements arise in the above statements—the number of older workers and their labor force participation rate (the percentages). As for the changing number of older workers in the United States and their labor force participation rates, Table 12 provides this data over the last 3-1/2 decades since World War II, with specific yearly data from 1970 to 1982.

Summarizing this data by decade and in terms of increments and decrements, we observe the following:

| | AGE 55-64 | | | | | AGE 65+ | | | | |
|---|---|---|---|---|---|---|---|---|---|---|
| | Δ NUMBER[a] | | | Δ PART RATE[b] | | Δ NUMBER[a] | | | Δ PART RATE[b] | |
| *TIME PERIOD* | *M* | *F* | *T* | *M* | *F* | *M* | *F* | *T* | *M* | *F* |
| 1950-60 | +606 | +1,147 | +1,753 | − 0.1 | +10.2 | −167 | +323 | +156 | −12.7 | +1.1 |
| 1960-70 | +724 | +1,167 | +1,897 | − 3.8 | + 5.8 | −123 | +149 | + 26 | − 6.3 | −1.1 |
| 1970-80 | + 40 | + 438 | + 478 | −10.7 | + 1.5 | −287 | + 88 | −199 | − 7.7 | −1.7 |

[a]Change in number of workers, in thousands
[b]Change in labor force participation rate

The number of workers age 55-64 has been increasing in each of the last three decades, but the smallest increase was during the 1970s. Moreover, the bulk of this increase stems from increasing numbers of women—in the 1950s and 1960s due to their increasing size and increasing labor force participation rates in the 1970s primarily due to their increasing size, since there was little change in female labor force participation rates during the 1970s. Equally noteworthy is the very large decrease in labor force participation rates during the 1970s for males age 55-64. In 1947, 89.6 percent of males age 55-64 were in the labor force; by 1982, 35 years later, the percentage was 70.2, a decrease of 19.4; moreover, 12.8 or two thirds of this 19.4 percent drop occurred in the last one third of the period, between 1970 and 1982. Hence, in terms of changes, increases in the number of workers ages 55-64 is not new. Rather, what *is* new is the following: (1) in the 1970s the size of the labor-force increase in the age 55-64 category was significantly smaller than any decade since World War II; (2) female labor force participation rates in the 55-64 age group had a small increase overall during the 1970s, although they were generally stable at 41 to 42 percent; and (3) male labor force

**TABLE 12. Numbers and Labor Force Participation Rates of Older Workers in the United States: 1947–82.**

| | AGE 55–64 | | | | | AGE 65 AND OVER | | | | |
|---|---|---|---|---|---|---|---|---|---|---|
| | NUMBER OF WORKERS+ | | | LABOR FORCE PARTICIPATION RATE | | NUMBER OF WORKERS+ | | | LABOR FORCE PARTICIPATION RATE | |
| *YEAR* | *TOTAL* | *MALE* | *FEMALE* | *MALE* | *FEMALE* | *TOTAL* | *MALE* | *FEMALE* | *MALE* | *FEMALE* |
| 1947 | 7,169 | 5,647 | 1,522 | 89.6 | 24.3 | 2,821 | 2,376 | 445 | 47.8 | 8.1 |
| 1950 | 7,633 | 5,794 | 1,839 | 86.9 | 27.0 | 3,038 | 2,454 | 584 | 45.8 | 9.7 |
| 1960 | 9,386 | 6,400 | 2,986 | 86.3 | 37.2 | 3,194 | 2,287 | 907 | 33.1 | 10.8 |
| 1970 | 11,277 | 7,124 | 4,153 | 83.0 | 43.0 | 3,220 | 2,164 | 1,056 | 26.8 | 9.7 |
| 1971 | 11,361 | 7,146 | 4,215 | 82.2 | 42.9 | 3,146 | 2,089 | 1,057 | 25.5 | 9.5 |
| 1972 | 11,362 | 7,138 | 4,224 | 80.5 | 42.1 | 3,107 | 2,022 | 1,085 | 24.4 | 9.3 |
| 1973 | 11,182 | 7,003 | 4,179 | 78.3 | 41.1 | 2,962 | 1,908 | 1,054 | 22.8 | 8.9 |
| 1974 | 11,187 | 7,030 | 4,157 | 77.4 | 40.7 | 2,921 | 1,925 | 996 | 22.4 | 8.2 |
| 1975 | 11,226 | 6,982 | 4,244 | 75.8 | 41.0 | 2,939 | 1,906 | 1,033 | 21.7 | 8.3 |
| 1976 | 11,279 | 6,971 | 4,308 | 74.5 | 41.1 | 2,974 | 1,816 | 1,058 | 20.3 | 8.2 |
| 1977 | 11,410 | 7,043 | 4,367 | 74.0 | 41.0 | 2,910 | 1,845 | 1,065 | 20.1 | 8.1 |
| 1978 | 11,555 | 7,087 | 4,468 | 73.5 | 41.4 | 3,043 | 1,923 | 1,120 | 20.5 | 8.4 |
| 1979 | 11,719 | 7,140 | 4,579 | 73.0 | 44.9 | 3,073 | 1,928 | 1,145 | 20.0 | 8.3 |
| 1980 | 11,755 | 7,164 | 4,591 | 72.3 | 44.5 | 3,021 | 1,877 | 1,144 | 19.1 | 8.1 |
| 1981 | 11,969 | 7,170 | 4,799 | 70.6 | 41.4 | 3,042 | 1,866 | 1,176 | 18.4 | 8.0 |
| 1982 | 12,062 | 7,174 | 4,888 | 70.2 | 41.8 | 3,030 | 1,845 | 1,185 | 17.8 | 7.9 |

+In thousands.

Data Sources: 1947–79, Tables 3 and 4, ***Handbook of Labor Statistics, 1980***, Bulletin 2070, Bureau of Labor Statistics; 1980, Table 4 (p. 166–67) ***Employment and Earnings***, January 1981; 1981–1982, Table 4 (p. 144–45) ***Employment and Earnings***, January 1983.

participation rates for ages 55–64 decreased dramatically in the 1970s in this early retirement age band from 83 percent to 72 percent, the sharpest decrease of any decade since World War II. As for a transition in the 1980s, deduced from labor force participation rates, it may be the opposite of that drawn by Harris. To the point, comparisons of the 1974 and 1981 Harris samples do not represent national shifts in labor force participation rates over this time period for the 55–64 age group and more representative data, such as BLS figures, which also provide the sex distribution, should be used when discussing such national shifts.[22]

A similar result holds for the population age 65 and over. As shown in the summary data above, the number of working males age 65 and over has declined in all three decades, the largest numerical decrease being during the 1970s, almost 300,000. Females increased numerically in all three decades, but by less than half of the decrease by males in the 1970s and, hence, during the 1970s there was for the first time since World War II a net decrease in workers age 65 and over.

Over the last 35 years, males' labor force participation rates in the age 65 and over population have declined from 47.8 percent in 1947 to 17.8 percent in 1982, a decline of 30.0 or 63 percent. In contrast, females age 65 and over began with low rates in 1947 (8.1 percent), increased to 10.8 percent in 1960, then declined to 8.1 percent again in 1980, and, subsequently, to 7.9 percent in 1982. For both sexes over age 65, then, there has been a somewhat uneven but fairly continuous decline in labor force participation rates since 1960.[23]

Before moving to preferences, we point out that the shifts in the United States discussed above correspond to those of other industrialized nations. Fisher (1975) provides a nine-nation comparison of the age-65-and-over population for 1950 to 1970; Cohen and Stewman (1982) provide a ten-nation comparison from 1965 to 1980 for age 60–64 and 65-and-over populations. From the latter study, for instance, France, West Germany, Finland, and Denmark had even higher percentage declines in labor force participation rates of the age 60–64 population of males than in the United States.

It should perhaps also be noted that some of the retirees are responding to corporate inducements to retire in conjunction with labor cutbacks and that others' retirement may spring from a plant closing, neither mode of which, of course, opens a job vacancy. At the aggregate NLM level, this problem is taken care of by using net job changes–growth/decline. Thus, it is problematic only in specifying more exactly the sources of the trigger mechanisms, since the net value overallocates exits and underallocates new jobs via its net job change character. Such specification is an important avenue to pursue and very preliminary evidence from Barfield and Morgan (1969) indicates that less than 10 percent of retirements

[22] Specific comparisons for 1974 and 1981 are as follows: *males* 77.4 percent (1974) to 70.6 percent (1981), a decline of 6.8 percent; and *females* 40.7 percent (1974) to 41.4 percent (1981), an increase of 1.3 percent. Overall, there is a clear net decline in labor-force participation between 1974 and 1981 for individuals aged 55–64. Additionally, the same result holds for more detailed age groupings: 55–59 and 60–64. Source: Bureau of Labor Statistics *Employment and Earnings*, January 1975 and 1982.

[23] As for specific 1974 to 1981 changes, the national CPS data show the following for ages 65–69: *males* 32.9 percent (1974) to 27.8 percent (1981), a decline of 5.1 percent, and *females* 14.4 percent (1974) to 14.9 percent (1981), an increase of 0.5 percent, again indicative of a clear overall net decline in labor-force participation rates of the population age 65–69. Source: Bureau of Labor Statistics, *Employment and Earnings*, January 1975 and 1982.

were for unexpected job reasons, whereas almost 30 percent were for unexpected health reasons.

### Health and Changing Preferences to Work or Retire

Rather than use the Harris data to obtain measures of national shifts in labor-force participation by older workers, perhaps a better use would be in an exploratory mode to examine preferences for work/retirement by retirees and to obtain information relating to their retirement decision. As it turns out, the data indicate that the health of the individual is a major factor for at least 25 to 30 percent of retirees.

In comparing the 1974 and 1981 surveys, Harris (1981) found that 37 percent of retirees reported that they were forced to retire in both years. More importantly, in 1981 a follow-up questionnaire asked, "Why were you forced to retire?" and 67 percent of the respondents gave disability or poor health as the reason. Hence, 27 percent of the retiree population cited health as a fundamental reason for their retirement. Note that this 27 percent is remarkably close to the figure obtained in the 1978 disability data for ages 55 to 64–25 percent report a severe disability (cf. Table 11). Moreover, when comparing labor-force participation rates of men and women ages 55-64, the 1978 disability data base corresponds to the national data reported in Table 12–a participation rate of 74 percent for males and 41 percent for females. Additionally, however, the disability data also have labor force participation rates for this 25 percent severely disabled population–for males it was 16 percent and for females 1 percent, with an aggregate participation rate of 8 percent (Lando et al., Table 8). The Harris data and the disability data are from different years (1981, 1978, respectively), but the basic thrust of these independent data bases points to a disabling health factor as a basic cause of retirement for at least 25 percent of the population.

In the 1974 Harris survey, a question not repeated in a 1981 survey was asked of the retired and unemployed portion (69 percent) of the population age 65 and over, namely, "Would you like to work?" Thirty-one percent answered affirmatively; once again an even more important follow-up question was asked of this 31 percent subpopulation–"What's keeping you from working?" Poor health was given by 57 percent of the persons. Hence, of the 21 percent (.69 × .31) of the total population age 65 and over who would like to work, 12 percent (.69 × .31 × .57) stated that they were unable to work due to health reasons.[24] Other reasons given were "too old" (6 percent), "job opportunities" (3 percent), "lose benefits" (1 percent), and "other interests" (1 percent), with multiple reasons permitted. However, all other reasons, exclusive of health, account for only 9 percent of the 65-and-over population. Obtaining such follow-up information is essential when interpreting such work preference responses. In fact, we might consider such questions as "Would you like to work?" as being asked in a contextual vacuum–as hypothetical, not taking into account the adequacy of income, the adequacy of

[24]See J. H. Schulz 1976, Chapter 3, for the initial observations along these lines. To obtain the total population not working for health reasons, one would need information on the 69 percent (1-31 percent) who answered either that they would not like to work or were not sure (.69 × .69 × A) where A is the health component.

health, family conditions, job and organizational conditions, and labor market conditions. In this case, with a follow-up question, we discover that most of those who "would like to work" are not available for work due to health reasons.[25]

A 1978 Harris survey (Harris, 1979) also inquired into work/retirement preferences of retirees and found that 46 percent preferred to work, 12 to 13 percent of whom were employed, leaving 33 to 34 percent of the nonworking retirees who preferred to work, a percentage comparable to the 1974 data of 31 percent. Unfortunately, no follow-up question or questions were asked of this subsample as to why their preferences were not being realized, Thus we conjecture, using both the 1974 and 1981 survey data, that possibly 57 to 67 percent of this 33 to 34 percent "would like to work." but were unable to do so due to health, leaving 10 to 13 percent of the total retiree population who "would like to work" but have no health-based reasons for not working. In brief, the 1978 survey results, in the first part, are quite similar to the 1974 results, and if there is a shift in work preferences, it is slight once the employed population is removed and the populations become more comparable; in the second part, it seems reasonable to think that the 33 to 34 percent is a hypothetical figure, assuming good health and that once health is taken into account a more realistic upper bound might be 10 to 13 percent.

Lastly, we will briefly discuss the relationship between health and the declining labor-force participation rates by both the age 55-64 and the age-65-and-over populations discussed in the subsection Retirement. First, the increased retirement at age 65 and early retirement, age 55-64, would not appear to be the result of declining health at the aggregate level. Aside from the declining mortality, increasing morbidity proposition, an alternative appealing line of research may be in the joint health/income effects; specificially in the issue of threshold effects and boundary conditions. Just as in physiological processes where there appear to be threshold effects (see Stafford and Birren's chapter, this volume), it seems reasonable to propose a joint health/income effect. For instance, Barfield and Morgan (1969) refer to a "threshold" level of retirement income for voluntary retirement decisions and, where health is not a primary factor (for at least 50 percent of the retirees of their study, cf. p. 69), such an income threshold may become an enabling condition for other factors or systems to take over. Indeed, Barfield and Morgan also propose it as an enabling condition when health becomes a problem. Of course, if we push the health threshold argument to its limit, namely death, the income threshold is irrelevant. Thus, there are clearly at least two limiting thresholds, with the health threshold much more clearly defined in its limit, but with both threshold concepts equally provocative once the subjective and normative (psychological and social) limits of each are considered. What are such limits and how might they interact such that under different health conditions the income limit is raised or lowered? Or alternatively, once beyond the baseline income threshold, what shifts in health behavior are sufficient to induce retirement?

[25]The point of the above remarks is *not* that such questions should be dropped, but that follow-up questions must also be asked and perhaps a battery of such follow-up questions, delimiting the conditions, environment, and degree of interest, for example. It is, indeed, unfortunate that Harris has not repeated at least these two questions in subsequent surveys in order to provide comparable information on time trends and the individual's environmental context.

Granovetter (1978) provides a provocative discussion on one class of demographic models of threshold processes. Different distributions of thresholds in a given population generate quite different and unexpected behavioral outcomes, stemming from sequential threshold effects that cause a diffusion type of chain reaction. Hence, we might speak of three types of processes, two of which have diffusion or sequential threshold triggers; the first generated by other persons' behavior, as discussed by Granovetter, and the second generated by the health-income threshold sequencing. And, of course, the third type of chain reaction is that caused by the exit from the labor market generating not a threshold chain reaction, but a job vacancy chain reaction, as discussed earlier in this chapter.

We also know little about unexpected retirements, about the time frame involved, and about the nature of the decisions to change retirement plans. For instance, the Barfield and Morgan (1969) data show that 48 percent of their retirees retired unexpectedly, not at the time they had planned to do so. Moreover, 29 percent did so for health reasons, 9 percent for job reasons, and 6 percent for family reasons (Tables B34a, p. 219). Such data help to explain why plans and preferences for later retirement[26] are not good predictors of actual behavior for the total population. But perhaps more importantly, such data indicate the theoretical gaps in our knowledge—what is the nature of the decision for this half of the population who retire unexpectedly? That health is a major factor inducing retirement for at least 25 to 30 percent of the population[27] seems a reasonable first approximation, and that it continues to keep a large proportion (50 percent or more) of retirees who might wish to work from doing so also appears to be true. Yet how are such health thresholds reached and in what time frame are they reached? What are the processes (social, economic, psychological, and physiological) for determining such thresholds? Do preretirement health thresholds also operate similarly in the postretirement behavior of those who would like to work? Just how large are these populations experiencing health thresholds? Is 25 to 30 percent a lower bound or a ceiling for the preretirement population? Are approximately half of all retirements unexpected as to the timing of such a decision? Expressed differently, are retirement preferences and plans as to the timing of the decision to retire only realized in half of the population? These would seem to be important avenues to pursue, for there seems to be little doubt as to the significance of health on retirement for a large segment of the population.[28]

[26] For example, Barfield and Morgan's (1969) 1966 survey indicates that 36 percent planned to retire before age 65; Harris's (1977 and 1981) 1974 and 1981 surveys indicate 23 percent and 24 percent had such plans.

[27] And possibly up to 50 percent once the income threshold is accounted for. The 25 percent figure arises from the disability data, a 27 percent value from the 1981 Harris survey, and 29 percent from Barfield and Morgan—those retiring unexpectedly for health reasons.

[28] Other important studies indicating health-retirement-mortality relationships are Parnes, Adams, Adrisani, Kohen, Andrew, and Nestel (1975) and Kingson (1981). See also Myers (1982) for a challenge to Kingson's analysis. Myers does not dispute the early retirement health linkage, but rather points to a possible heterogeneity issue in need of careful scrutiny when conducting mortality analyses. This exchange highlights the importance of pursuing such linkages in more depth. On a quite different tangent, Myers makes several reasonable points about survey research, but reaches an unnecessary conclusion as to survey data validity, and therefore, in part, detracts from his main point on pitfalls of scientific research. Surely if creative efforts are necessary in mortality analyses, they are also necessary in analyses of survey data, and quite likely such innovative, careful analyses will pay off handsomely, especially if such questions are pursued in depth, from different points of view, and in conjunction with other data sources.

### Preretirement Withdrawal from the Labor Market

Just as we may have postretirement entry to the labor market by older workers, we may also have preretirement withdrawal from the labor market by younger workers, the latter of which is particularly important for female exit rates. To more concretely grasp the magnitude of such exit rates, reexamine row 1 of Table 10, in which the five-year female exit rates by age range from 15 percent to 40 percent, with the average at 25 percent. Perhaps additional insight may be obtained by comparing the ratio of female to male exit rates by age. Three ratios are shown in Table 13—the ratio for leaving the labor market (row 1 from Table 10), the mortality ratio (row 4, Table 10), and the ratio for the combined withdrawal and mortality rates.

The withdrawal rate for females is five times as great as that for males in the teenage years, over 13 times as great in the twenties, almost eight times as great in the thirties, over four times greater in the forties, twice as great in the fifties, and 10 percent greater at age 60 and over. However, since more females survive at each of these ages, part of the sex differential in withdrawal rates is due to these higher survival rates. In column 2 of Table 13, the female worker mortality rate is 40 percent that of a male worker during the teens and twenties, 60 percent during the thirties and forties; half that of male workers in the fifties, and 80 percent that of male workers at age 60 and over. Thus, the exit ratios for these two *combined* primary exit modes are 4-1/2 times greater for female workers than for male workers in the teens, over 10 times greater in the twenties, about five times greater in the thirties, about 2-1/2 times greater in the forties, but only 30 percent greater in the fifties, once mortality differences are taken into account and, likewise, are equal once age 60 or above. Overall, by taking into account mortality differentials, the exit rate is twice that of males and is a major triggering mechanism for job opportunities.

The second part of the exit rate story, however, is that of preretirement reentry to the labor market by these same females. Using an increment-decrement demographic model, Smith (1982)[29] derived several important work-life expectancies from 1977 data on the United States, including the following:

| | | MALE | FEMALE |
|---|---|---|---|
| 1. No. of labor-force entries | – at birth | 3.0 | 4.5 |
| | – at age 25 | 1.1 | 2.7 |
| 2. Expected duration in labor force per entry | – at birth | 12.6 | 6.1 |
| | – at age 25 | 29.1 | 8.6 |
| 3. No. of voluntary exits | – at birth | 2.7 | 4.4 |
| | – at age 25 | 2.0 | 3.3 |
| 4. % workers expected to die while in labor force | | 27.0 | 9.5 |
| 5. Work-life expectancy | – at birth | 37.9 | 27.5 |
| | – at age 25 | 33.4 | 23.0 |

While the number of exits is much greater for females, so is their number of reentries. Hence, the expected work life of males is about 38 years and of females about 28 years. It is not one half that of males, as might be expected from the 2.1 exit ratio (withdrawal + mortality) noted earlier. Rather, it is about 70 percent that

[29] See Schoen and Woodrow (1980) also for increment-decrement working-life tables.

**TABLE 13. Ratio of Female to Male Five-Year Exit Rates in U.S. Labor Market (1965–70).**

| AGE GROUP | WITHDRAWAL RATIO | MORTALITY RATIO | WITHDRAWAL + MORTALITY RATIO |
|---|---|---|---|
| 16–19 | 5.1 | .4 | 4.6 |
| 20–29 | 13.3 | .4 | 10.1 |
| 30–39 | 7.7 | .6 | 4.9 |
| 40–49 | 4.2 | .6 | 2.4 |
| 50–59 | 2.0 | .5 | 1.3 |
| 60+ | 1.1 | .8 | 1.0 |
| Total | 3.3 | .7 | 2.1 |

of males. Not only is the female work force growing at a much faster rate than that of males, increasing the number of female workers, but the career length or number of years worked per female is also increasing substantially.

In addition to the magnitude of job openings generated by female exit rates, there is also the impact on career chances of multiple exits and reentries along with the duration times between such events. There is certainly no direct substantive analogy, but in terms of the effects on career chances of retirees reentering the labor market or of individuals with health-based exits and reentries, different ways of thinking about the multiple exit/multiple reentry process may arise from increased knowledge about female careers, as they are embedded in the labor market and interfaced with the five labor-market structures of the prior section.

## CONCLUSION

We have introduced the concepts of a dynamic model of labor markets, illustrating several basic labor market structures with data and measurements from the United States. The structures entailed both populations of jobs and of workers, thereby enabling the analyst to deal in a much more in-depth manner with demand processes such as growth of new jobs, chain reactions of job opportunities, employer hiring practice, and job redistributions and processes, with special attention to the aging, health, and sex of the labor force.

If we return briefly to the initial question in the introduction, we should now have some glints as to how to answer such questions; in some cases, the illustrations given in the discussion provide initial information bearing directly on them. For instance, what are the relative job opportunities of middle-aged and older workers? The notion that few older and/or middle-aged workers make major career changes should be dispelled and replaced since, in fact, many job opportunities are taken by such workers. We observed, for example, that of the 1970 male working population age 65 and above (60+ in 1965), 16 percent had changed to a different major occupation and 13 percent had reentered the labor market since 1965. Hence, almost 30 percent of male workers age 65 and over were new to their job. In total number of workers, this represents over 300,000 occupational shifts and over 250,000 new hires. The comparable female data total 345,000 workers. Thus, of the 3.1 million workers age 65 and over in the 1970 U.S. national labor market, over 900,000 were new to their job. Additionally, of the 18.6 million workers age 50–64 in 1970, almost 4.7 million or 25 percent were new to their job, having either changed to a different major occupation (over 2.5 million) or entered, generally reentering, the labor market (over 2.1 million) since 1965. From a labor market point of view, there are certainly massive changes taking place in the job-worker populations for middle-aged and older workers. That such findings are surprising attests to the need for expanding our class of theoretical models for viewing employment and aging. An even more compelling reason is that we may obtain still additional insights into other interrelationships heretofore left unanalyzed or, in some cases, analyzed singly or statically.

Lastly, we point out that one of the major triggering mechanisms for the labor market structures was worker exit rates, for which changes in health were themselves, in part, trigger mechanisms. Among the more important health changes discussed were health-induced retirements, disability, and death. Just as the labor market dynamics referring to entrance and job change indicate that there are many job opportunities for middle-aged and older workers, the exit rate behavior and, particularly, the health-retirement, health-disability, and health-death data which was reviewed indicate a disabling health factor as a basic cause underlying many exits. For instance, the joint Harris (1981), Barfield and Morgan (1969), and U.S. disability (Lando, Cutler and Gamber, 1982) data all point to a disabling health factor as a basic cause of retirement for at least 25 percent of the population. Regardless of the agreement about this 25 percent figure, there remains little doubt as to the significance of health on retirement for a large segment of the population, further underscoring the need for a wider class of theoretical models to study employment, aging, and health. In short, just as some segments of the middle-aged and older populations are fully involved in the ongoing national labor market, other segments are withdrawing–some by choice without current health as a major factor, but for others with health a major determinant. Thus, not only should this worker heterogeneity be taken into account, but such analyses should also relate the different worker behavior to the labor market structures and processes in which such behavior is embedded and/or is impacting.

## *REFERENCES*

BARFIELD, R. E., and MORGAN, J. N. (1969). *Early retirement: The decision and the experience.* Ann Arbor, MI: Institute of Social Research, University of Michigan.

BELL, D. (1973). *The coming of post-industrial society: A venture in social forecasting.* New York: Basic Books, Inc.

BIRCH, D. (1979). *The job generation process.* MIT Program on Neighborhood and Regional Change, unpublished manuscript.

BLAU, P. M., and DUNCAN, O. D. (1967). *The American occupational structure.* New York: John Wiley & Sons, Inc.

BLUESTONE, B. (1982). Deindustrialization and the abandonment of community. In J. C. Raines, L. E. Berson, and D. Mcl. Gracie (Eds.), *Community and capital in conflict.* Philadelphia: Temple University Press.

CLARK, C. (1957). *The conditions of economic progress.* London: Macmillan & Co., Ltd.

COHEN, H., and STEWMAN, S. (1982) An international comparison of the decision to work or retire: 10 nations. Unpublished paper, Carnegie-Mellon University.

DOERINGER, P. B., and PIORE, M. J. (1971). *Internal labor markets and manpower analysis.* Lexington, MA: D. C. Heath and Co.

EASTERLIN, R. A. (1968). *Population, labor force, and the long swings in economic growth: The American experience.* New York: Columbia University Press.

FAUNCE, W. A., and DUBIN, R. (1975). Individual investment in working and living. In A. Cherns and L. Davis (Eds.), *Quality of working life*, Vol. 1. New York: The Free Press.

FISHER, P. (1975). Labor force participation of the aged and the social security system in nine countries. *Industrial Gerontology*, Winter, 1–13.

FLINN, C. J., and HECKMAN, J. J. (1982). Models for the analysis of labor force dynamics. *Advances in Econometrics, 1*, 35–95.

GRANOVETTER, M. (1978). Threshold models of collective behavior. *American Journal of Sociology, 83*, 1420–1443.

GREENE, R. (1982). Tracking job growth in private industry. *Monthly Labor Review, 105*, 3–9.

HARRIS, L., and ASSOCIATES, INC. (1977). *The myth and reality of aging in America.* Washington, D.C.: The National Council on the Aging.

HARRIS, L., and ASSOCIATES, INC. (1979). *American attitudes toward pensions and retirement.* New York: Johnson and Higgins.

HARRIS, L., and ASSOCIATES, INC. (1981). *Aging in the eighties: America in transition.* Washington, D.C.: The National Council on the Aging, Inc.

HAUSER, R. M., and FEATHERMAN, D. L. (1974). Socioeconomic achievement of U.S. men, 1962 to 1972. *Science, 185*, 325–331.

HECKMAN, J. J., and MaCURDY, T. E. (1981). New methods for estimating labor supply functions: A survey. *Research in Labor Economics, 4*, 65–102.

HECKMAN, J. J. (1981). Heterogeneity and state dependence. In S. Rosen (Ed.), *Conference on Labor Markets.* Chicago: University of Chicago Press.

HECKMAN, J. J., and SINGER, B. (1982). The identification problem in econometric models for duration data. In W. Hildebrand (Ed.), *Advances in econometrics.* Cambridge: Cambridge University Press.

KAUFMAN, R. L., and SPILERMAN, S. (1982). The age structures of occupations and jobs. *American Journal of Sociology, 87*, 827–852.

KEYFITZ, N. (1973). Individual mobility in a stationary population. *Population Studies, 27*, 335–352.

KEYFITZ, N. (1982). Paradoxes of work and consumption in late twentieth century America. *Research in Human Capital and Development, 2*, 31–54.

KINGSON, E. R. (1981). The health of very early retirees. *Aging and Work, 4*, 11–21.

LANDO, M. E., CUTLER, R. R. and GAMBER, E. (1982). *1978 survey of disability and work: Data book.* Washington, D.C.: U.S. Government Printing Office.

MARCH, J. G., and SIMON, H. A. (1958). *Organizations.* New York: John Wiley & Sons, Inc.

MINCER, J. (1974). *Schooling, experience and earnings.* New York: National Bureau of Economic Research.

MYERS, R. J. (1982). Why do people retire from work early? *Social Security Bulletin, 45*, 10–14.

NADEL, S. F. (1957). *The theory of social structure.* London: Cohen & West.

PARNES, H., ADAMS, A. V., ADRISANI, P. J., KOHEN, P. J., ANDREW, I., and NESTEL, G. (1975). *The pre-retirement years*, Vol. 4. Manpower Research

and Development Monograph No. 15, U.S. Department of Labor. Washington, D.C.: U.S. Government Printing Office.
SAUVY, A. (1969). *General theory of population.* New York: Basic Books, Inc.
SAUVY, A. (1980). *La machine et le chomage: Le progres technique et l'emploi.* Paris: Dunod.
SCHOEN, R., and WOODROW, K. (1980). Labor force status life tables for the United States, 1972. *Demography, 17,* 297–322.
SCHULZ, J. H. (1976). *The economics of aging.* Belmont, CA: Wadsworth Publishing Co.
SMITH, S. J. (1982). New worklife estimates reflect changing profile of labor force. *Monthly Labor Review,* (March), 15–20.
SOMMERS, D., and ECK, A. (1977). Occupational mobility in the American labor force. *Monthly Labor Review, 100,* 3–19.
SOROKIN, P. A. (1927). *Social mobility.* New York: Harper & Bros.
STEWMAN, S. (1976a). Markov models of occupational mobility: Theoretical development and empirical support, part 1: Careers. *Journal of Mathematical Sociology, 4,* 201–245.
STEWMAN, S. (1976b) Markov models of occupational mobility: Theoretical development and empirical support, part II: Continuously operative job systems. *Journal of Mathematical Sociology, 4,* 427–478.
STEWMAN, S. (1982). Vacancy chains and Venturi tubes: The demand side of a demographic theory of labor markets, paper presented at the AAAS meetings, Washington, D.C., January.
STEWMAN, S., and KONDA, S. L. (1983). Careers and organizational labor markets: Demographic models of organizational behavior. *American Journal of Sociology, 88,* 637–685.
U.S. BUREAU OF THE CENSUS. (1973) *1970 census of population: Occupation and residence in 1965.* Washington, D.C.: U.S. Government Printing Office.
U.S. BUREAU OF THE CENSUS. (1975). *Historical statistics of the United States, colonial times to 1970.* Washington, D.C.: U.S. Government Printing Office.
U.S. BUREAU OF THE CENSUS. (1982). *Statistical abstract of the United States 1982–83* (103d ed.). Washington, D.C.: U.S. Government Printing Office.
U.S. BUREAU OF LABOR STATISTICS. (1966). *Employment and earnings,* (February). Washington, D.C.: U.S. Government Printing Office.
U.S. BUREAU OF LABOR STATISTICS. (1975). *Employment and earnings,* (January). Washington, D.C.: U.S. Government Printing Office.
U.S. BUREAU OF LABOR STATISTICS. (1980a). *Handbook of labor statistics 1980.* Bulletin 2070, Washington, D.C.: U.S. Government Printing Office.
U.S. BUREAU OF LABOR STATISTICS. (1980b). *Monthly labor review,* (January). Washington, D.C.: U.S. Government Printing Office.
U.S. BUREAU OF LABOR STATISTICS. (1981). *Employment and earnings,* (January). Washington, D.C.: U.S. Government Printing Office.
U.S. BUREAU OF LABOR STATISTICS. (1982). *Employment and earnings,* (January). Washington, D.C.: U.S. Government Printing Office.
U.S. BUREAU OF LABOR STATISTICS. (1982). *Occupational projections and training data,* Bulletin 2202. Washington, D.C.: U.S. Government Printing Office.
U.S. BUREAU OF LABOR STATISTICS. (1983). *Employment and earnings,* (January). Washington, D.C.: U.S. Government Printing Office.
WHITE, H. C. (1970). *Chains of opportunity: System models of mobility in organizations.* Cambridge, MA: Harvard University Press.

# 8

# THE HISTORICAL DECLINE IN LATE-LIFE LABOR FORCE PARTICIPATION IN THE UNITED STATES

Judith Treas

Two dominant explanations for the declining work rates of the elderly have co-existed for several decades. One explanation has emphasized structural changes in the economy which have reduced employment opportunities for the aged. The other explanation has focused on the arena of public policy and the increased availability of pensions that make retirement more attractive.

Declines in the work-force involvement of older American men may be traced as far back as the 1890s, an era that greatly predates the introduction of Social Security and the spread of private pensions. For this reason, conventional wisdom holds that early employment declines are attributable to industrial transformations of the economy, while more recent labor force developments are due largely to the financial inducements of retirement pensions. Buttressing this notion is the fact that corporate industrialism creates an economic surplus to finance income-maintenance programs as well as a labor surplus to require these programs.

From a practical and a theoretical standpoint, however, this chapter argues for reconsidering old-age pensions as probable determinants of our earliest retirement-based work force declines on record. First, discussions of retirement have failed to recognize Civil War pensions as an early and significant *de facto* system of old-age support in the United States. Second, the preoccupation with pensions as replacements for earnings has detracted from the role of pensions in the *institutionalization* of retirement. By institutionalization, I refer to the process by which (1) work-force withdrawal came to be normatively defined as appropriate behavior for the old, (2) a belief system compatible with work-force withdrawal was constructed and embraced as objective reality, and (3) structural arrangements supporting retirement were evolved. Little attention has been given to how the existence of special pensions for the elderly may have legitimated labor force withdrawal by establishing a practice of retirement, defining the aged (as a category) as too infirm to perform productive labor, introducing special economic provisions based on chronological age, and the like. Pensions may contribute to declines in late-life economic activity not only by giving people a financial alternative to work, but also by fostering cultural beliefs in retirement's respectability, desirability, feasibility and inevitability.

## THEORETICAL AND EMPIRICAL BACKGROUND

Both the structural and the earnings-replacement explanations of the rise in retirement rates are persuasive. Adherents to the structural argument have included both early social reformers (Epstein, 1928; Rubinow, 1913) and contemporary students of modernization (Cowgill, 1974; Cowgill and Holmes, 1972). According to this viewpoint, the march of industrialization renders older workers unemployable by introducing a factory system that emphasizes speed instead of experience; by continually demanding new job skills; by reducing opportunities for self-employment; and by giving rise to large-scale, bureaucratic work settings with inflexible retirement rules (Atchley, 1982). With modernization, generational job competition is fostered because longer lives mean that death is no longer as effective at creating job openings for the young by removing the old (Cowgill, 1974). The pension perspective, on the other hand, suggests that older workers have been enticed to retire by the growth of old-age pensions, particularly Social Security. Whether this expansion of old-age support represents an altruistic response to superannuation, a means of rationing jobs, or a tool of social control, it has certainly made it possible for millions of older persons to forego work in favor of leisure.

Impressive empirical evidence exists in support of both structural and pension influences on late-life labor force participation. Studies suggest that changes in industrial structure, particularly declines in agriculture, have acted to decrease the labor force participation rates of older men (Bowen and Finegan, 1969; Pampel, 1979). Similarly, numerous cross-sectional and panel studies have demonstrated that anticipated retirement income is a major factor behind individuals' decisions to retire or to keep on working (Barfield and Morgan, 1969; Boskin, 1977; Burkhauser and Tolly, 1978; Parnes, 1981).

As a force behind labor force declines, however, pensions are usually invoked only with reference to the last three or four decades. For example, Long (1958, 162–163) argues that pensions could not have accounted for late-life work force declines until fairly recently.

> Many elderly persons have dropped out of the labor force even when pensions were inadequate or nonexistent. They left in extremely large numbers in the United States during 1890–1910 and 1930–1934, when there were almost no government assistance and private pension plans....

To be sure, the turn-of-the-century declines in the economic activity of older males, the earliest national trend that can be documented, greatly predates Social Security, which did not pay out benefits until 1940. It also predates the post-World War II expansion of private pensions–indeed, in 1910, there were only about 60 corporate plans (Graebner, 1980, 133).

As argued below, however, the early declines do not predate the impressive system of Civil War pensions. Furthermore, such a pension system might prove to have been an important influence on retirement patterns, even if one concedes that transformations of the industrial structure were pivotal in shaping early stages of late-life labor force withdrawal, and that the availability of pensions as earnings replacements has emerged as the force behind labor force declines in recent decades. Pampel and Weiss (1983) note that initial declines in the work rates of the old may result from economic changes which "push" older workers out of the labor force, but financial inducements to retirement (that is, "pull" factors) have become more significant as retirement has become more fully institutionalized. This argument assigns an important role to early pension efforts. Even if such systems do not serve initially as financial inducements to behavioral changes in late-life labor supply, they warrant attention as components of the institutionalization of retirement.

This chapter takes a closer look at the institutionalization of retirement in America. In pointing to the importance of Civil War pensions as a *de facto* system of old-age support, the paper asks whether the policies of the federal nation-state served to reinforce any tendency of the changing economy to dislocate older workers. We hypothesize that the evolution of veterans' pensions may have served to cushion work force withdrawal and/or to legitimate chronological age as a reason for not working. The first section of this chapter describes the evolution and scope of military pensions in the United States. After charting late-life labor force trends, the second section presents a preliminary analysis of changes in the gainful employment of older men in the states and territories of the United States between 1890 and 1920. In addition to considering the effects on work rates of industrial structure, generational competition for jobs, and the availability of alternative sources of labor, the analysis considers whether existing data on each state's experience with military pensions can add to the explanation of turn-of-the-century changes in the labor supply of older men.

## CIVIL WAR PENSIONS: A BRIEF HISTORY

Civil War pension legislation began in 1862 as a fundamental law applicable to all claims for pensions arising from deaths and disabilities due to military service after March 4, 1861 (Glasson, 1918). The law provided for those who became permanently disabled as a direct consequence of military duty. Also protected were the dependents of soldiers who died from injuries received or illnesses contracted while in military service. The law, of course, applied to Union servicemen, not to those of the Southern Confederacy. Pensions were graded by military rank and by degree of disability, with a totally disabled private receiving eight dollars per month. Higher statutory rates were allowed for severe disabilities such as the loss of both hands. Gradual liberalization of the law expanded the list of severe disabilities and introduced functional criteria by which general health conditions might be judged. Thus, $25 per month was granted for disabilities requiring the regular aid and attendance of another person, $20 per month was paid for the incapacity to perform (even lighter kinds of) manual labor, and $15 per month was allocated for disability *equivalent* to the loss of a hand or foot.

Despite the modest beginnings of invalid pensions, the late nineteenth century witnessed an impressive expansion and liberalization of eligibility and benefits. This growth may be traced to bipartisan arrears legislation of 1879, which was designed to remedy certain inequities by providing substantial lump-sum back payments for veterans who belatedly filed claims (Sanders, 1980). This legislation encouraged a flood of new claimants. Growing ranks of former soldiers were mobilized behind the Grand Army of the Republic (GAR), a special-interest group that lobbied for still further extension of veterans' benefits. Grover Cleveland, elected in 1884 with the support of the Democratic Solid South, was a temporary impediment to expansion. Cleveland vetoed hundreds of private pension bills in addition to a Dependent Pension Bill designed to grant pensions to disabled veterans without questioning the service-relatedness of their disability (Billington, 1974, 49–51). The Republican Party, however, was more than willing to enter into a political marriage with veterans of the Republic. In return for favored treatment for the cause of former Union soldiers, Republicans cultivated a loyal political constituency while finding a way to reduce an unpopular federal budget surplus resulting from high protective tariffs (Sanders, 1980; Skocpol and Ikenberry, 1982).

Liberalization of benefits transformed Civil War pensions from a limited system of relief for those with war-related disabilities to a system of old-age support targeting middle-class and elite working-class aged. Since the service-relatedness of a condition was difficult to establish, legislation focused on this eligibility requirement. In 1890 a new law provided that pensions be paid to all persons who had served 90 days or more in the military or naval service of the United States during the Civil War, who had been honorably discharged, and who suffered from "a mental or physical disability of a permanent character, not the result of their own vicious habits, which incapacitates them from the performance of manual labor in such a degree as to render them unable to earn a support" (Glasson, 1918, 234). Since this law no longer required that a disability have a service origin and since it demanded only an incapacity for difficult manual labor, the pension committee of the GAR was able to boast that the new law offered pensions to "all the survivors of the war whose conditions of health are not practically perfect" (Sanders, 1980, 142).

Since young men fight wars, old age had not been a concern when the general law was drafted in 1862. By 1890, however, 9 percent of Civil War veterans were age 65 or older (U.S. Census Office, 1897, 573). Although there was no mention of age in the 1890 law, it was the practice of the Pension Bureau to administer the act as a service-and-age law. Examining physicians were instructed by the Commissioner of Pensions as follows:

> A claimant who has reached the age of 75 years is allowed the maximum rate for senility alone, even where there are no special pensionable disabilities. A claimant who has attained the age of 65 years is allowed at least the minimum rate, unless he appears to have unusual vigor and ability for the performance of manual labor in one of that age. The effect of partial senility should be considered with other infirmities, where there are such, and the aggregate incapacity stated (Glasson, 1918, 243).

In 1904, when the bulk of veterans were in their sixties and seventies, President Theodore Roosevelt reiterated this policy in Executive Order No. 78, which provided that a declaration of old age was sufficient evidence of disability even in the absence of other disabling conditions. Thus, a healthy 62-year-old was considered one-half disabled in performing manual labor and was entitled to $6 per month. A 65-year-old was entitled to $8, a 68-year-old to $10, and a 70-year-old to $12 (Glasson, 1918, 247).[1] Legislation of 1906 and 1907 recognized age as a disability while raising the payment schedule. Subsequent legislation also led to higher benefits.

In short, chronological age itself came to be proof of poor health and incapacity. This negative evaluation of old age was consistent with the contemporary theories of economics, medicine, and scientific management which underpinned age discrimination in the workplace (Achenbaum, 1978; Fischer, 1977; Graebner, 1980). Far from contesting this unflattering characterization of late life, groups serving the interests of older veterans (such as the GAR) sought to promote this equation of chronological age and physical deterioration.

The result of the liberalization of military pensions was a patronage system which rivaled in magnitude more universal old-age insurance programs. As social reformer I. M. Rubinow (1913, 404-405) wryly noted:

> (I)t is idle to speak of a popular system of old age pensions as a radical departure from American traditions, when our pension roll numbers several thousand more names than that of Great Britain. It is preposterous to claim that the cost of such a pension would be excessive when the cost of our pension is over $160,000,000, or more than three times as great as that of the British pension system. In the face of such a cost, it is childish to consider the system of war pensions as a sentimental problem only, and to speak of the millions spent for war pensions as the cost of the "Civil War." We are clearly dealing here with an economic measure which aims to solve the problems of dependent aged and widowhood.

The magnitude of this federal undertaking cannot be overemphasized. Although earlier wars had spawned military pensioners, restrictive legislation had limited their numbers. It is estimated, for example, that less than 4 percent of Americans over the age of 60 were receiving federal military pensions in 1840 (Achenbaum, 1978, 84). In 1913, on the other hand, federal veteran's benefits were paid to

[1]To be sure, there is no reliable evidence on which to gauge the actual incidence of impairment among the elderly in this era. Although 1900 was marked by lower life expectancy than today, most of this differential was due to the incidence of acute illness rather than the chronic conditions associated with disability in old age. Today, 44 percent of Americans 65 and older report a health condition limiting activity (U.S. Bureau of the Census, forthcoming, Table 6-3). Although it may be argued that these elders are healthier than those in previous generations, it may also be hypothesized that today's aged have higher levels of impairment: chronic conditions such as heart disease, diabetes, and high blood pressure may be more common today because medical advances permit the survival of persons with these health problems. In short, there is little reason to believe that the Civil War pension rule defining all persons 62 and older as disabled was an accurate assessment of the health status of the group as a whole.

roughly two thirds of native white men 65 and older and living outside the South, according to estimates by Rubinow (1913, 404).

As Figure 8-1 demonstrates, nearly a million veterans and survivors were on the military pension lists at the turn of the century. Not counting Alaska, one in every 77 persons in the continental United States drew a federal pension in 1900 (Glasson, 1918, 226). After a peak in 1902, the sheer numbers of pensioners began to decline as death claimed old soldiers. Outlays for pensions, however, continued to climb until 1913, because benefits were raised both by legislation and by the aging of the veteran population within a system where higher benefits were pegged to higher ages. To place pension dollars into perspective, it is helpful to note that pensions made up 42 percent of all federal expenditures in 1893 (U.S. Bureau of the Census, 1975, 1106-1149).

To place the administrative component of the pension system in perspective, we might note that the Bureau of Pensions was heralded by its commissioner in 1891 as the "largest executive bureau in the world" (Raum, 1958, 211). With 2000 clerks in Washington, 3800 examining physicians across the United States, and 400 agents who issued payments from 18 regional offices, few would dispute this claim. In short, federal military pensions represented an extraordinary federal effort, one which cushioned old age for a very substantial minority of aged Americans.

It is also worth noting that pension recipients were an economically priviledged segment of the population. By and large, federal military pensions went to white native Americans who were landed farmers or members of the urban middle

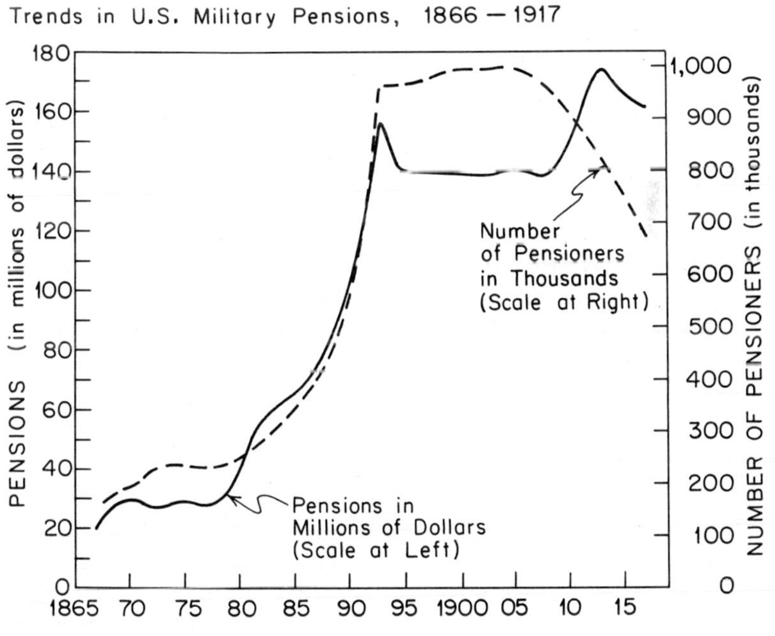


**FIGURE 8-1. Trends in U.S. Military Pensions, 1866-1917**

or upper working classes (Skocpol and Ikenberry, 1982). Pensions did not go to blacks, nor to the industrial working class founded on immigrants who had arrived since the Civil War. Also excluded were veterans of the Confederacy. Although southern states made some provisions for Confederate veterans (Lubove, 1968, 125; Squier, 1912, 231-232), the aged in the South were disadvantaged by the Civil War legacy of economic stagnation in the region. As Rubinow (1913, 408) lamented, federal military pensions did not go to those older persons who needed assistance the most. Rather, these moneys went to relatively affluent Americans, many of whom could probably lay claim in retirement to savings and family assistance to supplement their veterans' pensions.

From the perspective of the institutionalization of retirement, the Civil War pension system may well have played a pivotal role. As an institutional structure, the system was a highly visible, bureaucratic behemoth. It evolved to provide a uniform, federal response to problems of old-age dependency among a "respectable" and "deserving" segment of Americans. By basing pension eligibility on the attainment of a given chronological age, the system probably fostered a new age-consciousness in a society in which calendar age *per se* had been of little significance. By assuming all old men were disabled, the system legitimated late-life labor force withdrawal and contributed to the negative evaluation of the aged's capacities, thus perhaps undermining the elderly worker's position in the work place. If, as Myles (1984, 16) contends, "superannuating elderly workers at a fixed age without regard to physical or mental capacity" was an essential requisite in the social creation of old age, Civil War pensions loom large. These initial influences upon everyday understandings of old age must certainly have contributed to norms, expectations, and conventions of late-life economic activity. The pension income may also have had a direct influence on the employment status of pensioners.

Although military pensions were part and parcel of old age for many Americans, the adequacy of benefits is an important issue in gauging their possible short-run influence on late-life work and retirement decisions. In other words, could older persons afford to retire on Civil War pensions? One indicator of adequacy is the replacement ratio of the average federal military pension to the estimated average money earnings of factory workers. This ratio appears in Table 1 for selected years. Although varying over the period, this ratio stood at .38 in 1914. This is

**TABLE 1. Replacement Ratios for Civil War Pensions in Selected Years**

| | 1899 | 1904 | 1909 | 1914 |
|---|---|---|---|---|
| Average annual pension | $140 | $142 | $220 | $220 |
| Average annual earnings of factory workers | $446 | $483 | $557 | $576 |
| Replacement ratio | .31 | .29 | .29 | .38 |

Sources: Paul F. Brissenden, ***Earnings of Factory Workers 1899 to 1927: An Analysis of Payroll Statistics.*** Census Monographs X. (Washington, D.C.: Goverment Printing Office, 1929). William H. Glasson. ***Federal Military Pensions in the United States.*** (New York: Oxford University Press, 1918, 273).

somewhat below the .44 replacement ratio which Social Security currently affords the average earner (Hendricks and Storey, 1982), but it does suggest that pensions were not set at levels that were trivial by the wage standards of the day.

As is the case today, pensions alone were likely to offer insufficient income to get by on. Since pensioners were largely middle-class and upper working-class, however, they were probably in a better position than many older Americans to draw on savings, assets, and family support. Thus, Civil War pensions may have provided the extra margin of comfort and security that permitted retirement. To be sure, the receipt of Civil War pensions does not seem to have required that the veteran pass a strict retirement test. Many may have continued to work while drawing a pension. Nonetheless, research on older workers today suggests that the existence of a retirement or earnings test may have little effect on retirement decisions (Tracy, 1983). It is the level of expected retirement income that seems to be crucial. The Kansas farmer, growing too frail for the demands of farming, may have found that a few extra dollars from his U.S. veteran's pension tipped the balance toward a retirement decision.

## LABOR FORCE PARTICIPATION: TRENDS AND ANALYSIS

Let us begin by sketching in broad brush the work force participation trends of older persons in the United States. It is widely agreed that retirement was a rarity among early Americans (Atchley, 1982). The 1890 Census of the United States was the first to document the economic activity of older Americans at the national level. That census reported that 74 percent of men 65 and older were gainfully occupied (U.S. Census Office, 1897, Tables 3 and 83). Elderly blacks were more likely than the typical aged to be gainfully engaged; aged immigrants were less likely. By the 1920 census, however, gainful employment for aged males had slipped to 60 percent (U.S. Bureau of the Census, 1923, Table 15).[2]

In 1890, older working men were overrepresented in agriculture and the professions and underrepresented in domestic service, commerce, and manufacturing; 60 percent of all older working men were employed in the category labeled "agriculture, fisheries, and mining" (U.S. Census Office, 1897, cxxiii) as compared with 44 percent of all male workers. Older workers were certainly left behind in agriculture as economic activity shifted to urban industries. In farming and the pro-

[2] It is important to emphasize that the *gainful employment* concept differs considerably from the labor force definition used in the 1940 and subsequent censuses of population. Between 1890 and 1930, census schedules required that an occupation be stated for each person 10 years of age and older who was usually gainfully employed. Gainfully employed persons were, therefore, those for whom an occupation was reported. The concept is quite vague. It is very likely that some newly retired and permanently disabled persons reported a former occupation, while others who actually had a job did not, because they did not consider themselves to be engaged in their usual line of work (Walther, 1975, 35). In its evaluation of the 1930 Census of Population, for example, the Census Bureau estimated that there were 472,000 recently retired and disabled Americans who reported a gainful occupation, but who would not have been numbered among the labor force—that is, among persons working or looking for work (Durand, 1968, 198). Therefore, labor force participation trends for early decades in Table 2 have been adjusted downward from gainful employment statistics for comparability with the 1940 census (Durand, 1968).

fessions, however, self-employment also offered older men the opportunity to keep working, perhaps at a reduced pace.

The 1890 census furnishes little evidence of age discrimination. Older working men were less likely than their juniors to have reported a bout of unemployment during the previous year. Even in manufacturing, where the forces of industrialization would seem most likely to have pushed out the elderly, 24 percent unemployment among the aged was only marginally higher than the 22 percent reported for the prime-age workers, 25 to 34 years old (U.S. Office of the Census, 1897, 744).

Table 2 represents labor force participation trends from 1890 to 1980. The declines in men's rates are striking. Although 68 percent of men 65 or older were estimated to be in the labor force in 1890, only 19 percent were working or looking for work in 1980. Over half this decline occurred before implementation of Social Security in 1940. Indeed, the Depression of the 1930s had a devastating impact on the employment of the elderly. In comparison, the work rates of older men held steady during the 1940s due to the World War II mobilization of such "secondary workers" as the aged, teenagers, and married women. Subsequent drops coincided with further expansion of eligibility and benefits under public and private retirement plans.

The labor market experience of elderly women is distinctly different from that of men. Their labor force participation rates had stabilized at low levels for much of the period under study. Only in recent decades did the late-life labor force

**TABLE 2. Labor Force Participation Rates for Americans 65 and Older by Sex: 1890–1980.**

| | Men | Women |
|---|---|---|
| 1890 (June) | 68.3 | 7.6 |
| 1900 (June) | 63.1 | 8.3 |
| 1920 (January) | 55.6 | 7.3 |
| 1930 (April) | 54.0 | 7.3 |
| 1940 (April) | 41.8 | 6.1 |
| 1950 (April) | 41.4 | 7.8 |
| 1960 (April) | 30.5 | 10.3 |
| 1970 (April) | 24.5 | 10.0 |
| 1980 (March) | 19.1 | 8.1 |

Sources: U.S. Bureau of the Census, ***Historical Statistics of the United States, Colonial Times to 1970.*** Bicentennial Edition, Part 1, (Washington, D.C.: Government Printing Office, 1975). 132.
U.S. Bureau of the Census, "Population Profile of the United States: 1980," ***Current Population Reports*** Series P-20, No. 363. (Washington, D.C.: Government Printing Office, 1981).

participation of older women rise slightly. Due to secular increases in the labor force involvement for mature women (Oppenheimer, 1970), each new generation of women has moved into old age with a higher proportion who are actually working. The cohort phenomenon has apparently offset the trend to earlier retirement among working women—a trend that became clear during the decade of the 1970s (Treas, 1981). Since the level and direction of trends in older women's work force participation have probably been dictated more by the demand for female labor than by the situation of older workers, we limit attention in the analysis which follows to the employment trends for older men.

Although the pattern of declining work force involvement for older men is clear, the determinants of the initial decline remain a matter for investigation. In this analysis, we consider change between 1890 and 1920 in the percent of men 65 and older who were gainfully employed.

While the period of study is dictated by the availability of data, this era is of substantive interest. Men's work rates would decline more precipitously in some later decades, but the roots of these developments are certainly to be seen in the 1890–1920 period. Indeed, in 1920, levels of gainful employment among men 65 and older stood at only 82 percent of what they had been thirty years earlier. Furthermore, the period may be viewed as a pivotal one in the history of labor and the development of the economy.

As Gordon, Edwards, and Reich (1982) point out, wage labor, in supplanting slaves and independent producers, had become the "normal" condition of workers by the 1890s. As the rural landless, bankrupt craftsmen, women, children, immigrants, and others swelled the ranks of wage earners, labor could no longer be considered to be in short supply. That women could succeed children (or the foreign-born displace native labor) within industries suggests that the stage was set for the displacement of older workers by the young. In fact, during the 1890–1920 period, mechanization, together with the simplification and segmentation of tasks, increased the potential substitutability of workers.

The pacing and organization of work became increasingly a prerogative of management, implying fewer opportunities for the restructuring of work to accommodate the special needs of aged workers. As corporate mergers led to "monopoly capitalism" (Baran and Sweezy, 1966), the scale of production expanded and firm size increased. More formalized personnel relations were called for by the bigger scale of enterprises, and bureacratized work rules precluded personalized employment arrangements for the elderly.

To be sure, the transformation of industrial production and the reorganization of work were not complete by 1920. The era was a transitional one. The family farm, the small business, and the independent craftsman were still to be found. Many older Americans may have hung onto their jobs, even as the most modern sectors of the economy invented mandatory retirement, experimented with private pensions, and embraced "scientific" views of the elderly's incompetence. That structural transformations were uneven, that cultural patterns of late-life activity lagged structural changes, is not to deny that some changes in the work force behavior of the old may have been evident before retirement itself was entirely institutionalized.

In the current investigation, the unit of analysis is the states and territories of the continental United States, including the District of Columbia and excluding

Alaska. As we have indicated, 1890 presents the earliest available information on economic activity for older men in the United States, and comparable data are not published again by state until 1920. To be sure, comparability between any two censuses is affected by changes in the format of questions, the instructions to interviewers, the date of enumeration, and the social and economic conditions at the time of the survey (Miller and Brainerd, 1957). No attempt has been made to adjust the data for greater comparability because, as Lebergott (1964, 385) has argued, "(t)he Census in general should not be adjusted except where it is clearly in error as judged by long-term relationships or external data."

The analysis is based on ordinary least-squares regression. The dependent variable is the percent of men 65 and older gainfully employed in 1920. This variable ranged from a high of 78.9 for Mississippi to a low of 43.8 for Nebraska. Since our interest is in change, we include as an independent variable in our model the percent of older men gainfully employed in 1890 (EMP90). By introducing a baseline level of employment, we are essentially studying changes in employment rates. In evaluating other independent variables in the model, we are asking what their effects are on 1920 gainful employment rates, given the rates extant in 1890. In evaluating the regression coefficient for 1890, we are considering a host of work force determinants, unique to each state, which are not embodied by the other variables in the model. We expect, of course, that 1890 employment rates will be positively associated with gainful employment thirty years later.

Given their prominence in national life, the role of Civil War pensions is of considerable interest. One rough operationalization of this variable is dollars per capita received from federal pensions by the states and territories in 1910 (PEN). This variable ranged from $4.55 in the District of Columbia to 19 cents in South Carolina. An alternative operationalization is that of United States veterans as a percent of the male population (VET). Although 6.7 percent of males in Kansas were veterans, only one half a percent in Alabama and North Carolina were veterans of the United States.

Behind the inclusion of both versions of this variable is the hypothesis that the federal policy of pensioning aged soldiers promoted the decline in economic activity by older men. Admittedly, most veterans of the Civil War were dead by 1920. Thus the pension variable does not permit a test of the hypothesis that retirement income enabled older workers to retire. It is possible, however, that states which felt a substantial infusion of military pensions were, all things considered, those which more thoroughly *institutionalized* the practice of late-life withdrawal from gainful employment. The notion that old age equals incapacity—made explicit in pension policy—may have been more widely adopted as a norm by workers and employers in states with substantial exposure to the federal military pensions. If these pensions enabled earlier generations of older workers to retire, it is possible that employers turned to alternative sources of labor which would have continued to serve them in good stead in 1920. To be sure, the relentless march of modernization, industrialization, and demographic change may have provided the impetus to initial declines in economic activity among older workers, but it is worth considering whether Civil War pensions altered aggregate behavior in the long run.

To return to our earlier arguments, declines in late-life work force involvement have been attributed to structural changes in the economy as well as to pension development by the polity. The rapid industrialization that characterized the period under study is widely regarded as having worked to the disadvantage of the older worker. The new skills required by new technologies, the premium placed on speed, and the standardization of work tasks made it more difficult for the older worker to compete. The rationalization of personnel relations led to the introduction of mandatory retirement rules in industry, particularly as a response to labor's demands for a recognition of seniority rights (Haber, 1978). Reduced opportunities for self-employment, especially in agriculture, placed older workers at the mercy of the new demands of industry and employers.

To gauge each state's level of industrialization, we use the percent of gainfully employed persons engaged in manufacturing and mechanical industries in 1920 (MFG). This figure varied from 9 percent in North Dakota to 54 percent in Connecticut. We hypothesize that higher levels of industrialization will be associated with greater declines in the employment of elderly men. Conversely, we anticipate a negative relation between the work declines and the percent gainfully employed in agriculture, forestry, and animal husbandry (AGRI). This alternative measure of industrial structure ranged from zero in the District of Columbia to 70 percent in Mississippi.

In the modernization argument, a concomitant of industrialization affecting the status of the aged is the growth of the older population itself. Improvements in life expectancy, coupled with lower fertility, mean that the percentage of elderly in the population increases, leading to greater intergenerational competition for jobs in the work place (Cowgill, 1974). In our model, we measure this competition in terms of the percent of males 10 years of age and older who were ages 65 and above in 1920 (GEN). This measure considers how numerous the aged were relative to all males who, by census criteria of the day, were old enough to be counted among the gainfully employed. Although the figure for Wyoming is only 3.4 percent, 10.2 percent of Maine's male work force eligibles were 65 and older. According to the modernization thesis, we would expect the generation variable to be positively related to late-life employment declines.

To be sure, aged workers in the early twentieth century may also have faced competition from immigrants. For this reason, we include foreign-born whites as a percent of the total population in 1920 (IMM), anticipating a positive relation with late-life employment declines. In addition to taking account of job competition, this variable sharpens up our per capita pension indicator by controlling for the fact that the pension variable is depressed in states with large shares of post-Civil War immigrants. Since blacks did not typically receive Civil War pensions either, we consider them as a percent of the total state population in 1920 (NEG). It is also important to include this variable because the higher late-life labor force participation of blacks inflates the overall gainful employment rates for older men in states with significant minority populations. We expect less decline in work rates for states where blacks constituted a large share of population. The compositional differences in state populations were substantial. For example, more than half of Mississippi's population was black, but only half a percent were foreign-born whites. In contrast, 28 percent of Massachusetts' people were foreign-born whites, while merely 1 percent were black.

Lastly, prosperous states may have witnessed greater declines in the economic activity of the elderly than their poorer counterparts, if only because wealth may facilitate private savings and public as well as private relief efforts for the indigent elderly. As our indicator, we take the state's per capita income in 1920 (INC). Although South Carolina averaged only $295, the figures for California, Nevada, and the District of Columbia were all above $1,000.

The results of the analysis appear in Table 3. For the total and the non-Confederate United States, three equations are estimated. In order to test the sensitivity of the results to the variables included, different equations use different operationalizations of industrialization and of the scope of veterans' benefits.

Despite the intuitive appeal of the argument that a massive system of veterans' pensions contributed to the gradual institutionalization of retirement, the analysis offers support only for the null hypothesis that military pensions had *no* long-run effect on elderly males' levels of economic activity. Since none of the coefficients prove statistically significant, there is no evidence that states with greater exposure to the Civil War pension system saw greater declines in the gainful employment of elderly men than did states with fewer U.S. veterans and fewer pension dollars.

To be sure, the poor performance of the pension variables may be due to the inadequacies of the analysis, rather than to the unsoundness of the thesis. The per capita pension measure, for example, is not specific to the older male population. Furthermore, the analysis speaks to the long-run institutionalization of retirement, but the aggregate level of the data means that it is impossible to address the important question of whether individuals who received pensions actually quit working. Indeed, any income effect of pensions on retirement would have dissipated by 1920, because most veterans were dead by then. Although the present analysis does not

**TABLE 3. Determinants of Gainful Employment; United States[a], 1920**

| | CONTINENTAL U.S. | | | NON-CONFEDERATE U.S. | | |
|---|---|---|---|---|---|---|
| EMP90 | .86* | .91* | .80* | .93* | .96* | .89* |
| PEN | 2.01 | 1.01 | | 1.78 | 1.89 | |
| VET | | | .53 | | | .33 |
| AGRI | | -.31* | | | -.39* | |
| MFG | .32* | | .33* | .31** | | .32** |
| INC | -.01 | -.02* | -.00 | -.01 | -.02** | -.00 |
| GEN | -2.00** | -.95 | -1.34 | -1.70 | -.96 | -1.00 |
| IMM | -.06 | .07 | -.16 | .03 | -.03 | -.04 |
| NEG | .19** | .18** | .19** | .38 | .06 | .44 |
| Intercept | -2.60 | 15.37 | -1.31 | -10.53 | 15.21 | -10.18 |
| $R^2$ | .71 | .76 | .70 | .54 | .65 | .52 |
| N | 49 | 49 | 49 | 38 | 38 | 38 |

[a]including the District of Columbia and excluding Alaska
* $p<.01$
** $p<.05$

Sources: EMP90 (U.S. Census Office, 1897, Tables 3 and 83); PEN (Glasson, 1918, 269); VET (U.S. Census Office, 1897, clxxiv, 24-37); AGRI, PEN (U.S. Bureau of the Census, 1923, Table II); INC (Leven, 1925, 256); GEN (U.S. Bureau of the Census, 1923, Table 15); IMM, NEG (U.S. Bureau of the Census, 1923, Table 22).

indicate that the Civil War pension system left a legacy of institutionalized changes in aggregate employment practices, we cannot discount the possibility that pension income affected the retirement decision of veterans who received benefits.

The results do offer strong statistical support for the industrialization thesis. As predicted, declines in the employment of aged males were greater in states with a large manufacturing sector and smaller in states where agriculture held sway. These results are not merely a consequence of the income returns to industrial development since they hold when state income is controlled. Nor do they seem to be an artifact of the Confederacy's retarded economic development since they are replicated when these southern states are dropped from the analysis. Instead, it seems that work opportunities in old age were limited by the sectoral composition of the economy.

Although industrial structure appears to have been influencing the demand for older workers, there is little or no indication that late-life employment rates were affected by labor supply factors. I had argued (in the tradition of modernization theory) that work rates would show more precipitous drops when the aged constituted a larger share of the population. Contrary to expectations, the coefficients for the generational job-competition variable were negative across the six equations, and only one coefficient was statistically significant. The modernization argument assumes that the visibility of an aging population promotes generational job competition so that the aged are eventually squeezed out of the work force. The results of this analysis suggest that causation may run in the other direction. A scarcity of jobs may lead to an aging population for states where the young have moved on to better job prospects elsewhere, leaving existing opportunities to their entrenched elders.

Although immigrants certainly furnished a remarkable pool of surplus labor in the early years of this century, there is no evidence that they displaced older workers. The coefficients for the foreign-born population are statistically insignificant and unstable in sign. Although the percent of blacks is shown to be significant for the total United States, this variable seems to be tapping a general distinction between the old Confederacy and the rest of the nation. When the eleven Confederate states are dropped from the analysis, the race variable is no longer significant. In sum, late-life employment rates were not responsive to the presence of alternative sources of labor that might displace the old.

Lastly, we note that state per capita income is sensitive to the specification of the model, achieving statistical significance only when the agricultural indicator is employed as a measure of industrial structure. Although we had reasoned that retirement would flourish in prosperous states, the negative coefficients suggest that these states saw the least decline in late-life employment rates. Perhaps the very prosperity of such states created a demand for labor that made older workers more attractive.

In sum, the empirical results tend to be ambiguous, often deviating from theoretical expectations and proving sensitive to the specification of the model and the universe. The clearest finding, however, is that the industrial transformation of the economy is linked to late-life work force declines. That the best predictor of a state's 1920 employment rate was its rate 30 years earlier implies that the patterning of work and retirement is not entirely new, but rather an extension of previous norms of late-life economic roles.

## CONCLUSION

There is convincing evidence that the 1890–1920 drop in gainful employment among older men was a response to the distribution of the work force across industrial sectors. Whether we consider the entire United States or the non-Confederate segment, the industrialization thesis is upheld. Despite every indication that federal military pensions represented a federal undertaking of unprecedented magnitude, we are unable to reject the null hypothesis that veterans' benefits were of no long-run consequence to the economic activity of older Americans. In other words, the results of the analysis are consistent with the notion that historical declines in the labor force participation of older men were initiated by the industrial transformation of the economy, rather than by public innovations in pension policy leading to an institutionalization of retirement.

Contemporary public policy may certainly be informed by the historical developments discussed here. Today, for example, there is considerable interest in extending the work life in order to insure the fiscal integrity of pension systems, guard against a potential labor shortage, and promote meaningful social roles for an aging population. Worthy though these goals may be, this paper suggests that the trend toward earlier and earlier retirement may be difficult to stem. Late-life work force participation rates have been declining for almost a century. Since 1890 gainful employment rates so accurately predict their counterparts in 1920, it seems likely that the processes leading to older Americans' declining work force involvement may have been underway even *before* 1890. In other words, retirement has a lengthy and impressive history of institutionalization, and this institutional inertia may well continue to support retirement practices for years to come. Neither can there be any doubt that the United States has moved away from the economic structure which was most hospitable to older workers. Since farming and self-employment will never again dominate the American economy, the future of late-life employment will probably depend on older workers finding a place in the expanding service sector.

The discussion of Civil War pensions also underscores the point that old-age support programs in the United States have been rooted in interest group politics, shaped by a suspicion of the dole, and wrapped in the flag. Even today, old-age programs may be vulnerable to shifts in perceptions of the aged, their needs, and their worthiness. The equation of old age with incapacity is often denounced by advocates of the aged. While such stereotypes or generalities may act to exclude the able elderly from some spheres of life, these images of the aged as deserving unfortunates have justified special treatment of older persons in a nation slow to guarantee a minimum standard of living to all. Civil War pensions were justified on the grounds that the aged were too impaired to work. In securing old-age support for elderly veterans, military pensions reinforced the ageist ideology displacing the elderly from the work place. Current efforts to remove age barriers to employment have stressed the continuing capacities of older workers. In the long run, however, rosy assessments of the health and functioning of the aged might run the risk of undermining public sympathy for old-age support.

Efforts to end mandatory retirement have emphasized that ability, rather than age *per se*, is the best criterion for continued employment. This line of reasoning would also call for awarding retirement income on the basis of capacity to work instead of chronological age. There is an appealing logic to a social insurance program that would protect individuals from the contingencies of old age instead of rewarding them for merely growing older. As the case of Civil War pensions demonstrates, definitions of disability are themselves subject to political and fiscal considerations. Criteria for assessing disability for Civil War veterans were progressively liberalized in light of a budgetary surplus and partisan concerns. In turn, complaints of fraud, abuse, and mounting costs led to calls for tightening up military benefits. While recent Social Security legislation proves that age standards of eligibility are not inviolate, the administration of disability programs is even more vulnerable to political manipulation. Both retirement practices and social institutions which support them are subject to change and redefinition. The history of Civil War pensions and late-life employment declines suggests that such changes are often unwitting, constrained by the evolution of the economic structure, and questionably responsive (in the short run) to policy manipulation.

## REFERENCES

ACHENBAUM, W. (1978). *Old age in the new land: The American experience since 1890.* Baltimore: Johns Hopkins University Press.

ATCHLEY, R. C. (1982). Retirement as a social institution. *Annual Review of Sociology, 8,* 263–287.

BARAN, P., and SWEEZY, P. (1966). *Monopoly capital: An essay on the American economic and social order.* New York: Monthly Review Press.

BARFIELD, R. W., and MORGAN, J. (1969). *Early retirement: The decision and the experience.* Ann Arbor, MI: Institute for Social Research.

BILLINGTON, R. A. (1974). *American history after 1865.* Totowa, NJ: Littlefield, Adams, and Co.

BOSKIN, M. (1977). Social security and retirement decisions. *Economic Inquiry, 15,* (January), 1–25.

BOWEN, W. G., and FINEGAN, T. A. (1969). *The economics of labor force participation.* Princeton, NJ: Princeton University Press.

BRISSENDEN, P. F. (1929). *Earnings of factory workers 1899 to 1927: An analysis of payroll statistics.* Census Monographs X. Washington, D.C.: Government Printing Office.

BURKHAUSER, R., and TOLLEY, S. (1978). Older Americans and market work. *The Gerontologist, 18,* (October), 449–453.

COWGILL, D. (1974). Aging and modernization: A revision of the theory. In J. F. Gubrium (Ed.), *Late life. Communities and environmental policy.* Springfield, IL: Charles C. Thomas.

COWGILL, D. O., and HOLMES, L. D. (1972). *Aging and modernization.* New York: Appleton-Century-Crofts.

DURAND, J. D. (1968). *The labor force in the United States, 1890–1960.* New York: Gorson and Beach Science Publishers.

EPSTEIN, A. (1928). *The Challenge of the Aged.* New York: Vanguard Press.

FISCHER, D. H. (1977). *Growing old in America.* New York: Oxford University Press.

GLASSON, W. H. (1918). *Federal military pensions in the United States.* New York: Oxford University Press.

GORDON, D. M., EDWARDS, R., and REICH, M. (1982). *Segmented work, divided workers: The historical transformation of labor in the United States.* Cambridge: Cambridge University Press.

GRAEBNER, W. (1980). *A history of retirement: The meaning and function of an American institution.* New Haven, CN: Yale University Press.

HABER, C. (1978). Mandatory retirement in nineteenth century America: The conceptual basis for a new work cycle. *Journal of Social History, 12,* 77–96.

HENDRICKS, G. L., and STOREY, J. R. (1982). Economics of retirement. In M. H. Morrison (Ed.), *Economics of aging: The future of retirement.* New York, Van Nostrand Reinhold, 136–190.

LEBERGOTT, S. (1964). *Manpower in economic growth: The American record since 1800.* New York: McGraw-Hill.

LEVEN, M. (1925). *Income in the various states: Its sources and distribution, 1919, 1920, and 1921.* New York: National Bureau of Economic Research.

LONG, C. D. (1958). *The labor force under changing income and employment.* Princeton, NJ: Princeton University Press.

LUBOVE, R. (1968). *The struggle for social security, 1900–1935.* Cambridge, MA: Harvard University Press.

MILLER, A. R., and BRAINERD, C. P. (1957). Labor force estimates. In S. S. Kuznets and D. S. Thomas (Eds.), *Methodological considerations and reference tables.* Philadelphia, PA: American Philosophical Society.

MYLES, J. (1984). *Old age in the welfare state: The political economy of public pensions.* Boston: Little Brown.

OPPENHEIMER, V. K. (1970). *The female labor force in the United States: Demographic and economic factors governing its growth and changing composition.* Berkeley, CA: University of California.

PAMPEL, F. C. (1979). Changes in the labor force participation and income of the aged in the United States, 1947–1976. *Social Problems, 27,* no. 2 (December), 125–142.

PAMPEL, F. C., and WEISS, J. A. (1983). Economic development, pension policies, and the labor force participation of aged males: A cross-national, longitudinal approach. *American Journal of Sociology, 89,* no. 2 (September), 350–372.

PARNES, H. S. (1981). *Work and retirement: A longitudinal study of men.* Cambridge, MA: MIT Press.

RAUM, G. (1958). Pensions and patriotism. In L. White (Ed.), *The republican era.* New York: Free Press.

RUBINOW, I. M. (1913). *Social insurance with special reference to American conditions.* New York: Henry Holt and Company.

SANDERS, H. T. (1980). Paying for the "bloody shirt": The politics of Civil War pensions. In B. S. Rundquist (Ed.), *Political Benefits.* Lexington, MA: Lexington Books. 137–159.

SKOCPOL, T., and IKENBERRY, J. (1982). The political formation of the American welfare state in historical and comparative perspective. Paper presented at the Annual Meetings of the American Sociological Association, San Francisco.

SQUIER, L. W. (1912). *Old age dependency in the United States: A complete survey of the pension movement.* New York: The MacMillan Company.

TRACY, M. B. (1983). Older men's earnings tests and work activity: A six nation study. *Research on Aging, 5* (June), 155–171.

TREAS, J. (1981). Women's employment and its implications for the economic status of the elderly of the future. In S. B. Keisler, J. N. Morgan, and V. K. Oppenheimer (Eds.), *Aging: Social change.* New York: Academic Press, 561–585.

U.S. BUREAU OF THE CENSUS. (1923). *Abstract of the fourteenth census of the United States: 1920.* Washington, D.C.: Government Printing Office.
U.S. BUREAU OF THE CENSUS. (1923). Fourteenth census of the population: 1920. Vol. IV. *Occupations.* Washington, D.C.: Government Printing Office.
U.S. BUREAU OF THE CENSUS. (1975). *Historical statistics of the United States.* Part 2. Washington, D.C.: Government Printing Office.
U.S. BUREAU OF THE CENSUS. (Forthcoming). Demographic and socioeconomic aspects of aging in the United States. *Current Population Reports.* Special Studies, Series P-23, Washington, D.C.: Government Printing Office.
U.S. CENSUS OFFICE. (1897). Eleventh Census. *Report on population of the United States.* Vol. 1, Part II. Washington, D.C.: Government Printing Office.
WALTHER, R. J. C. (1975). *Occupational position and urban economic structure: An explanation for the employment experience of the immigrant.* Ph.D. dissertation. Berkeley, CA: University of California.

# AUTHOR INDEX

# SUBJECT INDEX